THE GREATEST
ROGUE IN ENGLAND
THE SHOCKING CAREER AND
DRAMATIC DOWNFALL OF
COLONEL FRANCIS CHARTERIS

Linda Stratmann

SAPERE
BOOKS

THE GREATEST
ROGUE IN ENGLAND

Published by Sapere Books.
24 Trafalgar Road, Ilkley, LS29 8HH
United Kingdom

saperebooks.com

ISBN: 978-0-85495-307-3.

To Elric

The greatest rogue that ever wore a head,
Curst when alive, and damned when dead.[1]

---

[1] 'On Colonel Charteris', in J. Maidment (ed), *Private Letters Now first Printed from The Original MSS* (Edinburgh, privately printed, 1829), p. 83

TABLE OF CONTENTS

AUTHOR'S NOTE

The name Francis Charteris is frequently misspelled Chartres, Charters or Chartris in contemporary documents, and Wemyss is often rendered as Weems. All original spellings have been retained in quotations.

Wherever possible, sources contemporary with the life and times of the infamous Colonel have been used. Several biographies of Francis Charteris were published as pamphlets shortly after his trial. Some of the stories they relate can be verified from other sources, some are based on truth but have probably been embellished by the teller, many are almost certainly untrue but give a fascinating insight into how his contemporaries regarded him, and most are far too good not to repeat.

LIST OF ABBREVIATED TITLES

Authentic Memoirs

    Anon, *Some Authentick Memoirs of the Life of Colonel Ch—s, Rape-Master-General of Great Britain* (London, Printed and Sold by the Booksellers of *London* and *Westminster*, 1730)

Don Francisco

    Anon, *The Life of* Colonel *Don Francisco* (London, Printed for the Author, 1730)

Scotch Gallantry

    Anon, *Scotch Gallantry Display'd, or the Life and Adventures of the unparralel'd Col. Fr—nc—s Ch—rt—s, Impartially related* (London, Printed for, and Sold by the *Booksellers* in *Town* and *Country*, 1730)

History

    Anon, *The History of Col. Francis Ch—rtr—s*, fourth edition (London, printed for the author, 1730)

The Case of Col. Francis Chartres

    Anon, *The Case of Col. Francis Chartres, as it appeared at his Trial, at the Sessions held at Justice-Hall, in the Old-Baily, on Thursday the 26th of February, 1729-30; for a Rape committed on the Body of Anne Bond, his Servant, November, 10, 1729* in *A Collection of Remarkable Trials* (Glasgow, Eighteenth Century Collections Online, *c.* 1739) (accessed British Library)

The Reprieve

Anon, *The Reprieve: An Epistle from J—ck K—ch to C—l C—s* (London, A. Moore, 1730)

Chesterfield

B. Dobrée (ed.), *The Letters of Phillip Dormer Stanhope 4th Earl of Chesterfield* (6 vols, 1932, London, Eyre & Spottiswoode Limited)

Applebee

Applebee, J. (ed.), *Select Trials at the Sessions-House in the Old-Bailey, for Murder, Robberies, Rapes, Sodomy, Coining, Frauds, Bigamy, and other Offences* (94 vols, London, J. Applebee, 1742)

Proceedings of the Old Bailey

THE PROCEEDINGS AT THE Sessions of the Peace, and Oyer and Terminer, FOR THE City of LONDON, AND County of MIDDLESEX; ON Wednesday the 25th, Thursday the 26th, Friday the 27th, and Saturday the 28th of February, 1730, in the Third Year of His MAJESTY'S Reign.

The Tryal of Colonel Francis Chartres

Anon, *The Tryal of Colonel Francis Chartres for a Rape Committed by him on the Body of Mrs. Anne Bond* (London, A. Moore, 1730)

Pepyat

Anon, *The Tryal of Colonel Francis Charteris for a RAPE Committed on the Body Of ANNE BOND, Who was tried & found Guilty at* Justice-Hall *in the* Old Bailey, *on Fryday the 27th of* February *1729-30* (London, Sylvanus Pepyat, 1730)

'The Case of Col. Francis Chartres'

Anon, 'The Case of Col. Francis Chartres, as it appeared at his Trial, at the Sessions held at Justice-Hall, in the Old-Baily, on Thursday the 26th of February, 1729 — 30; for a Rape committed on the Body of Anne Bond, his Servant, November, 10, 1729', in *A Collection of Remarkable Trials* (Glasgow, Eighteenth Century Collections Online, *c.* 1739) (accessed British Library electronic resources)

Percival

Viscount Percival, *Manuscripts of the Earl of Egmont. Diary of Viscount Percival afterwards First Earl of Egmont*, vol I. 1730-1733 (London HMSO, 1920)

Political State

Anon, *The Political State of Great-Britain* (60 vols, London, Printed for the Executors of Mr. Boyer, and sold by T. Warner, 1730)

Correspondence of Jonathan Swift

H. Williams (ed), *The Correspondence of Jonathan Swift* (5 vols) (Oxford, The Clarendon Press, 1963)

Pulteney

W. Pulteney, *An Answer to One Part of a late Infamous Libel, Intitled, Remarks on the Craftsman's Vindication of his two honourable Patrons; in which the Character and Conduct of Mr. P. is fully Vindicated* (London, R. Francklin, 1731), p. 36

INTRODUCTION: THE UNPARRALEL'D COL. FR—NC—S CH—RT—S[2]

On the morning of 26 February 1730, Colonel Francis Charteris, an ageing libertine, swollen by arrogance and the dropsy, was conveyed to the Justice Hall, Old Bailey to be tried for rape. The news of his indictment had roared through the capital like a flame devouring tinder, for the Colonel was one of the great celebrities of the day, his name synonymous with debauchery, avarice, spite and brutality. His contemporaries called him 'The Rape-Master General', and he was probably one of the most hated men in Great Britain. In every part of the great sprawling metropolis that had come to be known simply as 'London' from the heart of the teeming City to its quietest and most remote villages, all the talk was of Colonel Charteris. The nobles and gentry who clustered at the Royal Court, merchants, lawyers, artists and wits meeting in clubs and coffee houses, and the masses who sought oblivion a penny at a time, in taverns and gin-shops, all had, for many years, followed with amusement and horror the unsavoury exploits of the notorious Colonel.

The sight of Francis Charteris having to answer for his villainy was, for the eager spectators who crowded the public galleries and gathered in the courtyard outside the Justice Hall,

---

[2] Anon, *Scotch Gallantry Display'd, or the Life and Adventures of the unparralel'd Col. Fr—nc—s Ch—rt—s, Impartially related* (London, Printed for, and Sold by the *Booksellers* in *Town* and *Country*, 1730), title page

13

a pleasure long overdue, but the great marvel was, that it was happening at all. It was the latest scene in a life whose every action was marked by dishonour, but made remarkable for the success with which the Colonel had managed repeatedly to evade any serious consequences of his greed and depravity.

Rape was then a capital offence, the penalty, a long dance from a short rope at Tyburn in front of a howling mob, yet so confident was the Colonel of his acquittal that he had already made arrangements for a celebratory supper with friends that same evening. His confidence was not misplaced, since he had every advantage which had seen many another villain walk free — birth, money, influential friends, and a coterie of toadies and hangers-on who gobbled the crumbs from his lustful table and regarded perjury as merely a part of their duties.

The Colonel was descended from a Scottish family of great antiquity, who could trace their origins back to Norman France. The fact that one of his ancestors had been imprisoned and another beheaded, did not in any way besmirch the family reputation, rather it placed the Charteris clan at the centre of great events, and underlined the importance of its position in history. Francis Charteris was not born to great wealth, but had made it his business to acquire it by every means at his disposal apart from that of honest toil. As a young gambler he ruined those who failed to spot anything amiss with his cards and dice. Launched into society with tainted funds he added blackmail, usury, and fraud to his armoury of skills. By 1730 he was reputed to be worth £200,000. He maintained this fortune, not with any great business sense, but with an ineradicable streak of meanness. Rather than squander his money on expensive whores he maintained a number of houses in both England and Scotland as personal brothels, to which his procuresses brought unsuspecting girls for his pleasure.

Charteris had faced courts before — he had been dragged before Parliament to apologise on his knees for embezzling government funds, and many times had paid compensation to avoid being prosecuted for previous rapes, but the costs of making amends had, he calculated, always been outweighed by his gains. Over the years he had come to know the value of a well-placed bribe.

He was well-thought-of among a certain type of carousing man, who requires nothing more of his companions than the ability to tell a coarse story and match him drink for drink. One such, who never allowed his private pleasures to interfere with his public life, was the Kings chief minister, Sir Robert Walpole, who entertained Charteris at his country seat in Norfolk.

The Colonel had come to court well-prepared. There had been no witnesses to the rape, and his servants were all willing to swear not only that they had not heard the victim's screams, but that the girl was little more than a common strumpet, who had been seen in the Colonel's bed many a time, and afterwards entertained them with lewd jokes suggesting that the supposed rapist was actually impotent. There was also a forged letter to enter in evidence.

The young woman who had brought the complaint had none of the advantages of Colonel Charteris. Her name was Anne Bond, and she was a Lancashire girl, who had been the Colonel's servant maid. There were some past employers able to give her a good character, but as to the events leading up to and including the rape, there was only her word against Charteris and his many witnesses. She came armed with only her modesty, her honesty, and a firmness of purpose.

As the Colonel entered a plea of not guilty, it was with the confident knowledge that he would very soon be walking from the court a free man. The rape could not be proven, and the worst that could possibly happen was to be found guilty of an assault, and fined a few pounds. What followed was undoubtedly the trial of the decade, and one of the most extraordinary of the eighteenth century. Francis Charteris was about to discover that his career as a liar, cheat, cardsharp, extortioner, rake, whoremaster and serial rapist was over.

I: THE EXECRABLE SUBJECT OF THIS NARRATIVE[3]

It was common practice at Old Bailey rape trials of the eighteenth century to bring character witnesses for the defendant who would testify that the accused was a sober, honest and steady individual who would never have committed the crime with which he was charged. Colonel Francis Charteris wisely refrained from this ploy. His counsel must have known that testimony of this nature would have been greeted with astonishment and even an inappropriate hilarity, and would serve only to remind the court, if it needed reminding, of the many reasons why the Colonel was one of the most reviled men in Great Britain. There was an unseen silent witness at his trial, but one whose presence had a profound effect on its outcome; it was the history of Colonel Charteris, his cruelty, insolence, cowardice, and countless sexual and financial misdeeds. Many of his outrages were a matter of public record, and his appearance to answer for a capital charge must, for many observers, have seemed long overdue.

Francis Charteris' immediate origins lay in the solid and worthy middle classes of Edinburgh, then the largest city in Scotland, seat of the Scottish Parliament, home of the Royal Court, and a centre of overseas trade. His father, James was a lawyer who had been admitted as a Writer to the Signet (a Crown solicitor), in September 1671, placing him in the upper

---

[3] Anon, *The Newgate Calendar, or the Malefactors' Bloody Register* (London, T. Werner Laurie, 1932), p. 204

ranks of the city's flourishing legal profession. James' year of birth is unknown, but Writers were usually admitted in their mid-20s. It was probably in the early 1670s that James married Mary, the daughter of Francis Kinloch, Lord Provost of Edinburgh, and later 1st baronet. The future Colonel was baptised in Edinburgh on 4 April 1675.[4] The witnesses to this event reveal the importance of the Charteris family in the Edinburgh legal and administrative community — 'Francis Kinloch late Dean of Gild, Francis Kinloch, his son, Charles Charteris, late Baillie of Leith, and William Charteris Writer to his Majesties Signet, Mr Laurence Charteris, Advocat, and Mr James Rocheid, Town-clerk.'[5] James did not shine in his profession. He never achieved any office in the Society of Writers to the Signet and his only two mentions in the meeting minutes refer to his being fined for non-attendance. He was, however, '…of good Account and Reputation, and had oftentimes discharg'd the Duty of one of the Magistrates of the City of *Edinburgh*…'[6] After 1675, Mary Charteris disappears from the family history, her date and place of death unknown. There were no further children of the marriage and she may have died while her son was still very young.

Francis is said to have been educated at the village school in Prestonpans together with his first cousin Francis Kinloch (later 3rd baronet), a year his junior. If James Charteris expected his son to follow him into the legal profession, the boy might well have completed his education at the prestigious

---

[4] Appendix 1

[5] Hyde Park Family History Centre, Edinburgh Old Parochial Registers, film 1066663

[6] Anon, *Some Authentick Memoirs of the Life of Colonel Ch—s, Rape-Master General of Great Britain* (London, Printed and Sold by the Booksellers of *London* and *Westminster*, 1730), p. 4

Edinburgh High School. During the years when Francis may have been a pupil, the school boasted six classics masters, a writing master, and a teacher of bookkeeping, though for an additional charge those wishing to add some gentlemanly polish could hire a fencing master and a music teacher.

All the scant evidence on the subject suggests that Francis Charteris was not a good scholar and showed no youthful promise for any of the professions or indeed any inclination for hard work. '…His Father, who was a private Gentleman, took care to give him a liberal Education; but the Son made no great Progress in Learning…'[7] *The Life of Colonel Don Francisco* a satirical biography published shortly after the trial whose tales should be regarded with some caution as even its contemporaries regarded it as highly inventive, added '…he had an utter Aversion to Birch, as having often experienc'd the Severity of his Scholastick Discipline' since 'his roving Disposition would not admit of a Passive Obedience.'[8] The story of his visit, years later, to his old schoolmaster who berated him for playing truant and arranged for him to be beaten again by a violent posse of schoolboys is surely fanciful.

The acerbically critical poet Alexander Pope observed in 1738, '…*Chartres* scarce could write or read…',[9] however surviving documents show that Charteris, while not equipped by nature or application for great learning, could read, write and do arithmetic sufficient for his daily needs.

---

[7] *Scotch Gallantry*, p. 4

[8] Anon, *The Life of Colonel Don Francisco* (London, Printed for the Author, 1730), p. 6

[9] 'Epilogue to the Satires. Dialogue II' in J. Butt (ed), *The Twickenham Edition of the Poems of Alexander Pope* (10 vols., London, Methuen and Co Ltd, 1939-67), vol. 4, *Imitations of Horace, with an Epistle to Dr Arbuthnot and the Epilogue to the Satires*, p. 324

The most valuable lesson that Francis learned in his youth and the one that was to shape the whole of his future life, was the history of his own family. He was not, as he might have assumed, the product of a long line of dull but respectable Edinburgh lawyers. He was told instead of antique roots, a place in the landed gentry of Scotland, and, what he must have seen as most important, a past enjoyment of fame, power, rank and great wealth, which had been foolishly thrown away. Listening to this, he can only have felt cheated and angry.

The family origins lay with Robert de Carnoto a Norman knight from Chartres who had been granted lands in Dumfriesshire. From the thirteenth century the name was rendered 'Charteris' (pronounced Charters), and first became associated with the estate of Amisfield. In 1581 John Charteris, 10th laird of Amisfield married Agnes daughter of John Maxwell, Lord Herries. This alliance with a powerful, wealthy and noble clan elevated the Charteris family from relative obscurity to a position of prominence. John Charteris was knighted in 1605 on the accession of James VI, and to consolidate his status, built a new family residence at Amisfield, a handsome turreted tower-house, which still stands today. The 10th laird died in about 1616, and was succeeded by his eldest son, also called John, who proceeded to throw away most of what his predecessors had achieved. Land, wealth and influence had come easily to the 11th laird, and he soon acquired further estates and important judicial offices, but his recklessness with money gradually reduced the family to debt. A well-liked man might have smoothed over the situation, but John, known for his high handed arrogance and a habit of ignoring the letter of the law when it suited him, had offended so many people that when he was unable to pay his bills, the creditors rubbed their hands with glee and closed in. From

1634 he was obliged to borrow heavily and sell off parts of the estate, eventually — and this must have hurt — Amisfield Tower. John's youngest brother William had been known as William of Auchinstrowane after his estate near Amisfield. When the family fortunes disappeared, William was forced to sell his holdings and move to Edinburgh where he married a merchant's daughter, Catherine Marjoribanks, and became a burgess of the city. His eldest son was James Charteris. Two years after the birth of Francis, the 13th laird of Amisfield re-acquired the tower and a portion of the estate, but it must have been a struggle and the family was constantly in financial difficulties. Francis, pondering on the fate of his genteelly impoverished cousins, must have thought long and hard about what might have been.[10]

During the Civil War, the two sons of the 11th laird, John (later 12th laird), and Alexander, brought some unwanted notoriety to the family as loyalist supporters of Charles I. John, after sentence of banishment was passed on him by Parliament in 1646, supported the armed rebellion of the Marquess of Montrose, and was apprehended and imprisoned in Edinburgh Castle for two years. Alexander, also one of Montrose's men, was wounded and captured during the Marquess's final defeat in 1650, and was one of five officers selected for execution. He made a miserable end on the 'maiden' a precursor of the guillotine. His fellow officers faced death with dignity, but Alexander, at the suggestion of his friends, tried to save his life by reading out a long and unashamedly apologetic speech from the scaffold, in which he lamented the error of his ways. No

---

[10] In the nineteenth century the estate was again sold to pay debts and bought back once more but finally left the family's possession in 1904

sooner had he finished speaking than he was despatched. This pathetic scene may well have come back to haunt the memory of Francis Charteris eighty years later.

Family pride was never a bargaining counter for Charteris, and it is doubtful that he cared a farthing for his Norman ancestry. Long before he became Britain's most enthusiastic devotee of sins of the flesh, he learned to love money, and the power and prestige that came with it. He seems to have inherited more than a little of the arrogance of the 11th laird, though not his profligate ways. The youthful Francis determined two things, first that he would become rich, by whatever means were available to him, fair or foul, and secondly that once he had made his money, he would hold onto it. The loss of the bulk of the Amisfield estate clearly rankled, and the fortunes he later amassed were largely spent on land. It says much that when he purchased an estate near Haddington he renamed it Amisfield, and thereafter referred to himself as Francis Charteris of Amisfield. If his intention was to fool people into believing that he was a member of the senior branch of the Charteris family, and laird of Amisfield in Dumfriesshire, he succeeded beyond his wildest dreams as that confusion still exists today.

James must have realised early that his wayward and undisciplined son was not destined for the law, and entered him in the army as a cadet with the sixteenth regiment of foot under the command of Colonel Hodges. Accounts of young Francis' military career differ between the various contemporary biographies, and most of the incidents are undated. The possibility that some stories are pure invention should not be ignored in the compilation which follows. On the outbreak of war in 1689 the army embarked for Flanders where it fought against the French. According to *Scotch*

Gallantry Francis had not been there long before he was forced to run the gauntlet through the whole corps, for stealing a pair of breeches from an officer. He was then transferred to the twelfth regiment of foot under Colonel Brewer where he failed to achieve the promotion he felt he deserved. According to *Authentick Memoirs* his next crude attempt to redress the balance of his fortunes was to steal a piece of beef, for which he underwent the usual military discipline and was discharged. If these stories are true, they were early lessons in the foolhardiness of outright theft as a means of advancement. Returning to Edinburgh in disgrace, his father '…looking upon this as a juvenile Folly, entertained still some Hopes of him…'[11] and purchased him a commission as an ensign with the third regiment of foot guards under the command of Major-General Ramsay. He was soon back in Flanders, where his reputation for impudence, quarrels and petty crime had preceded him, and '…the Officers refused to inroll with him or keep him Company. The Prejudices ran so high against him, that he soon dispos'd of his Post, and took another Trip to *Edinburgh*, and so was a second Time returned on his Father's hands, like a leaden Shilling that *would not go*.'[12]

A Colonel Mcguill had been sent to Scotland to raise a regiment of foot for the service of the King, and so James Charteris '…had Interest enough to procure a Lieutenant's Commission for his *Wicked Frank*, as he used to call him…'[13] It was the last time Francis was able to rely upon that forgiving parent. Not long afterwards, James Charteris died and was buried in Greyfriars Kirkyard on 30 January 1691. He was probably in his forties, and his son was not yet sixteen.

---

[11] *Authentick Memoirs*, p. 5

[12] ibid

[13] ibid, p. 6

Some accounts suggest that Francis inherited a substantial patrimony, but no will or service of heirship can be traced to confirm this. *Don Francisco*, the most fanciful of his biographies, has Francis enlisting in a Dutch regiment of horse known as the Blue Guards, recently returned from the Battle of Aughrim fought in July 1691. He was '… admitted without Fee or Reward…'[14] since positions in that regiment were at that time neither bought nor sold. This suggests both a lack of personal finances and an understandable unwillingness on the part of his relatives to assist him.

As Francis grew to adulthood it became clear that he would never be good-looking — his face was coarse, with a prominent nose and fleshy sensuous lips, but he made up for that with a tall, well-built figure, and an abundance of superficial charm. 'His Air was lively and pleasant, his Shape compleat, tho' his Face not handsome…'[15] He must have looked every inch the soldier. 'It seems Fortune from the beginning design'd him for a great Man; a man of six Foot proportion'd every way, is a tall proper Person, fit for the Service of his Country, either in the Horse or Foot.'[16] But a trooper's income was '…a poor Allowance for an ambitious Man, a Person that had a mind to make a Figure in the World…'[17]

When the regiment was looking for someone to raise recruits they lighted on the young Lieutenant — robustly built and with an ingratiating air well-larded with self-confidence. He was entrusted with three months' pay and sent to England. On the

---

[14] *Don Francisco*, p. 7

[15] Anon, *The Genuine History of Mrs Sarah Prydden, usually called Sally Salisbury, and her Gallants* (London, Andrew Moor, 1723), p. 9

[16] *Don Francisco*, p. 6

[17] ibid, p. 8.

way over, he whiled away the time by gambling with a fellow officer, and lost every penny.

Here were two valuable lessons learned. First, that it was possible to make a lot of money very quickly by gaming with the right person, and second, that gambling was for fools unless matters had been arranged so as to make winning certain. While he digested that, he had more immediate problems to resolve. There are several slightly differing versions of how he managed to extricate himself from this situation, and if true, the story is the first recorded instance of a ploy he was to use many times during his life, with variable success. The device can be called 'pretending to have been robbed'. An accusation of robbery was then no trivial threat as it was a capital offence. It was an act he honed over the years until it must have been second nature, and it appears as part of his stock-in-trade in his dealings with Anne Bond.

Arriving at Harwich young Charteris proceeded to one of the best inns in the town, where, claiming that he liked to live well no matter the cost, he brazenly demanded the best in food, wine and accommodation that the landlord had to offer. He was conducted to a 'handsome Chamber'[18] where he was brought a dish of fish and two fowls. He also ordered nine bottles of the best French claret and invited the landlord to dine with him. Once the landlord had taken his leave and the house was quiet for the night, Charteris removed his breeches and put them on the fire. He then left the door of his chamber unfastened and went to bed. The next morning when the servant came to call him, he pretended to look for the missing breeches and not finding them, exclaimed loudly that he had been robbed of sixty pounds and his watch. The landlord,

---

[18] Anon, *The History of Col. Francis Ch—rtr—s*, fourth edition (London, printed for the author, 1730), p. 7

hearing the commotion, rushed up to the room, where his guest now threatened to ruin him by spreading the word among his influential friends that the business harboured thieves to steal from gentlemen in the night. The landlord was so alarmed at this prospect that he agreed to make compensation for the theft if his guest agreed not to tell of it. Charteris, whose style was all swagger and braggadocio was unable to keep his mouth shut about this adventure. 'Of this heroick Exploit he has often boasted, as his Master-piece; and he was as proud of it, as ever the greatest General was of a Stratagem, whereby he had gain'd a Victory…'[19] He did claim that he had later reimbursed the landlord with interest '…which I leave every one who knows him, or his Character, to believe, or disbelieve, like the *Apocrypha*,'[20] commented the *History*. He was also, when it suited him, to deny the story utterly. 'The Reverend Mr *Guthrie* having charg'd this Fact very home upon him since his Confinement in *Newgate*, the *Colonel* declared, *That as he hoped for the King's Mercy there was not a Tittle of Truth in this story*. Therefore every body must believe a Gentleman, after so solemn an Asseveration!'[21]

On the Peace of Reswick in 1697, 22-year-old Charteris shared in the general fate of officers and found himself back in Scotland on reduced pay. Far from disheartened, he had by now formulated his plan to become rich. 'He now gave himself entirely up to Gaming, and all manner of Licentiousness; and having uncommon Success, acquired great Sums of Money by it.'[22] Consistent and prolific success as a gambler suggests that he employed more than an unusual skill with cards. In *Don*

---

[19] ibid, p. 9 (misprinted 45 in fourth edition)
[20] ibid
[21] *Authentick Memoirs*, pp. 7-8
[22] ibid, p. 6

Francisco it is claimed that he frequented gambling dens and associated himself with card-sharpers to learn '…the Art and Mysteries of Gaming…'[23] and he is often credited as '…an admirable Proficient in the Art of *Legerdemain*…',[24] although simpler tactics such as marked cards or loaded dice may have also been involved. The card games he is said to have been most familiar with were ombre — a three-player game, the earliest to introduce the idea of bidding; piquet — a skilful two-player game with a shortened deck, still popular today; 'pharoh' (later called faro), a table betting game, and the infamous 'basset', where fortunes could be won or lost so rapidly that it was considered suitable only for the wealthier classes. He was also a player of 'hazard', a forerunner of the modern game of craps, where gamblers bet on the outcome of throws of the dice. These games, according to his contemporaries '…furnish'd him with such a Fund of *Learning* as laid the Foundation of his future Greatness.'[25] His other great skill was an oily persuasive charm. Seeking out dupes with more money than sense, he drew them, behind a mask of conviviality, and with liberal offers of drink, into gaming for amusement. Allowing them to win a game or two, he then suggested playing for money, and quickly stripped them of cash and valuables before their fuddled heads knew what had happened. With his winnings he acquired the clothing and accessories necessary to demonstrate that he was of a man of substance, and began to frequent the best coffee houses in town. '…Being a Person of a good Aspect, good Address, and a good Assurance withal…',[26] he was soon accepted into the

---

[23] *Don Francisco*, p. 8

[24] *History*, p. 3 (misprinted 43 in fourth edition)

[25] *Authentick Memoirs*, p. 4

[26] *Don Francisco*, p. 10

upper echelons of Edinburgh society. In elegant gaming clubs, he found himself in the company of gentry and nobility, whom he saw merely as a better class of dupe.

One bitterly cold winter's night, he was playing hazard in Edinburgh '…in Company with several Persons of the first rank, who had some suspicion of his not Playing like a man of Honour…' Watching him carefully, they caught him in the act of palming false dice. Infuriated, they insisted he refund them his winnings or else '…go thro' the Discipline of Blanket and Horse-pond, besides a good Bastinado…'[27] (caning the soles of the feet). He was obliged to reimburse them, but not satisfied with that, they resolved to teach him a lesson by requiring him to strip naked and to stand thus in the room the whole night. Before long he was suffering so much from the intense cold, that unable to endure the pain, he began to plead with them '…in the most pathetick Manner…'[28] to end the punishment. His companions took no notice of this, indeed they may well have enjoyed watching the incorrigible rogue suffer. After a time, certain rumblings in the bowels prompted another plea, and he asked to be allowed his liberty: '…Nature requiring a discharge backwards…' Knowing young Charteris, the players may have suspected this was a ploy to make his escape, and refused. It was no ploy, and '…he was forced to ease himself amongst them, the Stench of which was so very Offensive, that it made his Guards quit the Room, and so the Colonel got his Liberty.'[29]

In the right company, winnings could be very substantial. When the Duke of Queensbury was Commissioner to the Parliament of Scotland, Charteris smarmed his way into a card

---

27 *History*, p. 29
28 ibid, p. 29
29 *Scotch Gallantry*, p. 17

party with the Duchess. Whether by accident or his contrivance, the Duchess was seated near a large mirror so Charteris could see her cards, and he won £3,000 from her in one evening.

During his years in Edinburgh Charteris was to commence a lifelong, and as it later proved, important friendship with Duncan Forbes, a rising young advocate. No breath of scandal has ever attached itself to Forbes, known for his good humour, honesty and conviviality, although in his younger days he was renowned as a hard drinker, and drew about him a circle of unconventional friends. Even Charteris, who usually judged men according to how much he could make out of them, seems to have genuinely appreciated Forbes' kindness, and gentle nature.

Charteris also became a frequenter of horse races and having '…a good Judgement in Running Horses…'[30] obtained an entrée to the best racing circles. He was later to demonstrate considerable pride in the horses he owned, showing them more care and consideration that he ever gave a human being. His knowledge of horses recommended him to a Duke who was a great racing enthusiast, and through this connection, he obtained a post in a troop of Life Guards.

It would have been an unusual life for a wealthy young man of the time not to have devoted himself very thoroughly to sins of the flesh, however what is remarkable about Francis Charteris is that he was never, like so many of his contemporaries, a frequenter of brothels. 'The Accounts of the Colonel's Amours are many and various, and if we may believe the most credible Reports, his Adventures that way were chiefly amongst persons in Low-Life, and mostly *Servant Maids*, many of which, 'tis said, were ruin'd by him…'[31] He may have

---

[30] *Authentick Memoirs*, p. 6

had a taste for the servant class, but he was also exercising a wise caution, something of which he frequently boasted. Gonorrhoea and syphilis (then considered to be different stages of the same disease) were the ever present dangers of consorting with prostitutes. The treatment, injection with mercury, was painful and ineffective. More importantly, the process would put a firm halt to a gentleman's sexual adventures until the symptoms — which could go into remission — had receded and he believed he was cured. For this reason, a virgin, bought from a procuress was an expensive commodity. Meanness ran deep to the core of Chatteris' nature, and he would never have financed the silk gowns of painted whores or lined the pockets of procuresses when he could take his pleasures for free. Charteris had his own, cheaper way of finding untouched sexual partners — he hired them as servants, seduced them if they were willing, raped them if they were not, and once he had tired of them, turned them out into the street. Any notion of the rake as a romantic, dashing figure must be abandoned here. Charteris was not an adventurer but a predator, with a callous, vicious streak that even his libertine contemporaries despised. There is something of the psychopath about Francis Charteris. Women were to him a commodity, to be used and discarded. He was unable to see why he should not do exactly as he pleased with other people, and did so throughout his life, repeatedly and uncontrollably, even where he was likely to be observed.

On 6 August 1701 he assaulted a young woman called Katherine Ramsay on the public highway, an incident he later claimed he was unable to remember because he was drunk. On 15 September in the same year, he raped a girl only twelve or thirteen years of age, the only recorded instance of him abusing

---

[31] *Scotch Gallantry*, p. 6

a child. He admitted that he had offered her money to lift up her clothes, but two witnesses had seen him lying on top of her, and heard the girl cry out while he told her to '…ly still…'[32] Three months later on 16 December he attacked Janet Scott, a married woman. She had been on the road to Edinburgh when he had followed her, pulled her down off a stile, and '…abused her and lain with her Carnally…'[33] These cannot have been the only incidents of the kind, '…he being generally Noised over the Nation as a flagricious profligate person an Habituall Drunkard, forswearer, Curser, and a whore monger and as guilty of frequent assaulting women even on the high way for some of which he has been processed before the Judiciary.'[34]

The first of his known illegitimate offspring was born at this time. The parish register of Edinburgh Canongate records that 'Captaine Francis Charteris in ye hors guards had a child begotten in fornication with Margt Grahame…',[35] a daughter baptised Frances on 11 November 1701.

It was some months before anything was done to put a stop to his activities, and in the interval, he married. On 3 July 1702 in Edinburgh, Francis Charteris, then a Captain in her Majesty's Troop of Guards was married to Helen Swinton, 21-year-old[36] daughter of the late Sir Alexander Swinton, Lord Mersington, a member of the judiciary and Senator of the College of Justice in Edinburgh. The Swintons cannot have been ignorant of his reputation, but the events that led to this

---

[32] Scottish National Archives, Church papers, CG1/2/3/2, f. 226

[33] ibid

[34] ibid

[35] Hyde Park Family History Centre, Edinburgh Canongate Church baptisms, film 1067741

[36] The Swinton Family Society records state that she was born around 1681

marriage are unknown. The groom's personal fortune and winning manners could well have influenced them and it could also have been a device on his part to avoid serious repercussions from his brutal attacks on women by achieving a position of respectability. Love seems to be an unlikely reason on either side, on the Captain's because he was probably incapable of it, and on Helen's since although her swain was able to exert a brief charm, he was unable to maintain the fiction for long. A daughter, Janet, was born to the couple, the date and place of the birth a mystery, except that it did not take place in Edinburgh. It has been suggested[37] that the child was born in 1702 in Halyards, Fifeshire the home of her maternal grandmother, and it would not be a blot on Helen's reputation to speculate that she might have been seduced by the importunate young Captain, and married him in haste.

Unsurprisingly, it was not a happy marriage. 'No body applauded him for his good Usage of that Lady … but many accuse him of the contrary',[38] observed *Scotch Gallantry*, and *Authentick Memoirs* describes Helen as '…a Lady of good Family and Fortune, endowed with many excellent Virtues, who scarce hath met with any other Comfort since her Marriage, than that of an universal Commiseration.'[39] Helen stood by her husband as long as she felt able, but a great deal of their married life was spent apart. '…She long bore his scandalous Debaucheries and inhuman usage with exemplary Patience; but being at last quite weary'd out, she has at length

---

[37] International Genealogical Index. The provenance of this information is unknown. The index has several conflicting entries for Janet's birth.

[38] *Scotch Gallantry*, p. 5

[39] *Authentick Memoirs*, pp. 6-7

left him to his Evil Genius, and lives separate from him at *Edinburgh.*[40]

In September 1702 Charteris' early career as a serial rapist finally caught up with him and he was summoned before the General Assembly of the National Church on a charge of gross immorality. There was a lengthy hearing in which Charteris was questioned and witnesses summoned. There was little doubt of his guilt, and it was ordered that he should be publicly rebuked. The 1st Duke of Argyll under whom he had served in the guards and whom he had prevailed upon to write a letter in his support, was told bluntly '…How unseemly and offensive it is that such a Monster of Wickednesse should be in any publick employment…'[41]

When backed into a corner Charteris could perform humble contrition to international standards. On October 10, receiving his formal rebuke in church he '…behaved himself gravely and acknowledged his sorrow for all former miscarriages …' and promised a more '…Christian deportment…' in the future.[42] He cannot have meant a word of this apology and must have reverted to his old ways almost immediately.

The young Captain was soon drawn back into the military life. The War of the Spanish Succession, a major European conflict, broke out shortly after the death of the childless Charles II of Spain in 1700. With both French and Austrian claimants to the inheritance, most European countries took sides, and battle lines were drawn. British armies under the command of John Churchill, Duke of Marlborough, were involved until the Treaty of Utrecht in 1713. There are no details of Captain Charteris' career as a soldier, no accounts of

---

[40] *History*, p. 10
[41] Scottish National Archives Church Papers, CG1/2/3/2, f. 226 v
[42] ibid f. 216

battles in which he took part, of deeds done upon the field of war. It may have been during this period that he suffered an accident in which he broke his leg. In the best full length portrait of him, by Hogarth, he is leaning on a stick, and close inspection shows that the left leg is deformed. He may well have walked with a limp. It is doubtful that the injury happened in battle, or indeed in any way that might have brought him honour, or bore a retelling. The boastful young Captain would surely have tried to enhance his reputation with such a tale, instead of which he remained entirely silent about when, where or how he was injured.

Charteris had only one activity during his military career to which he devoted himself utterly — the making of money. With the army quartered at Brussels, gambling, both with cards and dice, was a popular pastime among the officers, and the young men learned to their cost that the Captain was a regular winner. Many were left uncomfortably short of funds, but soon found that the Captain was able to assist them in their distress. He lent them back their money, at 100 per cent interest, a rate not merely outrageous but illegal. When his commanding officers, John Campbell, 2nd Duke of Argyll, and John Dalrymple, 2nd Earl of Stair, discovered what was happening, they reported it to Major-General George Hamilton, Earl of Orkney. Hamilton took the matter to Marlborough who had Charteris arrested and court-martialled. The evidence was overwhelming, and he was obliged to return the interest money, and deprived of his commission. His sword was ceremonially broken and he was drummed out of the regiment in disgrace. Unrepentant, Charteris returned to Edinburgh, and continued to amass money by gambling and usury. A notable victim was William Morison of Prestoungrange, a member of the first parliament of Great

Britain, whose indebtedness to the card-sharping Captain eventually amounted to almost £17,000.

A bombastic liar on Charteris' scale could hardly avoid quarrels and he was well-known for high words, and explosions of rage which often led to scuffles and brawls. According to *Authentick Memoirs*, in 1705, he quarrelled with a miller in Edinburgh market place, and in the heat of the moment bit off a piece of the man's nose. The miller brought a suit against his attacker who was brought before the Lords of Session, and fined eighty pounds. Arrogant as ever, he '…thought this pretty reasonable, and in a sneering jocular Way, flung down a Bill of 90l. to pay the Fine, and was marching off; When the Officer of the Court call'd him to take his Change, he replied aloud, *That he gave the Overplus to the Lords to drink.*'[43] Their Lordships were so offended that he was ordered back into court and fined another £50 for contempt.

In February 1709 his gambling winnings enabled him to purchase a company in the first Regiment of Foot-Guards for three thousand guineas. Charteris never paid out money of this order unless he was sure of getting a handsome return. He was entitled to 16*s* 6*d* daily pay, but the enterprise gave him substantial opportunities to extract far more by fraud and extortion. He also achieved the rank of Colonel, reputedly by gambling with a Colonel of the Foot-Guards, who lost all his ready money and his commission.

The company had not yet been ordered to Flanders, and was called upon to muster in London. There were supposed to be sixty-five men and five servants, for each of which Charteris was paid 4*s* per week subsistence out of the public coffers, but the actual number of effective men was, as it later transpired, only thirty-eight. The remainder were what was then known as

---

[43] *Authentick Memoirs*, p. 28

'faggots', non-serving men hired simply to make up the numbers. The men who took on this role did so because they were in debt, and enlisting protected them from arrest. Two company Sergeants, Williams and Pitman, managed the 'Effectives'[44] but Charteris, assisted by a Sergeant Cook, managed the faggots, and every week he put their pay in his pocket. In addition to this, he extorted commission money from victualling houses, and further sums from the faggots themselves to excuse them from duty. On enlistment each faggot was supposed to receive forty shillings, but this went into the Colonel's pocket, as did the benefit of the clothes and arms assigned to them. By these schemes alone Charteris was pocketing on average £12 5s 3d per week. The men were too afraid of arrest to complain. Before admitting the faggots into his company the Colonel extracted from them a fee of £5 to £10 apiece, according to their ability to pay, promising that he would excuse them from going to Flanders. He later tried to claim in his defence that he would have required them to march there if necessary, but this was hardly possible. '…Besides their being generally broken Tradesmen, in no way us'd to Exercise or Discipline…'[45] some of them lived in counties as widespread as Gloucestershire, Worcestershire or Buckinghamshire, and others through age or infirmity were unfit for service. 'For when a Faggot is taken in for protection, it matters not whether he is Blind, old, or Lame; so he has 5 or 10 l. to give the Colonel, he will pass Muster.'[46] Charteris was

---

[44] P. Hurly, '*Demonstrative Proofs, that Lieutenant Col. Charteris hath by* False Musters, *and other Unwarrantable* Practices, *Defrauded the Queen and Publick of 12*l. 5s. 3d. *every Week since he bought his Company*' (London, printed for P. Hurly, 1711), p. 1
[45] ibid, p. 2
[46] ibid, p. 2

adept at cultivating people when they were of some value to him, but once that value was at an end, he disposed of them without a second thought. The poorest men, such as George Milsom fared especially badly. When Charteris was unable to squeeze any further funds out of Milsom or his distressed family, he sold the man to his creditors for £10, by discharging him out of the company without his knowledge, upon which Milsom was arrested and thrown into debtors' prison.

Some faggots were able to pay off their creditors and leave the company, in which case a fresh one was enlisted. In all, some forty-two men were enlisted as faggots in the eighteen months before the practice was exposed:

> ...By all these Arts he was enabled to make a handsome Figure, and paid his Tradesmen pretty tolerably for an Officer in the Army, he in some measure recover'd his Reputation, was look'd upon as a Man of Fortune, and for some time kept the best Company.[47]

Discovery was inevitable. Charteris often underestimated those he tried to cheat or abuse. He was not a calculating man in that he rarely seemed to weigh up his chances of success before acting, and never tried to tailor his schemes to the qualities of the victim. His only criterion was money. If he ever thought of the possible consequences, he probably acted on the principle that even if some of his victims rebelled he would come out a winner overall. Profit was everything.

The man who exposed the frauds was Patrick Hurly, a debtor who claimed that he had been obliged to enlist after losing his money through extravagant living. In March 1709, Charteris, who had spotted that Hurly was worth more than his initial fee, sent for him and said that if Hurly could not give

---

[47] *History*, p. 16 (misprinted 41 in fourth edition)

him five guineas and an effective man to serve in the company he could protect him no longer. In return he swore upon his honour that Hurly would be exempted from all duties except on muster-days. Hurly, afraid of his creditors, complied, but shortly afterwards discovered exactly what the Colonels honour was worth, when Charteris sent for him again and demanded payment of 2s 6d a week to excuse him from duty. Once again, Hurly paid up.

On 1 July 1710, Hurly was arrested by his creditors, who had obtained a note from Major General Tatton certifying that he was not, as he pretended, a soldier. Hurly, lodged in the Fleet debtors' prison, sent a note to Charteris via Sergeant Cook, begging him to perform his promises, which the Colonel refused to do unless he was paid another, £50. Hurly was unable to pay the £50, but at length persuaded a reluctant Charteris to accept a promissory note. On 7 July the Colonel appeared before Lord Chief Justice Parker and swore that Hurly was an effective soldier and did duty with the other men. Unknown to Hurly, Charteris judged the worth of the promissory note by his own standards, and was resolved to take no chances. No sooner had Hurly been released than he was hurried away by Sergeant Cook and kept in confinement at the Savoy (the old Savoy Palace in London, then used as a military prison) until he could give better security for the £50 than his own note. Hurly was obliged to lodge a mortgage of £400 for the Colonel's own use as security. Charteris had judged his man badly, for Hurly was more intelligent and resourceful than he suspected. As soon as Hurly was at liberty he took steps to escape Charteris' clutches, by mounting legal action regarding both the £50 and the mortgage. This was Charteris' most serious brush with the law to date, and as events unfolded, he revealed to what lengths he was prepared to go in his attempts to evade justice.

Finding himself charged with false musters, protecting men against their creditors and extortion, Charteris acted like a blunt instrument. His imagination would only ever permit him to see two ways out of such a situation — threats and bribery — and he was usually prepared to employ both tactics on the same people, unable to appreciate that someone he had initially threatened would be unlikely to trust him enough to agree to a later bribe. He first tried to have Hurly confined to the Savoy again, as his soldier, and offered to sell him to an officer recruiting for the West Indies, with the stipulation that Hurly was not to land anywhere until reaching his destination, and was not to be allowed pen, ink or paper on the way. Failing in this design, and discovering that Hurly intended to put his case before the House of Commons, Charteris next ordered that Hurly be listed in the Gazette as a deserter, swearing that he would do his utmost to have him condemned by a court-martial and executed. These scare tactics did not work, and Hurly exposed the entire scheme before Parliament, which appointed a committee of enquiry. Before any witnesses could be examined, Charteris changed tack and offered Hurly a thousand pounds to stop the action. Hurly, wise to the value of the Colonels promises, and by now probably more interested in justice than money, refused. Hurly was assigned clerks, pens, ink and paper, and spent three weeks examining the regimental muster rolls, coming up with a schedule of duty-men and faggots, which he presented to the committee.

By now, Charteris was so desperate that he was actually prepared to make a promise he would have to keep. On the night that the committee first sat, he appeared at the Speaker's chamber door with an attorney, and offered Hurly to pay all his debts and '…make him very easy in his Circumstances, provided he would say nothing to his prejudice, before that Honourable Committee.'[48] Again, Hurly refused. '…When Col. *Charteris* found bribes would not take off *Hurly*, he had Recourse to Bullying and Threatening, but with as little Success.'[49]

Hurly's first witness, George Kemble revealed that the Colonel had asked him to seek out tradesmen in debt and tell them about the scheme to protect them from their creditors. Sergeant Cook then testified that he had kept a pay book for the company, but that the Colonel had instructed him to cut out the leaves and hand them over. The committee also learned of the fate of George Milsom, who was still in debtors prison, '…in a most Deplorable starving Condition',[50] and there were numerous other similar cases. Hurly said he had '…Letters, with other Papers and Complaints, put into his Hands, proving the Colonel guilty of many infamous Cheats, Tricks and Extortions …',[51] some of which were in civilian life.

With things looking bad for him, the obvious course for Charteris was to bribe witnesses. He organised meetings with some of the faggots and other soldiers at the Nagg's-Head Inn, Haymarket, and offered them money to tell the committee that they had been well treated. Sergeant Pitman was given ten guineas to pay off the men, but soon afterwards gave evidence that the true muster was never more than thirty-eight. For this,

---

[48] P. Hurly, *The Case of Several of the Persons from whom Lieutenant Colonel Charteris extorted Money for protecting them from their Creditors* (London, printed for P. Hurly, 1711), p. 2

[49] ibid

[50] ibid

[51] P. Hurly, *An Answer to Col. Charteris's Second Libel which he Calls his Humble Representation* (London, printed for P. Hurly, 1711), p. 4

he was later beaten and abused by his enraged Colonel. Cook and Kemble were more compliant and after receiving bribe-money, both changed their stories. John Hare, a soldier, was produced by the Colonel as evidence against Hurly, but eventually confessed that the Colonel had hired him and five others to testify, telling them '…they need not boggle at saying any thing, provided they could make their Stories but to hang well together…'[52] This shows unusual appreciation of what was required for a convincing deception, something Charteris had evidently forgotten in 1730 when instructing his witnesses for the Old Bailey trial.

Wading in once more, Charteris tried his next line of defence — another ploy he was to use many times in the future — which was to blacken the character of his accuser. He claimed that the witnesses against him were lying because they hated him for refusing to protect them. Hurly was declared to be a low born individual, who had once stood in the pillory, which was then the standard punishment for perjury. In response, Hurly was able to prove that he came from a good family, had studied at University for five years, studied law for another four, and had been paymaster of the Irish Army in France for five years. The suggestion that he had once stood in the pillory was shown to be untrue and Charteris was obliged to withdraw it. It is still possible that Hurly's character may have been suspect. It was claimed that he was '… a Person of an infamous Character…'[53] notorious for committing frauds upon tradesmen, by ordering furnishings for his house and then selling the contents and absconding. Even if true this is a minor villainy compared with the Colonel's.

---

[52] *The Case of Several of the Persons*, p. 3
[53] *Don Francisco*, p. 13

Eventually, with fifteen of Hurly's witnesses still to give evidence, the committee decided that the facts had been so fully proved it was superfluous to hear any more.

Charteris was taken into the custody of the Serjeant at Arms of the House of Commons, and brought to the bar of the House was obliged to kneel to receive a severe reprimand. Arrogant to the last, 'When he was going to perform this last Ceremony, he desired to be assisted in it, as being an utter Stranger to the Custom; he having, as he declared, not been above four times on his Knees during the whole Course of his Life before; and then he said it was only to qualify himself according to Law, for the Posts he had in the Army.'[54]

Cashiered, he was ordered to pay a fine of a hundred pounds. Unlike his earlier convictions after which he had managed to buy his way back into the army, he was '…Disabled to hold any Civil or Military Office, or Employment…'[55] His military career was over.

Charteris was a bad loser, always wanting the parting shot, however petty and spiteful. He threatened revenge against Hurly, saying he would have him tried under martial law as a mutineer for complaining against his Colonel, but it was all bluster. Charteris probably enjoyed the military life, but what must have most embittered him was the loss of a position which had given him such easy pickings.

The Colonel now '…gave himself up to a Life of Luxury and Pleasure. He was so surprisingly successful in Gaming, that he generally stript all the Gentlemen he play'd with, and then advancing Money on their *Acres*, it was not long before he would get himself into the sole possession of them; by which Means he became seized of several Lordships and Mannors

---

[54] *Authentick Memoirs*, pp. 7-8
[55] *The Case of Several of the Persons*, p. 4

42

both in *England* and *Scotland*.'[56] The military man had become a man of property.

---

[56] *Authentick Memoirs*, p. 9

II: THE MOST POPULAR WHORE-MASTER IN THE THREE KINGDOMS[57]

In 1713 Francis Chatteris acquired an estate at Newmills in Haddington, some seventeen miles east of Edinburgh. The property generated an annual income of £3,000. With more than a touch of triumphant irony, he renamed it Amisfield after the ancient and impoverished seat of his ancestors. Another important acquisition that year was Hornby Castle in Lancashire. Four years later he added two more properties in that county, Holme and Preston Patrick, which included the mansion house of Preston Old Hall and 322 acres of land. By 1722, he owned the Lordship of Cockerham. His annual income from his Lancashire properties alone was £4,000.

It is not known when he bought Stoneyhill (also spelt Stonyhill, Stonniehill, Stoney-hill and many other variations) in Musselborough, but there is a reference in the town's papers to his having built a bridge over the nearby river Esk at his own expense in 1728. Even then, the mansion was old and in a state of some decay (it was pulled down in 1838). '…Behind it are the garden and orchard, enclosed by a gigantic buttressed wall, apparently of great age. A mulberry tree in one of the walks may well have been coeval with that of Shakespeare.'[58] Duncan Forbes occupied Stoneyhill as a tenant while Charteris was away.

---

[57] *Authentick Memoirs*, p. 9

[58] J. Paterson, *History of the Regality of Musselburgh* (Musselburgh, J. Gordon, 1857), p. 189

Other known acquisitions were a house and lands in the barony of Cranston, Edinburgh, and Carren-House, '...a stately and ancient Seat...'[59] once the property of a General Ramsay.

The Colonel travelled extensively to oversee his estates, lodging in country inns on the road, and everywhere he went, he left behind him stories of servant girls despoiled. These tales were told with some relish by the pamphleteers after his trial, and are repeated here with the usual caveat as to their truth.

Staying overnight at a Lancashire inn, he found the maidservant very much to his taste, and resolved to have her — as cheaply as possible, of course. This story illustrates another of the Colonel's favourite seduction techniques, one which he was later to try on Anne Bond, which might be called 'the barbed gift'. He '...made love to her very warmly, that is to say, *a-la-mode de Charteris*, for he came immediately to the Point, and offer'd her a Guinea, if she would be his bedfellow that night.'[60] A guinea, especially in a country district, might well have represented four or more months' wages to a maidservant. 'The Girl at first gave him a Repulse, and stood upon her Character and reputation, but at length his persuasions and the Guinea prevail'd...'[61] That night, when all was quiet, the girl crept into Charteris' room and stayed with him until morning, returning to her duties with the guinea in her pocket.

Once the Colonel was up and dressed, he called for his bill, and when the landlord brought it to him asked where the maidservant was who had waited on him the night before. 'I sent her to change a Guinea, and she has neither brought me

---

[59] *Authentick Memoirs*, p. 40

[60] *History*, p. 10

[61] *Scotch Gallantry*, p. 6

that nor the Silver.'[62] The Landlord at once sent for the girl and the Colonel demanded where the change was for the guinea. The girl blushed, not daring to say how she had really come by the coin. Collecting her wits, she gave a respectful curtsey, returned the money and said 'Here is your Guinea, Sir, but I could not get it chang'd'. Thus far, the close-fisted Colonel '...who never loves to do things by Halves...'[63] had done no more than cheat a poor servant girl of both her virginity and a guinea, a mean enough act, but next he showed the true extent of his spiteful nature. With the coin in his grasp he told the landlord everything that had happened the previous night. The maidservant was expelled from the house, and such was her shame that she was obliged to leave the county. To the Colonel this was no more than an adventure, an amusing piece of sport, but long after he had dismissed it from his mind the story remained widely known in Lancashire, and in the long run it was Charteris who was the loser.

When Charteris stayed at the Crown Inn, Cambridgeshire, the landlord, Mr Gardner, had no doubts about who the real villain was. The Colonel attempted to rape the servant maid, and when she cried out for help, Gardener not only came to her rescue, but turned the Colonel, his entire company and servants out of the house, obliging them to travel three miles on dangerous country roads late at night to find lodgings.

The tradesmen of Lancashire also had good reason to distrust him. He once wrote to '...an eminent Oil-Man, for 20 Gallons of Rack, to be sent to *Hornby*...'[64] The oil was duly delivered but when a man came to collect the payment, the

---

[62] ibid

[63] *History*, p. 11

[64] *Authentick Memoirs*, p. 52

Colonel denied he had ever written for any oil. The letter was produced, but he denied it was his and claimed it was a forgery. This was another favourite trick he was to try once too often. The oil-man was obliged to take legal action and eventually recovered his money with costs.

The Colonel's notoriety was enough to strike terror in small children, who viewed him as a kind of bogeyman. It is not hard to imagine parents and nursemaids threatening children with the terrible Colonel if they misbehaved themselves. Alexander Carlyle of Inveresk, born in 1722, never forgot seeing the Colonel in church: '...when I was five or six years of age; and being fully impressed with the popular opinion that he was a wizard, who had a fascinating power, I never once took my eyes off him during the whole service, believing that I should be a dead man the moment I did.'[65]

Hornby Castle, '...which was peculiarly devoted to his Amours...',[66] became a notorious place during the Colonel's ownership. He ran it like his own personal brothel, '...under the Inspection of a venerable Matron, who ... kept an extraordinary Decorum, and administer'd to her Master's Pleasures with Consummate Applause...'[67] This lady was Mary (or Moll) Clapham, mistress of the maids, '...she had a certain Sallary for her Services, with an additional Allowance for Linen and other Necessaries made use of in the Business of *Love*: She was, it seems, an able and experienc'd Woman, in every Respect qualified for the important Trust. All the Affairs of the *seraglio* were under her Directions, and she would often defy the *Great Turk's* to be kept in better Order than her Master's.'[68]

---

[65] J.H. Burton (ed), *The Autobiography of Dr Alexander Carlyle of Inveresk, 1722-1805* (Bristol, Thoemmes Antiquarian Books, Ltd, 1990), p. 6
[66] *Scotch Gallantry*, p. 10
[67] ibid

47

The Colonel's most constant servant was Jack Gourlay, known as Trusty Jack, a man who served him with great energy and fidelity for many years, as footman, coachman, messenger and valet-de-chambre and could be relied upon to satisfy his master's every whim, whether it be committing perjury, signing false statements or procuring girls for his bed. Both for practical reasons and as a matter of personal taste, Charteris ignored '…the *sublime* part of the Fair-Sex, he has an easier Method of obtaining those of a *lower* Station…'[69] and he preferred tall, well-built women, who were able to withstand the onslaught of his brutish appetite. His agents were ordered to enlist '…none but such as were *strong, lusty, fresh Country Wenches, of the first Size, their B-tt-cks as hard as Cheshire Cheeses, that should make a Dint in a Wooden Chair, and work like a parish Engine at a Conflagration.*'[70]

On one occasion a procuress brought him a girl called Sarah Wilkins '…a comely Person, of good Features, a brown Complexion, and an admirable Length, being rather above six Foot (the Colonel's Standard) and about seventeen years of age.'[71] When he complained that she was too young, and '…seem'd not to have Strength or Substance enough to go through the Fatigue of his Business…', the matron at once fell into a violent temper and spoke to the Colonel in a way that he would have tolerated from few other professions. She had, she said, gone to a great deal of trouble and expense to bring the girl to him, and asked him to think again, or she would be obliged to offer her elsewhere, '…and few Gentlemen would care to make choice of what he had rejected; so that the

---

[68] *Authentick Memoirs*, p. 10
[69] ibid, pp. 9-10
[70] ibid, p. 10
[71] ibid, p. 15

Creature might lie on her Hands, and she, at long run be compelled to wagon her to London, and dispose of her to some Player or Barrister for a Song, and so make a hackney Harlot of her in a Week or Fortnight at farthest.'[72]

Relenting, the Colonel asked the girl to walk about the chamber, which she did, the old woman commenting throughout on her '…brisk and engaging Motions, together with many other shining Qualities and Perfections.'[73]

At length he ordered the girl '…to be scour'd and sent in that Evening…',[74] and was so pleased with her that he retained her services long enough for her to bear him three children, all of whom died young. She eventually shared the common fate of all his mistresses, and was dismissed without a thought to what eventual doom he cared nothing.

When he had set his mind upon a conquest he was very persistent, but his preference for large women may explain why on some occasions, despite his size and weight, he found it hard to overcome his victims. Having determined upon a '…very handsome tall Maid…' who lived with her grandmother less than three miles from Hornby Castle, he pursued her for six months. '…All his Engines had been at work without Effect, yet nothing could satisfy or divert him from the Chace.'[75] Eventually he was able to bribe one of the girl's relations to inveigle her away from her grandmother, and '…one *Sunday* in the Afternoon, she was brought in triumph, on Horseback, from her Parish Church…'between Trusty Jack and Moll Clapham. It was a very wet afternoon, so by the time the trio reached the castle, all were thoroughly soaked. The

---

[72] ibid, pp. 15-16

[73] ibid, p. 16

[74] ibid

[75] ibid, p. 12

Colonel ordered the gates to be opened, '…and the Joy he conceiv'd on her Arrival might be read in his Face.'[76] The girl was at once taken to the kitchen, where she was dried before the fire. This done, she was conducted to the butler's pantry for refreshments. The Colonel then called for her to be sent to his room. She had hardly been there six minutes when the '…House was in an Uproar with the most dreadful Shrieks that could be heard…'[77] The servants knew their places, and not one of them dared to enter the room until their master rang the bell. There they found that the girl had put up so strong a resistance that the Colonel, '…not being then able to overcome her … was under the necessity of adjourning his Passion to the time that she went to Bed.'[78]

The girl left the room in floods of tears, insisting she go home to her grandmother that night, but her captors would not allow her to leave. To ensure that she did not escape the Colonel ordered his servants to lock all the doors. It was probably not the first time and most certainly not the last that the Colonel, with the connivance of his servants, kept a woman prisoner in his home.

Moll Clapham took the unhappy girl to another room for the night, and tried to comfort her, saying she was sorry for what had happened but it was too late to think of going home. She reassured her reluctant guest that she would share her room that night and then early the next morning, before the Colonel rose, she would send her home to her grandmother. Soon after the two had gone to bed, the Colonel appeared, having entered the room by a trapdoor specially contrived for such an occasion. The girl screamed, and when Moll tried to abandon

---

[76] ibid, p. 13

[77] ibid

[78] ibid

her to her fate, she grabbed her supposed protector's shift and held on to her fast, begging her for God's sake not to leave her. But Moll knew her own business and that of her master too well to be moved by tears and entreaties. The Colonel leapt into the bed, while Moll Clapham stood beside it, telling the girl that she should reconcile herself to what was about to happen and ought to behave like a woman, '…for that she was at Years of Discretion, and not a silly raw Girl…',[79] and other similar inducements. At length her words had their effect, the victim surrendered to her fate, and Moll withdrew from the chamber, leaving the pair in bed together.

The next day the Colonels new mistress was up and about early, her tears of the previous night dried up. Her grandmother, having discovered where the missing girl was, came to the castle, but was refused admittance, and the Colonel continued to enjoy his new conquest without further hindrance. As the master's now willing favourite, the girl was well treated, given every luxurious comfort, and promises of fine gifts. Perhaps she was deluded into believing that she was his first and only choice, who would be kept in splendour for the rest of her days. Typically, however, her lover, having taken six months to satisfy his desires, tired of her in three weeks. Satiated, and with '…a new Amour presenting…',[80] he dispatched the girl to a neighbouring village where she was boarded at eighteen-pence a week. Here she was visited by her master's valet (presumably Trusty Jack), and was soon pregnant by him. What then became of her is unknown.

The Colonel was happy to share his sexual comforts with his visitors — at a price. Having met a gentleman of fortune at a gambling house, he hoped to draw him into his net, and

---

[79] ibid, p. 14
[80] ibid

invited him to dine at the castle. When dinner was over, the Colonel suggested a game of cards, which his visitor, perhaps seeing where matters were tending, refused, saying he wished to return home. The Colonel was prepared for this argument, and told his guest that he must stay to supper, since the stable doors were locked and he would not be able to get at his horses. Reluctantly, the gentleman agreed. The hospitality continued and '...the Glass going merrily about, the Colonel ply'd the Gentleman so warmly, that he was forced to take up his Quarters there that Night.'[81] Conducting his tipsy guest to a bedchamber, the Colonel retired. The gentleman undressed, but on drawing back the bed curtains, was astonished to find the bed already occupied by an attractive young woman. At first he thought he must have mistaken the room, then he recalled that the Colonel himself had shown him there. Knowing his host's character it was not hard to deduce that his bedfellow was '... design'd to compleat his Entertainment.'[82] Climbing into bed, he proceeded to take advantage of this unexpected bonus. His companion left him early the following morning but not before he made her a generous gift of five guineas. Impatient to be on his way, he was soon dressed and went downstairs. No one else seemed to be awake except a 'Dirty Wench who was scouring the Irons...,'[83] and he asked her the way to the stables. There was something familiar about the girl's voice, and he tried to get a glimpse of her face which she did her best to hide, but eventually he was able to see enough to satisfy himself that this was the young woman to whom he had not long given five guineas. Blushing, the girl admitted that he was right, and that he was not the first of the

---

[81] *Scotch Gallantry*, p. 8
[82] ibid
[83] ibid

Colonel's guests who she had entertained, and from whom she had received a gift '...but you don't know my Master,' she exclaimed.

'Not know your Master? What do you mean, Child?... I think if you can get five Guineas so easily, you need not clean irons.'

'Ah, Sir ... that's true, but I have only but half a Crown for my Part, and the Colonel has the rest.'[84]

When servants who had given long and faithful service reached an age when they were no longer able to continue their duties, it was the usual practice for a good master to reward their labours with a handsome gift to enable them to retire in comfort. Charteris had his own way of showing his appreciation. Mary Clapham, '...this industrious Wretch, notwithstanding all her Care and Fidelity, was basely rewarded by her ungrateful Master, who dismiss'd her at a Minute's Warning; and 'tis said, the poor Woman is now driven to the necessity of Bawding and Pimping for the Ensigns of the Guards, and that too for a very low Hire.'[85]

Charteris' Lordship of Hornby gave him an entrée into public life, and he became one of the Deputy-Lieutenants for the Duchy of Lancaster. One of his duties was to assist the Lieutenant in maintaining the county militia. He would have seen the role as an opportunity for advancement, a way to gather some glory to his name, and hopefully one day to add a title. What he was not anticipating was that he might be expected to lead an army into battle. In 1715 supporters of James Stuart, the Old Pretender attempted to restore him to the throne in what later became known as the First Jacobite Rising. From August that year armed men were massing in

---

[84] ibid, p. 9
[85] *Authentick Memoirs*, pp. 10-11

Scotland and the North of England, and in November they marched on Lancaster where they believed they would find new recruits.

As the forces approached Lancaster, Charteris and another officer proposed blowing up the bridge over the River Lune that led into the town, hoping to stop the troops entering. The townspeople refused. They pointed out that such an action would not hinder the invasion, since the river was passable by foot or horse at low water, and boats could easily be found. The main effect of destroying the bridge was that the town would have to pay for a replacement. Giving up on that plan, Charteris and his associate then found a large quantity of gunpowder in the possession of a merchant, and ordered that it should be thrown down the well in the market place to prevent it falling into enemy hands. The one tactic they do not seem to have considered in the defence of Lancaster was opposition by force of arms. When the Jacobite army arrived it marched into the town centre unhindered, and assembled in the market place where a trumpet was blown and the Pretender proclaimed. The troops were mainly billeted in the town, but a party of English soldiers led by Colonel Oxburgh took over Hornby Castle. Robert Patten, a Jacobite chaplain and eyewitness of the occupation of Lancaster reported that no harm was done to the Colonel's home and apart from the men helping themselves to wine and beer, nothing was taken. He added that had the Scots paid Charteris a visit instead, they would not have scrupled to set it on fire, '... so well is he respected by them; and that not on account of his Affection or Disaffection to the one side or other, but on Account of his own Personal Character, which is known not to have been very acceptable to those who are acquainted with him.'[86] Charteris

[86] R. Patten, *The History of the Late Rebellion* (London, J. Warner, 1717),

later sent Colonel Oxburgh a bill for £3 6s 8d, for provisions taken '...for man and horse...'[87] Oxburgh responded by sending a promissory note for the sum '...payable when his master's concerns should be settled...'[88]

The invaders moved on to Preston after two days, where they were surrounded by the King's forces and obliged to surrender. Charteris, loudly declaring himself to be on the side of the winners, claimed that the rebels had seized and carried off thirty of his horses, and demanded that he should be able to recompense his loss by taking thirty horses of his choice from those of the Jacobite army. The rebels said that they had not taken any of his horses, but it was impossible to prove he was a liar, and so the demand was indulged. It was later alleged that Charteris had offered his services to both sides, '...by which means he was judg'd so Insignificant, that neither would lay any stress upon him...',[89] and his offer was declined.

Some respectable people were willing to associate with him if they thought it was to their advantage. Many of them came to regret it. When the Colonel was travelling from Hornby Castle to visit his estates in Scotland, he was taken ill with a '...pleuritick fever'[90] (pleurisy) while staying at an inn in York. A clergyman of that city hearing of the Colonel's plight, invited him to stay at his house to recover his health before continuing his journey. He may have hoped that by ingratiating himself with a wealthy man who was the owner of many estates, he might secure a valuable living. The clergyman had young

---

pp. 90-1

[87] W.O. Roper, *Hornby Castle, Lancashire* (Liverpool, Thomas Brakell, 1890), p. 17

[88] ibid

[89] *Scotch Gallantry*, p. 16

[90] *Authentick Memoirs*, p. 35

daughters, but must have thought they were safe from the Colonel's usual attentions, firstly because his guest was unwell and also because there were so many other women in the household that there was no possibility of his having any opportunity alone with one of the girls. He clearly underestimated Francis Charteris, who recognised no obstacle in his pursuit of a sexual conquest. Within three days of his arrival he had struck up a bargain with the clergyman's second daughter '…for the *last favour*…',[91] the only question being where the two could meet undisturbed. It was the girl who found the answer, saying that she had a friend in the city who for a small consideration would allow them the use of an apartment in her house. The Colonel and the clergyman's daughter went to the house on Whit Sunday, and were in bed by three in the afternoon, a time when most people would have been in church. Everything was quiet, but by a quarter past three the entire street was in turmoil. The couple next door who ran a carpenter's shop had gone out, leaving their children behind, who, playing with wood shavings, managed to set the house on fire. The Colonel can hardly have achieved his desire when smoke and flames began to attack the room in which he lay. The conflagration spread so fast there was no time to dress and it was impossible to escape any way but by the window. The alarm was given and citizens poured out onto the streets to assist. Seeing that there were people trapped in the house, feather beds were hurriedly brought and laid on the ground. The Colonel and his new mistress, dressed only in their shifts, jumped for their lives to the great hilarity of the onlookers.

---

[91] ibid

The Discovery of the Intrigue gave great Diversion to the whole County, particularly to the Ladies: Not a Visit, not a Tea-table, but what rung of it for a Twelvemonth. Soon after, the late Counsellor *Hungerford* coming to *York* Assizes, the young Woman's father advised with him about the Affair; and asking his Opinion, *Whether an* action *would not lie against the* Colonel *for this Injury to his Daughter?* The Counsellor, who was well known to be a very facetious Gentleman, answered, *That he had better go home and take more care of the rest of his Children, for he believed his Daughter had had too much Action with the* Colonel *already.*[92]

While Francis Charteris was spending much of his time apart from his family, his daughter was growing into a young woman, and by 1720 had reached marriageable age. Janet Charteris seems to have shared her mother's opinion of her disreputable father. Thus, while the Colonel was investigating both the money and flesh-pots of London, or carousing with his personal whores in Lancashire, Janet stayed with her mother in Edinburgh. Her portrait shows a tall, slender, graceful girl, who had unfortunately inherited the long nose and fleshy mouth of her father, but, from all accounts, none of the unpleasant side of his personality.[93] She was also her father's only legitimate descendant, and in view of the coolness between her parents, this was likely to remain the case. Her marriage prospects were excellent, but she was potentially the target of fortune-hunters, from which the constant presence of a strong father might have protected her. Janet was young, pliable and romantic. Wooed by the eligible Earl of

[92] ibid, pp. 36-7

[93] The portrait of Janet Charteris is in private hands but a facsimile may be viewed by prior arrangement at the National Portrait Gallery of Scotland

Strathmore, she was also pursued by a poorer but more active rival who declared himself to be in love with her; James, Earl of Wemyss, a man who was to become a major figure in deciding the Colonel's eventual fate.

James Wemyss was born on 30 August 1699, and on 15 March 1720 succeeded his father as Earl of Wemyss. Sir Robert Douglas in his *Peerage of Scotland* writes glowingly of his character, as '...a man of great merit, universal benevolence and hospitality,'[94] while a family member, William Wemyss, praised James for 'His humanity and integrity, his affability and gentleness of temper, his veracity and fortitude of mind, his benevolence and compassion...'[95] The young Earl could certainly be charming if he wished, but the journals of his eldest son, David Lord Elcho, reveal that James' chief motivation was a pressing need for money. James, who was later to advise Elcho that if he wanted money he should seek out a wealthy wife, was a natural spendthrift and incapable of managing his finances, which were always in a muddle that caused great distress to his family and friends. Armed with his new earldom, he romanced Janet into agreeing to marry him, and easily obtained Helen's approval, but the Colonel was another matter. Francis Charteris both disliked and distrusted James Wemyss. The idea of a man known to be careless with money getting access to his strongly guarded fortune must have appalled him. He may also have known that James' father had had Jacobite leanings and suspected his son of the same views. Janet, he must surely have thought, could do a great deal

---

[94] Sir R. Douglas, 'The Peerage of Scotland' (Edinburgh, R. Fleming, 1764), p. 692.

[95] Sir W. Fraser, K.C.B. LL.D. *Memorials of the Family of Wemyss of Wemyss*, 3 vols. (Edinburgh, no publisher, 1888), vol. 1, *Memoirs*, p. 358

better. James, knowing that he had powerful rivals for Janet's hand, made plans to marry her secretly while her father was on one of his visits to London. When the Colonel did not leave Edinburgh on the appointed day, 17 September 1720, Janet still managed to sneak away. The wedding took place that evening, and was not discovered by the new Countess's parents until the following day. The wedding was later the subject of a saccharine ode by poet Allan Ramsay, and one must wonder if there was a touch of sarcasm in his reference to 'The beauteous CHARTERISSA...'[96] and the 'Thrice happy parents...'[97]

It was not a happy marriage, but it was held together by the Earl's hope of money to come. In August 1721 Janet gave birth to a son, David, later Lord Elcho, but it was the second son, born on 21 October 1723 and baptised Francis, who became the Colonel's especial favourite, and for whom in due course he made a substantial provision in his will. Another son, James, and four daughters were to follow.

When, in February 1730 the Colonel was brought before the Old Bailey charged with rape, one of the things that must have occupied the minds of the jury was whether he had been guilty of earlier rapes for which he had never been punished. The incidents of 1701, although the subject of official records, had faded from memory and never entered the London rumour-mill. One story of which the jurors cannot have been ignorant was the tale of the miller's wife of Musselborough, which appears in *Scotch Gallantry*, *Authentick Memoirs* and the *History*.

---

[96] A. Ramsay, 'An Ode with a Pastoral Recitative, on the marriage of the Right Honourable James Earl of Wemyss and Mrs Janet Charteris', in *Poems by Allan Ramsay* (2 vols, London, J. Clarke, 1731), vol 2, p. 84

[97] ibid, p. 86

The story goes that while travelling south from Edinburgh Charteris encountered the woman, '...a jolly likely Dame, and of the Colonel's size (for he lov'd Strappers)...',[98] carrying a sack of corn from the mill to one of her husband's best customers. Aroused by the sight of such a strong young woman, and having had no sexual encounters for a week past, he determined to have her. Ordering his servants to go ahead with the baggage to an inn, he said he would join them later. The Colonel alighted from his horse, and drawing the woman into an innocent conversation, soon made his desires known. Words alone did not sway her, so he offered her a purse of gold. When she continued to refuse, he drew out his pistol, pointed it at her head and swore that 'if she did not immediately lay down her Sack, and afterwards lie down upon it herself, he would end her Days upon the Spot...'[99] It was half a mile from any house, and no help was at hand, so the lady, '...since she must suffer by one of the Colonel's Weapons, chose to take that which she thought would not prove Mortal.'[100] When she returned home, she told her husband of the encounter, and he at once went to Edinburgh and swore a complaint. By then the Colonel was back in England, and so he was found guilty of rape in his absence, at a Scottish court, and formally condemned. Back in London, and unable ever to return to his native land, for fear of execution, Charteris complained to '... many Great Men...'[101] of '...this inhuman and vile Treatment by his own Countrymen; saying, *She was the most D—d faw* [gypsy] *dirty piece of Fornication he ever met with in his Life*, and that *it was the Deel of a Hardship to be*

---

[98] *History*, p. 35
[99] *Scotch Gallantry*, p. 21
[100] ibid
[101] *Authentick Memoirs*, p. 38

brought under such a Dilemma *for it.*'[102] He pestered all his friends to make an intercession for him for a pardon, but '...they all rather banter'd than pitied him. One Great man advis'd him to go down and reverse the Attainder, by his personal Appearance, and take a fair Trial for it. *No, Deel d—n me, Mon,* cries the Colonel, *if I do.* But said, *If he once had his Pardon in his pocket, he'd gang down among the rascals, and shew his A—se at the very Cross of* Edinburgh.'[103]

The story concludes by stating that King George I '...having the Case represented to him in a favourable Light, thought fit to grant him His Most Gracious Pardon...'[104] This was presented to the Colonel on New Year's day 1722 (25 March under the Julian Calendar then used in Britain), and was said by him to be the most welcome New Year's gift he had ever received. He spent a fortnight thanking all his friends, '...to some of whom he promised an Amendment of his Life; and to others, less soberly, *That he would be reveng'd of all the Bitches in* Great-Britain *for it.*'[105] So the story goes, and while no documentary proof of it has come to light, it is very probably a garbled version of an incident for which there is.

On 2 January 1722 Charteris was on the highway near Dunwoody Green in Annandale, Dumfriesshire, on his way back to England, probably after a visit to his cousins at Amisfield, when he encountered Janet Watson, wife of James Carruthers. (It was customary in Scotland for married women to be referred to by their maiden surname). She was not carrying a sack of corn, for though Carruthers was a miller, he was a 'walker' employed at a fulling mill in Wamphray which

---

[102] ibid, pp. 38-9

[103] ibid, p. 9

[104] *Scotch Gallantry*, p. 21

[105] *Authentick Memoirs*, p. 39

processed cloth. What preliminaries there were, if any, are not reported, although it is likely that the Colonel as was his usual practice, tried first to overcome her by persuasion and bribery, and was refused. What is known is that Charteris violently seized the woman, and despite her struggles and cries for help, dragged her some distance from the roadway into the cover of the broom. As she lay dazed upon the ground he threw up her clothes, pulled down his breeches, and committed a savage rape, oblivious to her screams and struggles. By the time the crime had been reported, and an investigation commenced, he was back in England, and as a result there was a considerable delay in resolving the enquiries. The matter was eventually placed before the public prosecutor, Robert Dundas, His Majesty's Advocate, who published a list of six witnesses, and on 14 December, issued a summons for Charteris to appear at the Tollbooth Criminal Court Edinburgh to answer the charge, which the Colonel ignored. For reasons which were never made clear, Dundas withdrew consent to the prosecution, but James Carruthers refused to accept this situation. He petitioned the King, complaining that the Colonel '…in the most violent and barbarous manner that can be imagined committed a rape upon [Janet Watson] notwithstanding all the struggle she could make and Cryes she could utter.'[106] The Colonel's methods of escaping punishment must have been well known for Carruthers anticipated them '…your humble petitioner apprehends the said Colonel Francis Charteris may upon a misrepresentation of the state of this atrocious fact apply to your majestie for a pardon in order to cover himself from Justice and to evade the punishment that so high a crime deserves.'[107] He begged the King not to grant a pardon but to

---

[106] Public Record Office, Petition of James Carruthers SP35/34/151
[107] ibid

issue an order to apprehend the Colonel and have him brought back to Edinburgh to stand trial. When this was unsuccessful, Carruthers was able to raise enough money to bring a private action for damages, which was heard on 4 April 1723. It is not clear whether Charteris was present at this hearing. Strong objections were raised on his behalf, in particular the delay in bringing the action, the fact that the action was not taken until Carruthers received money, and the withdrawal of the public prosecutor, but these were brushed aside. Charteris' counsel then introduced a new argument, one that would be used again in 1730 when the Colonel was charged with raping Anne Bond, that he could not have committed the crime as he was physically incapable:

> …He had not, and could not, have committed a rape on the prosecutor's wife; for she was a strong young woman, he an infirm unwieldy man, who had had the misfortune to break his leg long ago, which had rendered him lame, as must be very obvious to every person that looks at him; besides, when he met this woman he was in his boots and great coat.[108]

He also claimed that the prosecution was '…instigated by his enemies, who had bribed this prosecutor…'[109]

There was, however, good evidence that the rape had taken place, since the spot to which Charteris had dragged his victim was not as isolated as he had supposed. Apart from Janet there were five witnesses, George Hamilton, a merchant, Samuel Greensheils, a 'farmourer's son', Thomas Lambert servant to

---

[108] 'Carruthers v Charteris' in J.M. Lord Dreghorn, *Arguments and Decisions in Remarkable Cases Before the High Court of Judiciary and Other Supreme Courts in Scotland* (Edinburgh, printed for J. Bell and E.&C. Dilly, London 1774), pp. 67-8
[109] ibid p. 68

the Earl of Hopetoun, Robert Lockie, servant to the Laird of Munchies, and Lockie's wife, Margaret, who had seen and heard the encounter. Charteris' counsel tried to explain this away:

> Crying and resisting is natural to the sex when willing; and no man would be safe if these were sufficient to infer a rape.[110]

The court did infer a rape. 'In this case she struggled to the last, and that is clearly sufficient.'[111] The case was referred to the assize court where it was heard on 12 November, and after examining the witnesses found it proven 'by plurality of voices...' that the defendant was '...seen lying above Janet Watson, the complainer's wife...' and '...while they were on the ground together, the said Janet Watson was heard to cry out.'[112] Six days later the court awarded damages of £300 and ordered that Charteris be imprisoned until he made payment. From then on, there seems to have been a fixed idea in the Colonel's head that £300 was the going rate for a rape.

Charteris was spending increasing amounts of his time in London where he lodged with a gentleman in Poland Street, in elegant St James' Parish Westminster. Money and panache could take him anywhere, and he slipped easily into fashionable society which revolved around the royal court, parliament and the great houses of the aristocracy. As early as 1714, Erasmus Lewis, MP and Secretary of State, writing to Jonathan Swift, named the Colonel as a runner employed to spread evil reports about the Earl of Oxford by his political enemies.

---

[110] ibid p. 70
[111] ibid
[112] ibid

It was not long before he had established a reputation in London for debauchery and quarrelling. Accused of fathering two illegitimate children, in one case he was able to escape the consequences, but in the other, the woman was cook to a nobleman who helped her obtain a warrant from a justice. When a constable arrived to serve the warrant, the Colonel, seeing the man was armed only with a stick, drew his sword and took a cut at him. The constable, who had probably dealt with rougher brutes in his time, easily avoided the cut, '...knock'd him down with his short Staff, and after breaking his Head very handsomely, to the Colonel's great Terror, overpowered him with his *Posse of Myrmidons*, as the Butchers do a mad Ox, and led him in Triumph before the Justice, who made him, before he got loose, pay a good Composition for his unlawful Embraces...'[113] It was the kind of minor event which the Colonel had long learned to shrug off without a thought.

In 1716 Charteris quarrelled with an army Major at the gaining table. Satisfaction was demanded, and in the heat of the moment, they agreed to fight a duel in Marylebone Fields. Once there, the cold light of day revealed unwillingness on both sides to proceed, and much time was wasted arguing about the ground and the method of combat and who had the sun in his eyes, before either was prepared to admit that he didn't want to fight. Ultimately, to save what honour they thought they had left, it was agreed that the fiasco would be resolved by each giving the other a slight wound. The next argument was about who would go first, which went on at such length, that at last, the Colonel, making to draw his sword, boldly declared that it was well known he was a man of honour and if the other would not trust his word, he was

---

[113] *History*, p. 22

prepared to take his chances on the duel. It was far from being a courageous act, since he well knew that in the heat of a quarrel the act of offering to draw his sword would usually escalate matters to the point where the other man would back down. As calculated, this bombast induced the Major to agree to submit first, and trustingly offered his sword arm for a cut, whereupon the Colonel delivered a deep and vicious gash. The pain was so violent that it was some time before the Major was able to speak, when, complaining bitterly, he demanded to know where his opponent would agree to be wounded. 'Nowhere, by God!' exclaimed the Colonel, and told the Major he might go and tell of his ill-treatment if he dared, since it would involve them both in equal disgrace.[114] He had judged the man right, as the Major was too ashamed of the escapade to relate the story. Not so the Colonel who dined the same day at the King's Arms in Pall Mall and boasted to the noblemen present that he had fought with and disarmed the Major, and generously granted him his life. Nevertheless, rumour spread the contrary story, and the Colonel's reputation being well-known, it was generally believed that the men had agreed to settle the matter with slight wounds, '…to save what neither of them had — *their Reputations.*'[115]

While a man may enjoy notoriety it can become a burden, and in Scotland and Lancashire the kind of ill-repute that attached itself to the Colonel, especially where it involved money, had become a hindrance to his way of life. Even on those rare occasions when he performed an unselfish act, his detractors naturally looked for a deeper motive. In 1725 there was a fire in the Lawnmarket, Edinburgh, and Charteris was the only private individual to subscribe to a fund for the relief

---

[114] *Authentick Memoirs*, p. 29
[115] *Scotch Gallantry*, p. 14

of the victims. The amount was four guineas, and Edinburgh historian Robert Chambers observed 'Uncharitable onlookers would probably consider this as intended for an insurance against another fire on the part of the subscriber.'[116]

By 1725 the Colonel had decided to move his main sphere of action permanently to London, and purchased a house in fashionable Bond Street, described in a contemporary survey as '...one of the longest and best built Streets in Town.'[117] Located on the east side of the street his new residence was seven houses and two stable yards north of the corner of Bond Street and Maddox Street, a stone's throw from the homes of the gilded nobility in George Street and Hanover Square.[118] There, he felt poised to take full advantage of everything London had to offer.

---

[116] J. Grant (ed), *Cassell's Old and New Edinburgh* (3 vols, London, Cassell & Co., 1884-1870), vol. 3, p. 366

[117] J. Mottley, *A Survey of the City of London and Westminster* (2 vols, London, J. Read, 1733-5), vol. 2, p. 666

[118] Westminster Archives, St George Hanover Square Rate books, Conduit St Ward, C1-8/433

III: THE MOST NOTORIOUS BLASTED RASCAL IN THE WORLD[119]

The polar extremes of London society in the eighteenth century were the well-born and landed gentry, often referred to as the Quality; and the poor, who lived a short, violent and hand-to-mouth existence, and were known as the Mob. The Mob hated the Quality, yet aspired to be like them, aping their manners and wearing their cast-offs several times removed. The Quality despised the Mob, fearing its anarchic lawlessness and only appreciated its members when they provided a brief moment of theatre at Tyburn. These distinct groupings had one thing in common, the passionate pursuit of pleasure. Gentlemen of the Quality gathered at the tables of gambling clubs, fought duels, kept expensive mistresses, drank the best wines in abundance, and disported themselves at whorehouses where any taste could be accommodated at a price. Men of the Mob gambled in the streets and at fairs, pimped for their mistresses, drank whatever they could, thieved for a living, and rarely went out of doors without getting involved in a fight. Sandwiched uncomfortably between these diverse yet similar classes were the honest tradesmen, artisans, scholars and professional men, who tried to live quiet lives, and largely turned a blind eye to the criminal and immoral behaviour of both the Quality and the Mob.

---

[119] B. Dobrée (ed), *The Letters of Phillip Dormer Stanhope 4th Earl of Chesterfield* (6 vols, 1932, London, Eyre & Spottiswoode Limited), Vol. 4, letter 1684, p. 1484

The second driving force of London society was money. In the commercial heart of the city swarmed increasing numbers of jobbers, brokers and speculators, greedy for quick and easy profits, while the prospect of fortunes to be won was attracting the once aloof aristocracy into dabbling on the stock exchange. A greedy man can be a fool with his money, and the Colonel knew how to seek out such fools and take advantage of them.

The third great stimulus of London society was news. The town was constantly buzzing with the latest and most intimate tales of popular and unpopular celebrities. Rumour — faster than a letter or newspaper, unregulated by any censor, untraceable to its source, a medium devoid of any notion of decency and restraint — only rumour had the speed, piquancy, and freshness to feed the impatient hunger for satire and scandal. Its hubs and clearing houses were the popular meeting places of the city — taverns, theatres, coffee houses, parks, the street — while behind elegant facades, gossip crackled like lightening over the tinkling teacups and in the sweat and steam of kitchens. If the story became embellished in the telling and re-telling, if speculation and spiteful invention were transmuted into 'fact' then so much the better, as the final product was a thousand times more amusing than reality.

Every day, the collectors of news were '...running among Clerks to Justices, Turnkeys of Prisons, Coachmen to Physicians, footmen to Quality, Servants to Undertakers, Writers to Ship-Brokers, Waiters at the *Court* and *Royal-Exchange* Coffee-Houses, Porters to the Lord-Mayor, and private Acquaintances, for Intelligence...',[120] then repaired to taverns the same evening to write up their copy before taking it to the printers. The contents of these newspapers were the

---

[120] Anon, *Low-Life or One Half of the World Knows not how the Other Half Live* (London, printed for the author, undated *c.* 1753), p. 85

subject of lively debate wherever people gathered, and the Colonel, it soon appeared, was not so much a consumer of news, as a fount of the kind of sensational stories of which the public never tired.

The intimate affairs and private correspondence of the Quality were under the constant scrutiny of their servants, who delighted in passing on the latest scandal.

> The Quality, who fly about with their sumptuous Equipages, imagine themselves to be the Admiration of the Vulgar Sort, On the contrary, they are the only Objects of their Ridicule, as they being too well acquainted with their most private Affairs. Many of the Quality falsely judging themselves secure, in their most secret Vices, from the seeming Ignorance of those about 'em; for it is notorious, that a louring, awkwardly Fellow, with a *West Country* Countenance, whom no Body would suspect no more than the Devil, shall be able to carry off the whole Conversation of a Tea-table, and report it *Verbatim* to half the Ale Houses in Town. A Man of Quality's Letter to a *Matron* upon the subject of broaching a Girl, or to his *Mistress*, are frequently expos'd to a Third of the Parish, before they reach Directions…[121]

By contrast, the Colonel's trusty coterie of servants showed extraordinary loyalty to their master, and actively connived in his debaucheries. There was a bonus for anyone able to bring him a fresh, handsome and innocent wench.

London gossip linked the Colonel's name with that of others noted for their depravity, and to attack someone's character it was enough just to say that he or she had dined with Charteris. The only woman ever known to have been passionately

---

[121] Anon, *A View of London and Westminster, or, the Town Spy* (London, T. Warner, 1728), pp. 5-6

devoted to him was Sally Salisbury. Born around 1690 she was beautiful, witty and vivacious, but with a rebellious and termagant spirit. She had sold fruit and vegetables in Covent Garden before being noticed and taken up by one of the procuresses of the district then famous for its brothels and bath-houses. A game girl, one of her tricks when entertaining three gallants at once was to stand on her head naked, her legs apart, supported by two of the gentlemen while the third tossed gold coins at her nether money-box. All she could catch she could keep. Her slender build was not to the Colonel's taste, but she was drawn to his easy charm and pursued him, making sure to be in all the public places he frequented, where to her frustration she saw him surrounded by her rivals. Eventually, however her persistence paid off, and winning him over, she became his mistress, or at least, one of them. In Sally, Charteris found a woman who could match him for drinking, gambling, foul language and playing cruel tricks on others, so their association lasted longer than most, but at length like all his bedfellows, she was dismissed. In December 1722 Sally's temper got the better of her and she stabbed a man during an argument. Tried the following April, she was sentenced to a year in Newgate prison, but died there in February 1724.

Charteris was reputed to be a regular companion of Phillip Duke of Wharton, from whom he is known to have purchased an estate. Wharton, born in 1698, was in many ways the antithesis of Charteris, since he started life with every advantage — handsome, intelligent, charismatic, witty, heir to both a fortune and a title — and then proceeded to throw it all away. A libertine, heavy gambler and drinker, he was possibly the only man to be both a Grand Master of the Freemasons and president of the notorious Hellfire Club simultaneously. When his infant son died of smallpox — a tragedy for which he blamed his wife as she had brought the child to London during an outbreak — his rage and grief were such that all sense of control was abandoned and he plunged into every kind of excess, destroying his health and dissipating his fortune. Charteris was no doubt on hand to drink his wine and help him lose his money. Wharton spent the years between 1718 and 1725 in London, where one of his diversions was to go out on drinking sprees with his friends, and roam the streets at night banging on people's doors to wake them up. Whether Charteris limped along with this youthful rabble is unknown but it doesn't seem like his style. Charteris may have joined Wharton at the taverns where the Hellfire Club met. There, members drank, swore, ordered a dish called Holy Ghost pie, gambled on a Sunday, derided religion, and thought themselves very daring. Wharton was eventually outlawed by the Government for his support of the Old Pretender, and died in Spain, destitute, in 1731.

The procuress and brothel keeper Elizabeth Needham was said to be another of the Colonel's associates. She had started her professional life as an orange seller, but became a prostitute at the age of fourteen. Even at such an early age, she had a sound head for finance. '…Contrary to the common Practice of Whores, she saved a good deal of Money, so that before she was turn'd off, she had an abundance of fine Clothes, and a House well furnish'd; by the means of which she became a Procurer, and used to assist others when She was herself past the Game.'[122]

Needham's method of luring unsuspecting virgins into prostitution is immortalised in plate 1 of Hogarth's series of engravings 'The Harlot's Progress'. A wagon carrying virtuous

---

[122] Anon, *Mother Needham's Elegy* (London, publisher unknown, *c.* 1730)

young girls looking for suitable employment has just arrived in London from York, drawing up outside the Bell Tavern, in Wood Street, Cheapside, and a clergyman has come to offer them what appear to be religious tracts. He is oblivious both to the corruption happening behind his back or to the fact that his horse has knocked over some pots, a metaphor perhaps for broken maidenheads. One of the girls, the subject of the later plates in the series, has descended from the wagon and has been met by Mother Needham, who caresses the face of her prey appreciatively. Nearby, on the steps of the tavern, under the sign of the Bell leers a middle-aged rake. With one hand he leans on a walking-stick, but the other is thrust suggestively into his clothing. By his side, fawns a servant. These figures are Francis Charteris and 'Trusty' Jack Gourlay. Below Charteris in the picture is a basket from which lolls the neck of a dead goose, a symbol, perhaps of his declining virility.

According to the anonymous author of *Mother Needham's Elegy*, 'If we may credit Fame, she has helped Col. Ch—s to above 100 Country Maidenheads which she picked up at the Carriers... Her way of Life was to delude young Women, and decoy young men, of both which she has ruin'd some hundreds, by Usury, Bribes and Corruption...'.[123]The Colonel is unlikely to have paid good money for virgins when he could hire them for nothing, but it is easy to imagine him and Mother Needham swapping stories over a bottle or two of burgundy, while striking a deal for the procuress to take some of his tearful cast-offs.

Thomas Woolston was a theologian whose writings challenged the literal interpretation of the Scriptures, arousing the fury and derision of the Church. It was said that he had dined with Charteris and at his host's request brought along

---

[123] *Mother Needham's Elegy*

copies of his recently published *Discourses on the Miracles*. After dinner, the Colonel offering his guest a woman, was told that. His '…Inclinations lay quite another Way…'[124] Woolston later angrily denied that this unlikely meeting ever took place, and it seems probable that his opponents spread the story to damage his reputation.

The Colonels most powerful friend, said to have benefited from his generosity with the favours of female servants, was leading Whig politician Robert Walpole, who for much of his career was, in essence although not in name, Prime Minister of Great Britain. The minister enjoyed company, drink and women, often shocked friends with a coarseness of language they thought unfitting for a man in his position, and was no stranger to the art of bribery. 'He was the first minister that taught corruption systematically,' observed Lord Chesterfield. '…He maintained that every man was venal, and had his price…'[125] One of Walpole's most strident critics, William Pulteney, accused him of '…The Profusion of the publick Treasure on a worthless Crew of *Pimps*, *Spies*, *Projectors* and *abandon'd Scribblers*, for thy own secret Service …',[126] and Charteris was undoubtedly one of Walpole's crew.

Walpole's friends and family strongly disapproved of the association. Laurence Charteris (probably a cousin and son of

---

[124] *Authentick Memoirs*, p. 45

[125] P.D. Stanhope, P.D, 4th Earl of Chesterfield, *The Characters of George the First, Queen Caroline, Sir Robert Walpole, Mr. Pulteney, Lord Hardwicke, Mr. Fox, and Mr. Pitt, Reviewed* (T. Davies and T. Cadell. London, 1777), pp. 18-19

[126] W. Pulteney, An Answer to One Part of a late Infamous Libel, Intitled, Remarks on the Craftsman's Vindication of his two honourable Patrons; in which the Character and Conduct of Mr. P. is fully Vindicated (London, R. Francklin, 1731), p. 36

the Laurence who was present at Francis' baptism) wrote in 1723: 'H.W. [Horatio Walpole, younger brother of Robert and Laurence's patron] and all the friends of the family are extremely angry att his having so much of R. W. countenance: But notwithstanding all the affronts and Rubbs he gives, he will be there every day when in towne.'[127]

In 1730 Swift referred to Charteris as '...that continuall favourite of Ministers.'[128] In his poem *On the Death of Dr Swift*, written in 1731, Swift satirises the reactions to his own death and places the Colonel in the thick of the social scene:

Now Chartres at Sir Robert's levee,
Tells with a sneer the tidings heavy.[129]

He himself:

Despised the fools with stars and garters,
So often seen caressing Chartres.[130]

The editor adds in a footnote:

Chartres is a most infamous vile scoundrel... He had a way of insinuating himself into all ministers, under every change, either as pimp, flatterer, or informer.[131]

---

[127] National Archives of Scotland, papers of Clerk of Penicuik, GD18/5245/4 letter 11, 26 November 1723

[128] H. Williams (ed), *The Correspondence of Jonathan Swift* (5 vols) (Oxford, The Clarendon Press, 1963), vol. 3, p. 405

[129] 'On The Death of Dr Swift', in W.E. Browning (ed), *The Poems of Jonathan Swift, D.D.* (2 vols, London, G. Bell and Sons, Ltd., 1910), vol. 1, pp. 252-3

[130] ibid, vol 1, p. 258

[131] ibid, vol 1, p. 252 fn 4

It was public knowledge that Walpole used his influence to get his friends out of scrapes. A letter to Duncan Forbes from an unknown correspondent in 1726 gives an account of one of the Colonel's more puerile quarrels, in which Walpole became personally involved. It occurred at Whites gaming club, and was between Charteris and 'Churchill' — probably Charles Churchill — loyal friend and aide to Walpole. The Colonel tried his old trick of putting his hand to his sword, but Churchill was not cowed, and the two men had to be physically parted by their friends. Hearing of the incident, Walpole went to the Colonel's house and had him arrested, and gave orders for Churchill to be confined. Eventually the two men were brought to Walpole's house in Chelsea, where not without some difficulty the quarrel was settled with grudging amity.[132] Charteris, who could never leave well alone, took Churchill to court over the matter in the following year and lost.

Following the Colonel's trial in 1730, many stories were circulated about his seduction and rape of maidservants. According to *Scotch Gallantry*, a pretty young girl, newly arrived at the Swan Tavern near Holborn Bridge, was offered the position of chambermaid for £5 a year. The new maid was '…wonderfully pleased with the fine Appearance and glittering Furniture of her Master's House.'[133] Her employer questioned her kindly, and gave her half a guinea, which he said was not an advance on wages, but a gift to encourage her. If she proved to be a good girl, he promised he would raise her wages accordingly. The next morning he called her to him, and instead of issuing instructions as to her work, began to praise her appearance, and even made to feel her breasts, saying that

---

[132] D. Warrand (ed) *More Culloden Papers* (5 vols, Inverness, Robert Carruthers and Sons, 1927), vol 3, p. 5

[133] *Scotch Gallantry*, p. 26

it was a pity such a comely young woman should undertake the drudgery of housework — she was made for something better — not a servile place, but the post of housekeeper.

The servant who had procured the girl completed the process by saying that her master was a generous man, and if she would only humour him her place might be worth as much as £50 a year. '…and I don't doubt but you may ride in your Chariot [an elegant lightweight closed carriage] before you dye…'[134] The girl was thus an easy conquest, and in due course gave birth to one of the Colonel's numerous illegitimate offspring.

Sometimes the Colonel liked to scout his game himself. More than one biographer reported that Trusty Jack drove him around town in his chariot from which he could survey the street for women who pleased his fancy, and take immediate action to assuage his lust. On one such occasion, passing through St Alban's Street Charteris saw '…a masculine young Woman…'[135] — from this description presumably tall and strong — selling old clothes. He at once signalled Trusty Jack to stop and ordered him to pursue the woman and decoy her into a public house on the pretext of having some suits to sell. With this ruse Jack brought the woman to the Scotch Arms Alehouse in nearby Pall Mall, and told her that if she waited there he would send a valet who had a great many of his master's suits to sell. He then ran back to the Colonel and advised him of what he had done. Soon afterwards, Charteris entered the house via the back door in Little Warwick Street, and pretending to be a valet suggested that he and the woman retire to a private room where the clothes would be brought for her to view. It was not long before his real intentions were

---

[134] ibid, p. 28
[135] *Authentick Memoirs*, p. 17

made plain, but having chosen a sturdy woman found that she was not easy to overcome, and he was obliged to threaten her with his sword. Her cries of 'Help, Help, Murder, Murder'[136] aroused the whole house and the landlord rushed into the room, '...where he found the Colonel with more Weapons than one drawn, and the Woman almost spent in defending herself...' The Colonel's only comment was that '...if he had thought she had been such a virtuous Bitch, the Deel should have taken her before he would have given himself so much trouble to so little purpose.'[137] Once again he had made the mistake of assaulting a married woman. Her husband visited him and the Colonel '...very handsomely asked his Pardon for the Mistake, saying *It was his known Resolution never knowingly to meddle with Wives, or common Prostitutes, for that he had ever been averse to* Salivations [treatment for venereal disease] *and* Criminal Conversations [adultery conferring a right on the husband to sue for damages]. This generous Declaration, with a Purse of Twenty Guineas, made an amicable End of the Matter.'[138]

There are several stories in which the Colonel committed or attempted rape at pistol point. *Don Francisco* with unusual precision, which suggests some foundation in fact, reports a deposition made by a country girl, Sarah Selleto, on 15 April 1725 before Justice Ellis. Procured by one of the Colonel's servants to work as a maid, she resisted both his bribes and his advances until he told her plainly that he must lie with her, adding the tempting promise '...there is no Woman that I debauch, but I make a handsome Provision for them afterwards.'[139] He then threw her on the bed, and when she

---

136 *Scotch Gallantry*, p. 19

137 *Authentick Memoirs*, pp. 17-18

138 ibid, p. 18

139 *Don Francisco*

continued to resist, he put a pistol to her breast and threatened to shoot her if she did not instantly submit. When she pleaded with him to delay carrying out his design until the following day, he gave orders that she was to be locked in her room overnight, and next morning arrived with the pistol, and terrorised her into compliance. She remained a prisoner for several days, but when freed, having nowhere to go, she stayed in the house, where her new lover provided her with money and clothes. In due course she found herself to be pregnant and he promised to take care of her, but when it drew near to her time, he picked a quarrel with her and turned her out of doors. As a result of her complaint he was ordered to maintain the child.

The Colonel's biographers loved stories where his vile intentions were thwarted, one of the best being the tale of the parson's daughter. This '…bouncing Country Wench…'[140] had resolved to be maidservant only to respectable women, and was hired on the pretence that she was to wait upon his lady. No sooner was the girl in his house than he ordered her upstairs to his chamber, threw her upon a couch, pulled up her clothes, '…and without any ceremony, was going to gratify his vicious Inclinations…'[141] (In another account, probably embellished, the maid discovers the Colonel in bed, wearing a suit of women's night-clothes, like the wolf in Red-Riding-Hood.) She fought him so strongly that he resorted to the pistol which he held to her breast, saying '…with the most bitter Execrations…'[142] that he would kill her if she did not consent. Thinking quickly, she pacified her attacker by agreeing

[139] *Don Francisco*, p. 50
[140] *Authentick Memoirs*, p. 24
[141] *Scotch Gallantry*, p. 22
[142] *History*, p. 37

to submit, but added with some dignity that she would not lose her maidenhead except between a pair of sheets. Reproaching him for taking up arms against a weak woman, she urged him to lay his weapon aside and use a manlier one. With only one thought on his mind, the Colonel put down the pistol, undressed as quickly as he could, and got into bed, but instead of his new conquest following as he expected, the girl snatched up the pistol and swore by all that was sacred she would send him to the Devil if he dared to move. She rang the bell, and when '…the Servant, who was Confident of all his Villainies…'[143] appeared, she clapped the pistol to his chest and said that if he did not go down stairs before her and let her out by the street door, she would instantly dispatch him. Parson's daughter she may have been, but she obviously meant business with the pistol, and was able to make her escape. The Colonel is said to have lamented this event as one of his greatest losses, saying 'A Woman that had such a large Share of Courage when on her Heels, must have a vast deal more when between a Pair of Sheets.'[144]

Although not a frequenter of whorehouses, the Colonel was a regular visitor to fashionable gambling clubs, notably White's Chocolate House in St James' Street, where he made useful contacts, chiefly wealthy individuals whom he could fleece at gaming, or with whom he could do business. His meanness became legendary. 'This colonel is one of the greatest and most known rogues in England,' wrote Viscount Percival, 'and by his villainies had amassed an incredible estate. His practice was to owe abundance of mean debts and never pay any till arrested and forced by law, and being asked why he would act so meanly and suffer so much trouble for trifles, he answered

---

[143] ibid, p. 38
[144] *Authentick Memoirs*, p. 25

that for one who arrested, there were twenty that did not, and so he was a gainer.'[145]

The Colonel was always looking for ways to add to his fortune, and the great commercial maelstrom of London, seething with a lust for gain that must have warmed his avaricious heart, was alive with possibilities. On 27 March 1720 he was at court where he chanced to meet Sir James Carmichael, Second Earl of Hyndford. Their conversation naturally turned to the burning topic of the day, the South Sea Company, which had been formed in 1711 chiefly as a vehicle for the funding of government debt.

In 1719 the company, with £12 million of public debt already on its books, proposed a new and audacious scheme to purchase a further £31 million. Robert Walpole supported a competing offer from the Bank of England, but the company responded by raising its bid and sweetening the deal with handsome bribes. In 1720 Parliament approved the South Sea Company's scheme. There was feverish excitement on the Stock Exchange, and the shares, which had been £130 a hundred, rose rapidly in value. By the time Hyndford and Charteris met the price was £320. Charteris owned a substantial block of South Sea Company shares, although exactly how many and what he paid for them is unknown. Hyndford, short of ready money, but eager to buy 5,000 of Charteris' shares, suggested that he be allowed to defer payment for a year. Charteris agreed, but at a price. There was a little gentlemanly haggling. Charteris wanted £420 a hundred, Hyndford countered with £400, and the deal was done at £410.

---

[145] Viscount Percival, *Manuscripts of the Earl of Egmont. Diary of Viscount Percival afterwards First Earl of Egmont*, vol. 1,1730-1733 (London HMSO, 1920), p. 75

In return for the shares, Charteris received a bond for £20,500 over Hyndford's estates and those of Sir John Anstruther, his guarantor, payable in one year. All through the summer, stocks rose in a frenzy of speculation, with Charteris no doubt kicking himself as he saw the price of a hundred shares peak at £1,000. Hyndford, a sad victim of the mass delusion, used the inflated value of his shares as security to borrow nearly £27,000 from the South Sea Company, probably to purchase more shares. By August, however, confidence was evaporating, and shareholders began to sell. The value of the stock declined rapidly and by the end of September a hundred shares were selling for £150. It was the first huge speculation in which the aristocracy had joined the hysteria, and many were ruined. They were very angry, they wanted revenge, and saw it as Walpole's job to take action against the promoters. Walpole, preferring calm to chaos, ignored the clamour for a public enquiry and set about restoring financial stability. He was widely reviled for screening the culprits from retribution, and became known as 'the Skreen-master General' (a pastiche on his office of Pay-master General of the armed forces), a nickname he was never able to shake off. Later, the association of Charteris and Walpole in the public mind led to this form of words being adapted to create the Colonel's famous nickname.

Hyndford, unable to pay the bond, tried to void the agreement, on the grounds that the excessive charge amounted to usury, as it was then illegal to charge more than 5 per cent interest a year. The case was eventually heard before the House of Lords in March and June 1723. Acting for Charteris was his old Edinburgh friend, Duncan Forbes. The Court held that the bond was usurious, but did not void it, ordering only that the amount payable should be reduced accordingly. Hyndford's wife was obliged to write begging letters to save the family from ruin. Charteris lost £3,700 and his expenses, but he had still made a profit on the deal, and was one of the few men who escaped the South Sea madness unscathed.

There was one thing that Robert Walpole would never do for his crony. Charteris was useful as a messenger, spy, and *agent provocateur*, but the minister who was notorious for promoting his family and friends to positions of power, and who could have engineered a seat in Parliament for the Colonel had he wished, notably failed to do so. And Charteris did have political ambitions. In 1722 Laurence Charteris, who had had little to do with the Colonel since he had been rude to one of his friends, received a surprise gift of twenty guineas. He should have been suspicious, but unwisely he accepted the gift and called on the Colonel who was politeness itself. '...Att [sic] first' wrote Laurence, 'I was willing to make myself believe that he was changed and willing to doe [sic] good natured things...'[146] He was soon to regret that naïveté. The Colonel's object in approaching Laurence was to establish good relations with Horatio Walpole, and Laurence reluctantly agreed to carry some messages to his patron. But the Colonel was unable to dissemble for long, and his true nature soon re-asserted itself. He pestered Horatio with constant demands, and eventually insulted him. When Laurence suggested to Charteris that he give up all thought of becoming a member of parliament the Colonel flew into one of his rages. Later Charteris pretended contrition and tried to heal the breach but he had gone too far and Laurence never spoke to him again.

---

[146] National Archives of Scotland, papers of Clerk of Penicuik, GD18/5245/4 letter 11, 26 November 1723, Laurence Charteris to John Clerk, p. 1

'... All the actions of his life terminate in Nothing But in his Interest,' wrote Laurence, 'gold is his Chief passion ... He is of a Imperious restless, unconstant & uneasy temper and there's nothing so slavish mean and unworth of a Man that he will not doe to obtain his ends and to gratifie his Lust and Vile appetitites, and would have any body about him subservient to him in all his lusts. His conversation is the Language of the Stewes and Morality Virtue and honour is by him termed Cant & pimping is entering into the passions of great Men. I can find no words strong enough to express his Unworthiness: And war I to tell you all I know about him I must write a pamphlet not a letter: My patron: H.W ... Abominates and detests him: Can not speake of him wt patience, & affronts him frequently, and my Lady says she trembels at the sight of him ...'[147]

William Aikman, the portrait painter, describing the Colonel as '...but a big Ruffian att best...', approved of the breach since 'H.W ... abominates the Col'l ... and also to save himself from risqueing his own character by being so much with such a monster.'[148]

Many of the Colonel's frequent quarrels escalated into fights, '...from most of which he was forced to extricate himself, either by undergoing the Discipline of the Cane, or the Foot, or by asking of Pardon.' The opinion of his contemporaries was divided about his courage, '...some having allow'd him to be a Man of Bravery, and others having reported him a mere Coward ... the most favourable Verdict that can be brought in, is, that his Courage has been discretional...'[149] His height and

---

[147] ibid, pp. 1-2

[148] National Archives of Scotland, papers of Clerk of Penicuik, GD18/4590 Letter to Sir John Clerk from William Aikman, 3 December 1723

[149] *Scotch Gallantry*, pp. 12-13

weight gave him confidence, and as a classic bully he would take on anyone he thought he could beat, but sometimes, unexpectedly, he met his match. He once received a severe caning from a young man he had often fleeced, and hoped to fleece again. He bore it with such patience that he was asked the reason for such passive obedience, to which he replied 'Deel tauk me Mon but I'd tauk twice as much, before I'd lose such a gu'd Benefice.'[150]

Charteris probably told a good fight better than he actually performed one. He was visiting the Duke of Wharton at his estate in Winchendon Buckinghamshire, when the conversation turned to the subject of courage and whether it was natural or acquired. 'My Lord Duke,' said Charteris, 'there is nothing in it, if a Gentleman once takes but a little to the practick Part of the Sword, Courage becomes habitual to him, as I have found by Experience. The Reason why most great Men are Cowards … is, because they seldom attempt any thing further than the theory.'[151] In a real fight he was less confident. He was dining at the Thatched House tavern, when words arose between him and another gentleman, and swords were drawn. The rest of the company decided to expose the Colonel's cowardice, and insisted that satisfaction must be given. If either refused to fight he could never again be admitted into the company of any man of honour. They then withdrew from the field of battle, fastening the door. One can imagine them clustered outside, listening and stifling sniggers, with Charteris wishing '…them and all Men of such nice Honour, heartily damn'd.'[152]

---

[150] *History*, p. 25

[151] *Authentick Memoirs*, p. 30

[152] *History*, p. 27

The Colonel's 'habitual' courage rapidly deserted him. His opponent advanced vigorously, and '...the Colonel thought his last fatal Period was really come, and retreated more nimbly than the other could follow.'[153] At this the other swordsman called out that if he did not want to become an eternal laughing-stock he must advance and let him feel his sword, as he was sure there were men planted at the door who would expose him. The Colonel was obliged to edge forward a little, but his boasted skill was not apparent, since he received a slight wound to the belly, presumably the part of him that most protruded. Terrified, he dropped his sword, begged his opponent's pardon, and demanded to be carried home in a sedan chair where he called the physicians and was a very troublesome patient.

When a general election was announced in June 1727 Charteris saw a chance to enter parliament, and decided to oppose Sir Thomas Lowther and Christopher Towers, the sitting members for Lancaster. 'His caracter, which was not good in all parts of England and Scotland, he had hoped to retrieve and declared him selfe a candidate for this town',[154] commented Lancaster man, William Stout.

The Colonel's cruel cheating of the Lancashire maidservant was still so bitterly resented that '...he could hardly get a Lodging in the Town, much less be chose for their Representative.'[155] When he eventually did find somewhere that would have him, '...not a Woman would appear, or come near him, but all avoided him like the Plague, so that he was forced to have so much as his Bed warm'd by his own

---

[153] ibid

[154] J.D. Marshall (ed), *The Autobiography of William Stout of Lancaster 1665-1752* (Manchester, the University Press, 1967),p. 198

[155] *Scotch Gallantry*, p. 7

Servants, which was no little Mortification to a Man of the Colonel's amorous Disposition.'[156]

It was claimed that during the election debates an attorney had heated words with a shopkeeper whom he was unwise enough to describe as '...a mere Ch—s...'[157] So offended was the shopkeeper at this slur on his reputation that he brought an action against the attorney who was obliged to pay substantial damages.

Not all the locals were too proud to take his money. Realising that the usually stingy Colonel would be good for bribe money, they reacted accordingly. '...Many innkeepers and inferior, poor and drinking freemen, about 100 on horseback, and as many on foot, went to Hornby to invit him, which soe much elevated him that he spent at least 100 a day for a weeke, which caused a great cry. And he stood a pole till Lowther and Towers had each about 300 voats and he but 90; soe he gave up, having spent near 1000 pounds...'[158]

Despite this ignominious and expensive defeat he hadn't quite given up on a political career. A private letter in September of that year reported: 'Colonel Charters has offered £1000 sterling to Selkirk, which has two votes, and 10,000 merks to Linlithgow, which last is refused...'[159] Presumably Selkirk also turned him down, and eventually he got the message.

There is such a thing as becoming too well known, and Charteris eventually found that his reputation as a cheat was so

---

[156] *History*, pp. 11-12 (p. 12 misprinted 46 in fourth edition)

[157] *Authentick Memoirs*, p. 32

[158] William Stout, op. cit.

[159] J. Maidment (ed), *Private Letters Now first Printed from The Original MSS* (Edinburgh, privately printed, 1829),John Boyd to Reverend Wodrow, letter XXXIX p. 54, 2 September 1727

widespread among the Quality and merchant classes of London that it was becoming increasingly difficult to get anyone to do business with him. As the Earl of Chesterfield observed in a letter to his son written in 1750:

> Colonel Chartres, whom you have certainly heard of (who was, I believe, the most notorious blasted rascal in the world, and who had, by all sorts of crimes, amassed immense wealth), was so sensible of the disadvantage of a bad character, that I heard him once say, in his impudent profligate manner, that, though he would not give one farthing for virtue, he would give ten thousand pounds for a character; because he should get a hundred thousand by it: whereas he was so blasted that he had no longer an opportunity of cheating people.[160]

The Earl's response was said to be that if Charteris had been able to buy a good character, 'It would certainly prove the worst Purchase he ever made in his life ... Because he would forfeit it again the next day.'[161]

No decent girl would knowingly work for him, and he was obliged to adopt a false name when in search of new game. Using this ploy one day at Epsom, he agreed with '...a Jolly Country Girl, Daughter to a Farmer ... to serve him in quality of Chamber-Maid.'[162] The girl agreed, and was not long in the Colonel's house before she was persuaded into his bed. When her father discovered Charteris' true identity, he hurried to London and applied to a Justice of the Peace for a warrant to apprehend the Colonel for seducing his daughter. The justice agreed, but since the Colonel was a man of substance,

---

[160] *Chesterfield*, vol. 4, letter 1684, p. 1484
[161] *Authentick Memoirs*, p. 4
[162] *Scotch Gallantry*, pp. 10-11

informed him of the warrant before it was issued, to give him the opportunity to come before the court voluntarily. Charteris, typically, '...did not think it worth his while to give his Attendance, whereupon a proper Warrant being issued out, the Colonel was brought by a Posse before the Justice.'[163] The farmer swore his complaint, saying he would not have let his daughter step a foot within the Colonel's doors had he known his real name, and demanded compensation. The Colonel and the Justice withdrew to another room for a private conversation, where gold was heard to chink. When the Justice emerged he tried to persuade the farmer to drop the action since the Colonel, being '...a Man of a great Estate and Interest...'[164] would undoubtedly succeed in any lawsuit. When the irate farmer insisted on continuing, the Justice was obliged to bind over the Colonel to appear at the next sessions. Charteris only avoided the Old Bailey on that occasion by paying compensation, and later complained '...that between the Justice and the Farmer the Business had cost him almost 600 l.'[165]

In August 1728 occurred one of the greatest commotions ever seen in elegant Westminster. Trusty Jack had inveigled a country girl into his master's service, unknown to her relations. Her sister hearing where she was, and '...having had a scandalous Character of the Colonel...'[166] came to the house intending to warn the girl about her new master and try and persuade her to leave. At the front door she demanded to see her sister, but the servants refused to admit her and denied that such a person was in the house. She persisted that she knew

---

[163] ibid, p. 11

[164] *History*, p. 21

[165] *Authentick Memoirs*, p. 12

[166] *Scotch Gallantry*, p. 23

her sister was there, a fact which was corroborated by the neighbours. Still, she was denied entry, but by now the noise had attracted considerable attention, and the news had spread. Roused by a thirst for entertainment, '…an infinite Mobb was immediately raised, who began to storm the House by throwing Stones, Brickbatts, &c. threatening to demolish it if the Woman was not immediately produced.'[167] '…'tis computed,' the newspapers later wrote '…near 1000 People assembled, casting stones at the windows…'[168]

Soon, the Colonel himself came to the door '…with an intent to Harangue the Populace…',[169] but with missiles flying around his ears like hail, and the windows and shutters smashed, he was forced to duck back in again. He was dining with a Scottish member of parliament, who was twice struck on the head by stones coming through the windows. Someone alerted the authorities and several constables and headboroughs (parish officers) arrived to discover the reason for the disorder and try to smooth things over. The Colonel invited the High Constable into his parlour, and complained of the 'intolerable Hardship' that a gentleman who paid his taxes '…could not keep a Whore in his house, without running the hazard of having it pulled down about his ears by a parcel of Scoundrels?'[170] He added that if they treated other people's houses the same way for the same reason there would not be more than twenty left standing in the whole parish. The High Constable agreed, and promised to arrest and punish the rascals, but for all the officers' efforts the clamour continued

---

[167] ibid, pp. 23-4
[168] 'Wye's letter verbatim, London Aug 8', in *The Caledonian Mercury*, 13 August, 1728, p. 7317
[169] *Scotch Gallantry*, p. 24
[170] *Authentick Memoirs*, p. 43

until it was decided that the only thing to do was bring the girl downstairs and ask her if she preferred to stay where she was or go home with her sister. To everyone's surprise the maid stated that her choice was to remain with the Colonel. 'The Sister, quite ashamed and confounded, to see her tender Care so basely rewarded, went away in Tears, with a mob of an hundred Men, Women and Children after her.'[171]

On 8 August 1728 by John Scrope secretary to the Treasury wrote to his friend Duncan Forbes:

> ...Only your crony Charters hath lately incurred the displeasure of the mob & his house had met with Dan Campbell's fate, had not the civil magistrate interposed. I think his windows were demolished.[172]

Campbell was a Glasgow M.P. whose house was invaded and the contents destroyed by a mob in 1725.

Charteris had long given up any thought of a title. It was said that he once complained to '...a great Minister of State [presumably Walpole] ... of the many who had less Merit and Fortune than himself, that were loaded with Titles and Badges of honour, while he, who had been an *humble Slave* and *Disciple*, continu'd no more than plain *Frank Ch—s.*' The 'Great Man' is said to have replied, 'That he thought him already sufficiently dignified, by a Title of his own acquiring, which was that of *Rape-Master General* of Great-Britain.'[173]

It was a title in which the Colonel may well have taken some pride. 'We hear,' reported *Fog's Weekly Journal,* in December 1728, 'a certain Scotch Colonel is charg'd with a Rape, a

---

[171] ibid, p. 44
[172] *More Culloden* Papers, Volume III, p. 31
[173] *Authentick Memoirs*, p. 3

Misfortune that he has been very liable to, but for which he has sometimes obtain'd a *Noli prosequi*. It is reported now, that he brags that he will sollicit for a Patent for ravishing whom he pleases, in order to put a Stop to all vexatious suits which may interrupt him in his Pleasures hereafter.'[174] No more is heard of this incident, and one suspects that the sum of £300 may have changed hands.

The Colonel was naturally an object of the prevailing taste for satire. In July 1729 Lady Hervey wrote of a display of satirical pictures she had viewed. One was called 'A Piece of Devotion' by Col. Chartres, to which the comment is added 'This irony needs no explanation.'[175]

As the Colonel entered his mid-50s it became apparent to those who observed and commented on society that he was declining in vigour. The anonymous author of *A View of London and Westminster*, a satirical account of people and manners, makes no allusion to Charteris in the 1725 edition, but three years later, writing of the '... vast Numbers of *Milliners* and *Chamber-Maids*' of St Martin in the Fields, he adds 'A certain *Scotch Colonel* was formerly a great Benefactor to them, but Age and Infirmities having advanced very briskly upon him, his Loins have failed.'[176]

A further indication that by 1729 Charteris was in physical decline, is that the anonymous pamphlets published shortly after the trial estimate that he was between nine and eleven years older than his actual age.

---

174 'London', 'December 28', in *Fog's Weekly Journal*, 28 December 1728, Number 14, p. 2

175 Anon (ed), *Letters to and From Henrietta, Countess of Suffolk*, 2 vols. (London, John Murray, 1824), vol. 1, p. 344

176 Anon, *A View of London and Westminster, or, the Town Spy* (London, T. Warner, 1728), p. 11

His youthful vigour gone he was beginning to feel the effects of a lifetime devoted to pleasure. His increasing girth must have told upon him, and his father's early death may have weighed upon his mind. In June 1729 the Colonel made his will.

He is supposed to have told his acquaintances that his constitution was so impaired that he would reduce the number of women in his house and alter his course of living, '…doing some good and notable Acts for the Benefit of the Kingdom…'[177] His proposals — and this was probably satirical nonsense — were reported to establish a charity school for all his illegitimate children, and build twenty four almshouses for the whores who had '…spent their Youth and strength in his Service.'[178] If he had suddenly developed good intentions it was only because he felt he was nearing the end of his life, and wanted, far too late, to try and tip the scales against his inevitable descent into the inferno of Hell. Trusty Jack was also seeing the beginning of the end. He had made enough money to purchase an annuity of £40, and asked the Colonel if he might retire from his service. This, his master refused to permit. Charteris did not have the power to force a servant to work for him, but if Jack had been promised a gratuity on his retirement it would have been a strong inducement to remain. Charteris is reputed to have said that '…it was unjust, as well as unkind, to desert him when Age was advancing upon him, and that *as he had D—d his Soul for him, his Body should not quit his House till such time as the Devil fetch'd both away together.*'[179] With this enticing prospect before him, Jack agreed to stay.

---

[177] *Authentick Memoirs*, p. 40

[178] ibid

[179] ibid, p. 42

Charteris was suffering from dropsy, an accumulation of fluid in the tissues nowadays known as oedema, not a disease in itself, but the symptom of an underlying disorder. His friends must have noticed the pallid complexion, puffy swelling of the feet and ankles, and shortness of breath, and heard him complain of coldness and lassitude. If he was retaining urine, he would have suffered '...heaviness and pain in the region of the loins.'[180] In 1729 he travelled to Flanders once more, where it was rumoured he had designs on a nunnery in Brussels, but illness slowed him down, and instead he sought a cure from a monk. The usual treatments for dropsy at that time were herbal, and may have included diuretics, laxatives and stimulants. Rest and a wholesome diet would have done the rest and before long he pronounced himself cured.

He decided to complete his recovery in Aix la Chapelle (now Aachen), a popular spa town, which in the eighteenth century attracted visitors both for the superior class of its prostitutes and its mineral water treatment for syphilis, where he went '...to try if those Waters would prop up his declining Carcase.'[181] Even there his celebrity pursued him, and '...abundance of Foreigners flock'd thither to see so remarkable a man...'[182] Among them was a German Count, who arrived in a handsome berlin, a fashionable four-wheeled carriage, drawn by a set of fine Flanders mares. Charteris, with an eye on this splendid vehicle and its horses, drew the Count into his select circle, and enticed him into gaming, eventually relieving the Count of his berlin, the mares and all his ready money. These prizes were brought back to England, where the Colonel made

---

[180] W.M.D. Lowther, *A Dissertation on the Dropsy* (London, J. Cooke, 1771), p. 14
[181] *History*, p. 39
[182] *Scotch Gallantry*, p. 24

a very great show of driving about in his new equipage. His health restored, any good intentions he may have had were quickly forgotten.

IV: BEING MOVED BY THE INSTIGATION OF THE DEVIL[183]

In early eighteenth century London the rapid expansion of the commercial middle classes and the building of substantial townhouses for the idle Quality created a demand for industrious and respectable servants. London-born domestics were viewed by potential employers as unsavoury at best; criminal, drunken, and vicious at worst; unsuitable retainers for the wealthy. The ideal servant was country-bred, the son or daughter of a farmer — able to read and write, modest, well-behaved, hardworking, and ready-trained in a variety of household skills. The advantages worked both ways, for London offered better wages and prospects than the country. It was possible for a diligent young servant to earn a trusted and well rewarded position, while gifts and recommendations from a grateful master could ultimately mean leaving a life of service to set up in business; a tavern perhaps or a coffee house. Some were attracted to the city as a glamorous, exciting place, having heard stories of fine houses, fashionably dressed beaux, and elegant carriages. Even servants, it was said, could aspire to dress in clothes so fine they were often taken for the Quality.

Every day, wagons rolled in from the country, bringing migrants to the city. Those seeking work came to inns which

---

[183] 'Francis Charteris, esq; for a Rape, February, 1729-30' in Applebee, J. (ed), *Select Trials at the Sessions-House in the Old-Bailey, for Murder, Robberies, Rapes, Sodomy, Coining, Frauds, Bigamy, and other Offences* (4 volumes, London, J. Applebee, 1742), vol. 3, p. 196

served as hiring centres, others already had a place to go through the recommendation of a friend. London's population was growing by some nine or ten thousand a year, but this increase was due solely to the constant influx of new arrivals. The death rate in early Hanoverian London was then greater than the birth rate. Poverty, malnutrition, disease, filth, and an abundance of cheap gin, were picking off the indigenous population faster than they could be replaced.

The only thing known for certain about the origins of Anne Bond, who prosecuted Colonel Francis Charteris for rape in 1730, is that she was born in Lancashire. The Colonel believed she came from Cockerham, a village on his estate. There was a family there with that surname, and an Anne Bond was baptised there on 5 December 1708. After the trial, a newspaper report stated that she was born near Lancaster which is six miles to the north of Cockerham. Anne firmly denied that she had ever lived in Cockerham, but it is possible that she was born there and grew up somewhere very similar, an agricultural village with less than a thousand inhabitants. Her family would have worked the land, and whether her father was a farmer or a simple labourer, he had made sure that his daughter was educated. Anne was able to read and write, and had received sound religious and moral instruction.

There is no portrait of Anne, and no description of her appearance apart from the Colonels mention that she was 'pretty' however, his interest in her suggests that she matched his known taste in women. The Colonel's servants and procuresses, directed to find a fresh face and a young body to stimulate his flagging equipment, would have sought someone attractive, of more than average height, and robustly built. Imagination conjures up a picture of a tall sturdy girl with good features, and modestly dressed.

Anne arrived in London at the beginning of July 1727. Her journey, almost certainly shared with other young women, would have taken well over a week, jolting along rough country roads in a covered wagon normally used to convey coal or turnips, sleeping in cheap inns overnight, two or three to a bed. Walter Besant in *London in the Eighteenth Century* reports that three girls travelling to London from York, a distance of 188 miles, took ten days by wagon, and Lancaster, if that was Anne's starting point is some fourteen miles more distant.

Anne came to London at the request of a Mr and Mrs Bell. They had known Anne in Lancashire and must have been impressed by her good character and diligence, for they had invited her to leave her family to work for them. When Anne arrived in London, therefore, she already had employment and a home waiting for her, and did not need to go to one of the hiring inns, or she might have encountered the Colonel a great deal earlier than she did. The Bells were well pleased with Anne, and employed her for a year.[184] It is not known what work Anne was employed to do, but she was probably a general housemaid, cleaning rooms, staircases and hearths; polishing and dusting.

She would have learned quickly about the strict hierarchy of London domestics and her place in it. The 'upper servants' as they were called, were skilled, held supervisory positions, wore livery, were well paid and dined almost as well as their masters. 'Lower servants', of which she was one, did the unskilled manual work. All Anne's time was at the command of her

---

[184] Some versions of the trial evidence state that Anne's first employer was a Mrs Harwood. It is assumed here that *Select Trials at the Sessions-House* described by the publisher as taken verbatim, is the more accurate

employer, who required application to her duties, strict obedience and a meek demeanour. In return she could expect to receive wages of perhaps £5 a year, twice the going rate in Lancashire, with clean lodgings, probably in an attic room shared with another maidservant, plain but adequate food, and work clothes — a plain stuff frock and apron; but she might if fortunate also receive cast-off clothing from her mistress. If her master entertained a good deal, she could double her income through a system known as 'vails', receiving tips from visitors to the house. There was no obligation for her to remain if the position did not suit her. If she was dissatisfied then she was free to leave, and the constant demand for good servants in London meant that she would have no difficulty in finding a new place.

The greatest challenge that Anne had to face was London itself. Coming from a rural village to a city of nearly three quarters of a million people, the first things that would have struck her on arrival were the crowds and the noise. She had probably been warned not to go out after sunset, for even though the streets were lit by oil lamps on the darker nights, or by the torches of hired link-boys, there was a constant danger of footpads, pickpockets and highwaymen. It was a time when drunken youths staggered back to their lodgings, housebreakers looked for opportunities, and whores and their pimps loitered at street corners. Any man on lawful business carried a sword or a cudgel or had to be prepared to use his fists. On her first day in the capital, Anne would have seen the city shrouded in the smoke of thousands of newly-lit fires, and perhaps might have wondered just what lay in store for her in this dark and unfamiliar place.

Even in daylight there were whole areas of London where the honest citizen would have been most unwise to wander.

Every thoroughfare teemed with a great multitude, traders with baskets on their heads, lice-ridden beggars, thieves and tricksters, men carrying sedan chairs wrangling over the right of way, messengers and parcel carriers hurrying about their business, and rudely jostling others aside. A contemporary writer commented that the town was '…a kind of large Forest of wild Beasts, where most of us range about at a Venture, and are equally savage, and mutually destructive of one another.'[185] Cries of the vendors mingled with the profanities of brawlers, the clatter of wheeled vehicles, the creaking of metal signs, jingling of horse-bells, the drums horns and fiddles of itinerant musicians, and the shouts of gamblers. The streets were awash with mud and dust, rotten eggs, dead cats, scraps of food and animal entrails, ordure of every kind, and the spatter of blood from the previous night's battles between constables and drunken carousers. Down the centre of the street, a gutter ran with filth which splashed from the wheels of passing carts, dirty water dripped from roofs when it rained, the clothing of pedestrians was smeared with blood from butchers' trays or soot from passing chimney sweeps, rubbish lay everywhere in malodorous heaps, and there were the ever present dangers of tiles falling from decaying buildings, cellar doors left open, and mad dogs. Everywhere the entrances of taverns, Geneva shops, gambling dens and bawdy houses gaped to ensnare the unwary. Everywhere was the stink of corruption, coal, dung, tobacco and gin.

Sometimes Anne might have seen a hint of another life, as the velvet lined sedan chairs of the idle rich passed by; a fop with powdered and rouged face grooming his curled wig with an ivory comb, or ladies in low cut gowns of silk and brocade

---

[185] Anon, *The Tricks of the Town Laid Open; OR A Companion for Country Gentlemen*, 2nd edition (London, H. Slater, 1747), letter IV, pp. 13-14

on their way to play cards or meet their lovers. Perhaps there were occasions when she was able to walk in the formal squares and see the town houses of the very wealthy, where the pavements were wide and laid with broad flat stones; or gaze at the elegant shops of the Strand, where the Quality bought their fans and gloves, perfumes and lace.

Anne's reasons for leaving the Bell family after a year of service are unknown, but her employers reported nothing to her detriment, so she may have decided to improve her fortunes by finding a better paid position. Her next employer was a Mr Harwood in Clapham where Anne stayed for nine months. He, too had a high opinion of her character, but Anne left that employment because she '...could not bear the Rudeness of some Watermen...'[186] It would have been March 1729 when Anne was next employed by a Mr Allen, who, according to a statement made by Mr Harwood, was also entirely satisfied with her, but she moved on again, not for any misbehaviour, but '...by Reason of other Matters that were not agreeable to her.'[187]

Anne's fortunes were temporarily at a low ebb. She had no employment, and claimed that she had been ill — the nature of the illness was not described — and had not been making any effort to seek another place. She was living in lodgings but had been obliged to pawn some clothing to meet her expenses. A good servant, and there is no evidence to suggest that Anne was anything less, should not have been in this position. A master who did his duty by his servants would have taken care of them when they were ill. Mr Allen did not appear at the Colonel's trial to give evidence — he pleaded illness — and it may be wondered if Mr Allen or someone in his household

---

[186] Applebee, p. 208
[187] ibid

was the reason that Anne had left, and he did not wish it to be made public. Perhaps her experiences had temporarily made Anne wonder if London service was such a good idea. Perhaps she had not been ill after all, and this was merely the polite excuse she had made to leave Mr Allen's household.

One day in late October 1729 Anne was sitting on a bench at the door of her lodgings, when a woman who was a stranger to her approached and started up a conversation. (Anne could not remember the exact day but thought it was around the 24th, however she knew that it was a Monday, which makes the 27th the most probable date.[188]) Anne's new acquaintance revealed that she was '...very serviceable in helping Servants to Places...'[189] and asked the girl if she wanted employment. Trustingly, Anne said that she would willingly embrace a good service. 'If you will go along with me,' said the woman, 'I will recommend you into a good Family. There is one Colonel Harvey, a very honourable Gentleman, and a good Master, that wants a Servant at this present Instant, and if you please to go along with me, I will introduce you; and I do not doubt but you may get the Place.'[190] If any further persuasion was necessary, Anne was no doubt told that Colonel Harvey lived in a fine house, and paid his servants handsomely. Anne had no reason to be suspicious of this approach. She must have known that many servants were hired straight from the country wagons with no way of the employer judging how effective they might be other than outward appearance. If she suspected anything at all it might have been that the woman was hoping to be paid a commission by the generous Colonel Harvey for

---

[188] Appendix 4

[189] Applebee p. 197

[190] Anon, *The Tryal of Colonel Francis Chartres for a Rape Committed by him on the Body of Mrs. Anne Bond* (London, A. Moore, 1730), p. 4

bringing him a strapping country girl to clean his elegant town house.

Anne, '…happy that Providence had taken such Care and had so well provided for her,'[191] thanked her new friend and accepted the offer. The woman asked Anne to follow her, and thus the girl was conducted to the Colonel's house, completely unaware of that gentleman's true identity.

Anne had of course, heard of the notorious Colonel Charteris, and there may have been servants' gossip of the angry mob which had gathered outside the Colonel's home in Bond Street in the previous year. The Colonel, however had been looking to move up in the world, and had cast his eyes north east of Bond Street. In Hanover Square, the handsome four storey brick houses with the new style sash windows, were occupied by the cream of London society, and the view from the square down George Street was held to be one of the finest in the city. Here, he must have felt, was a home fit for a Charteris. He was still living in Bond Street in May 1729, his home then having an annual rental value of £50, but later that year, he purchased two adjacent houses on the west side of Great George Street, standing on the very lip of the south side of Hanover Square. One property, with an annual value of £90, he rented to a Mr John Harris, the other, valued at £150, he occupied, and furnished it sumptuously.[192]

---

[191] Anon, 'The Case of Col. Francis Chartres, as it appeared at his Trial, at the Sessions held at Justice-Hall, in the Old-Baily, on Thursday the 26th of February, 1729-30; for a Rape committed on the Body of Anne Bond, his Servant, November, 10, 1729', in *A Collection of Remarkable Trials* (Glasgow, Eighteenth Century Collections Online, 1739) (accessed British Library ECCO catalogue), p. 119

[192] Westminster Archives, St George Hanover Square rate books,

As the two women approached George Street, Anne would have been both dazzled and delighted by the prospect of making her new home there. '...the Street is broad, well-paved, and clean, suitable to the buildings that compose it ... well illuminated, both in Summer and Winter Nights, all the Year round, as most of the Streets and Squares in this Part of the Town are, by the Chrystal Lamps, which hang before the Doors of People of Quality...'[193]

The houses of George Street were narrow, but deep and lofty with high ceilings. The stately exteriors would have boasted ornamented doorways with rich carvings and pilasters, and handsome iron railings. Inside there were marble fireplaces, oak panelled walls, decorated plaster ceilings, and elegant staircases. A 1732 inventory of another house in the street describes accommodation on three floors, with three garret rooms, two upper bedrooms and a dressing room, a dining room, another bedchamber and dressing room, two parlours, a sitting room, kitchen, scullery, cellar, servants' hall, and larder. No description of the interior of the Colonel's house is available, but it is known that he did not stint himself when it came to comfort and elegance.

Anne's companion knocked at the door, and they were readily admitted. She asked if the Colonel was at home, and being told he was, said that she would like to speak with him, as she had brought him a young woman that wanted a place, and could recommend her as an honest industrious and good servant. This message was taken upstairs to the Colonel's room, and on receiving it, he came down immediately, and was well able to allay any nervousness Anne may have felt by his good manners and kind demeanour. Looking her over, he

Conduit St Ward, C1-22/434

[193] *A Survey of the City of London and Westminster*, vol 2, p. 666

seemed pleased with what he saw. Since maidservants were not normally part of a householder's public display of wealth, their attractiveness should not have been a factor in their employment. Perhaps Anne thought he was appreciating her clean, neat appearance, and strong, capable build. He asked her a few questions. The nature of these was never revealed, but this was probably where he learned that she was from Lancashire, and where she was previously employed. These formalities disposed of, Anne was hired as a maidservant on a salary of £5 a year. The Colonel then sent his footman with Anne to her lodgings to fetch her box and clothes, and she settled happily into her new home.

Anne's precise role in the household is unknown, but she was probably employed as a chambermaid, a position the Colonel was said to have assigned to his potential conquests on previous occasions. Her main duties would have been to look after the bedrooms, to keep them dusted and swept, to make up the beds in the morning and see they were warmed at night, and to light and tend to the fires. It must have well suited the Colonel to engage a maidservant whose duties lay in the bedroom, as there was no need to entice her into any room she was not expecting to enter. Anne would have reported directly to the main female upper servant, the housekeeper, Hannah Lipscomb. She would also have met John Gordon, the clerk to the kitchen, a senior upper servant, responsible for ordering and managing all the household supplies. The footman who had gone with her to get her possessions was John Gourlay, her Master's personal servant. His nickname of 'Trusty Jack' was almost certainly not revealed to the new arrival.

Anne must have expected to be assigned a garret bedroom to be shared with one or two other maids, and was greatly taken aback when Hannah told her that she must sleep in a truckle bed in the Colonel's room. Humble as her position was, Anne was not a girl to meekly submit to any irregularity and protested that '…this she could not relish nor easily digest because it seem'd awkward to undress herself before a Man.'[194] Hannah quickly allayed Anne's concerns, explaining that it was necessary because the Colonel was indisposed, and '…she might safely do it without any Blemish…'[195] because the curtains would be closely shut about the Colonel's bed and she would have another maidservant, Mary White, as her bedfellow. With some misgivings, Anne did as she was told, and at first, as promised, nothing untoward occurred.

Undoubtedly the Colonel's servants were all complicit in Anne's fate. No-one warned her about the true reason she had been engaged or even revealed her employer's real name. Anne cannot have been there long, however, before she noticed a laxity of behaviour among the other servants; drinking, gambling, profanity and promiscuity, which she had probably not seen to that extent elsewhere. All would however have been kind to her, so as not to frighten her away, and none would have attempted to draw her into their less savoury activities before the Colonel had tasted her unsullied delights.

On the following day John Gourlay went with Anne to the pawnbrokers with money provided by his master to redeem her property. He was also instructed to buy a quantity of Holland cloth, plain unbleached linen then much in use for aprons, household goods, and simple dresses. When they returned to the house, the Colonel ordered that Anne should have the linen, saying that it was a general rule with him to give his servants such a necessary commodity. Smiling, he promised that she should have a clean shift every day. Modestly Anne

---

[194] *The Tryal of Colonel Francis Chartres* (A. Moore), p. 4
[195] ibid

refused, saying that she was '...provided already with a sufficient Quantity suitable to her Station.'[196] Had Anne already learned to be dubious of employers who offered more than she believed was her due?

Charteris next introduced his old ploy of the barbed gift, offering Anne something valuable which he never intended her to keep and which could be used later to substantiate a false charge of theft, if necessary. It was a snuff-box, an expensive trinket, but when he tried to get her to accept it, she refused. He further pressed it upon her, saying that he was giving it to her only to keep it for him, and she must take care of it, for if it was lost she would have to pay for it. On that understanding, Anne took the snuff-box from him, and put it in her pocket.

Anne never denied that in her first few days in the Colonel's employ she was treated very well, and not once during that time did she see any rude, uncivil or immodest action by her Master. She was not confined to the house and was free to go out when her duties permitted. The whole charade was part of the Colonel's standard campaign, making the victim feel at home and happy with her surroundings, to increase the chances that she would comply willingly when he tried to seduce her.

Having, as he thought, prepared her with kindness and generosity, the Colonel made his next move. Four nights had passed during which Anne had slept in the truckle bed in her Master's room without incident. All that was about to change. In the middle of the fifth night the Colonel suddenly called out to Anne's companion to come to bed with him, which she willingly did, but she had not been there long before he called out to Anne, 'Come hither, Nanny you Bitch, come to Bed to me, that I may lie in State.'[197] When Anne refused to comply,

---

[196] *The Tryal of Colonel Francis Chartres*, p. 4

the Colonel lost his temper, and cursed and swore at her. She was so terrified that she quickly put on her petticoat and shoes, and ran downstairs to the kitchen. There she stayed for the rest of the cold winter's night. Bitterly, the Colonel ordered that '…since she would not condescend to lye with him, she should have no other Bed, but that she should sit in the Cold as a Punishment for her Obstinacy.'[198]

Having failed to bring the girl into his bed by persuasion or bullying, he next resorted to bribery, offering her a purse of gold and many fine clothes if she would grant him the favour he desired. Anne was not the kind of girl to be lured by the glitter of gold and finery, the outward show of the whore. Very sensible of the double standards of the day, she was determined to preserve the one thing that was of true value to her — her virtue. As a contemporary writer put it:

Man, the lawless libertine, may rove
Free and unquestioned through the wilds of love:
But woman, sense and nature's easy fool,
If poor, weak, woman swerve from virtue's rule,
If strongly charmed, she tempt the flowery way,
And in the softer paths of pleasure stray,
Ruin ensues, remorse and endless shame,
And one false step entirely damns her fame:
In vain with tears the loss she may deplore,
In vain look back to what she was before;
She sets, like stars that fall, to rise no more.[199]

---

[197] ibid

[198] ibid, p. 5

[199] W Jackson (ed), 'Narrative of the Trial of Sarah Prydden otherwise called Sally Salisbury, who was convicted of an assault', in *The New and Complete Newgate Calendar* (6 vols) (London, Alexander Hogg, 1795), vol. 1, pp. 336-7

This extract of a speech from Nicholas Rowe's *The Tragedy of Jane Shore* was considered so accurate a description of the rules of society that it was sometimes appended to stories of women who had 'swerved'. It was quoted in the publication of the trial of the Colonel's old flame, Sally Salisbury.

Firmly and with dignity Anne refused the Colonel's offers, saying that she had nothing but her reputation to depend upon. Perhaps it was this part of the game that Charteris liked best, the negotiation for a maidenhead. Like his friend Robert Walpole, the Colonel believed that every person had their price, and it was just a matter of finding Anne's. He increased the stakes, and since he had no intention of giving her anything, he could, of course, offer whatever he liked. Aware that she was concerned about her fate if cast upon the world as a ruined woman, he brushed aside that little difficulty by saying that he would help her to a good husband, and even give her a house, of which he owned a great many.

Anne obstinately persisted in her denials. She told him that '...she would take none of his Money on any such Account: That she came not thither for any such Purpose; that if she did not do his Work to his Mind, he might turn her away...'[200] Concealing his excitement and frustration he pressed her no further for the moment, but his determination was unabated. He would have the prize, whether given willingly or not.

The possible consequences to Anne if she had capitulated were far more than just a loss of reputation. Maidservants who became pregnant usually lost both employment and home at once, and were left with little option but prostitution in order to survive. There was another, more desperate temptation. The majority of women tried for infanticide in that period were servant maids, and many were hanged.

---

[200] Applebee, p. 197

Anne did not attempt to leave the house at this point, though she was clearly considering it. Her place at George Street was probably by far the best she had had in London, and she was loath to give it up. So far there had only been attempts at persuasion, and offers of lavish gifts. Nothing suggested that her Master might become violent. Anne may well have mentioned the solicitations to her fellow maidservants not realising that they were in collusion with their Master. The other young women seemed content enough. As far as she was aware only Mary White was sharing the Colonel's bed, presumably in return for financial reward, but the rest clearly did not perceive themselves to be in any danger. Reasoning that they would have told her of any threat to her virtue, Anne stayed on. It may have been soon afterwards that the Colonel called Anne up to him to show her off to two gentlemen visitors, saying that he had '…got a pretty *Lancashire* bitch…'[201] and each of the gentlemen, presumably in anticipation of future pleasures, gave her half a guinea. She put the money in the snuff-box.

The Colonel must have thought that it was only a matter of time before Anne gave in to him, but the days passed and still she preferred to sleep in the cold kitchen rather than enter his bedroom. He continued trying to persuade her into bed, but eventually, irritated at her repeated refusals, he exclaimed, 'Well, you Bitch, you will not always find me in a Humour to indulge your vanity!'[202]

Thus far, Anne was unaware of her employer's identity, but all was made plain when she overheard a visitor who knocked at the door of the house ask for Colonel Charteris, and she realised that she was in the hands of a monster. She went at

---

[201] ibid, p. 200
[202] *The Tryal of Colonel Francis Chartres*, p. 5

once to the housekeeper, saying she had thought her master's name was Harvey, and that she had heard a bad character of Colonel Charteris, and would never have come to work for him if she had known his real name. She then said that she was not well and would leave the house immediately. (It should be remembered that this was the same excuse she gave when leaving the house of Mr Allen.) Hannah brought Anne before the Colonel where the girl made a formal request to leave. Typically, he flew into a rage. Once he had determined to enjoy a woman he could never voluntarily let her go but must pursue her by increasingly violent means. Refusing her request, it may have been then that he used the whip on her for the first time, uttering many savage threats to her life. He then called the other servants to him and ordered them to keep a constant watch over her movements. The doors were to be kept locked and Anne was not to be allowed to leave the house. From that moment on, she was a prisoner. The key to the front door was held by Mr Gordon, and if he went out it was passed into the keeping of either the housekeeper or the butler. Anne continued to do her household duties, and hoped that in time she would be able to escape, but none of the other servants would help her. She was utterly, defencelessly, alone.

Eventually the Colonel ran out of patience with Annes refusals. The conflict between them was no longer about desire or even sex; it was about authority, power and revenge. Between seven and eight o'clock on the morning of Monday 10 November, Anne was sitting forlornly by the kitchen fire, when the Colonel rang the bell. John Gordon went up to him, and was ordered by his Master to '…call the Lancashire bitch into the Dining-Room…'[203] On his return, Gordon told Anne to go up to her Master. As soon as she entered the room, the

---

[203] Applebee, p. 198

Colonel, who was in his night gown, told her to stir the fire, and as she did so he moved behind her and locked the door. He then suddenly caught her up in his arms, threw her violently onto a large couch which stood by the fireside, and pressed the great weight of his body upon her. Anne, knowing that the servant's hall was next door, cried out for help, but no-one came. The room had windows looking directly onto the street, and the shutters were open, so to stop her screams the Colonel took off his night-cap and stuffed it into her mouth.

Anne's desperate struggles were no match for the bulk of the Colonel, a man well practised in methods of subduing an unwilling girl. He pulled up her petticoats, and took her by brute force. When the rape was over and she was freed from his grasp, Anne was, for a time, overwhelmed with distress. The Colonel probably expected her to lie on the couch helplessly bemoaning her fate, and then, eventually, be mollified into joining his stable of mistresses as so many others had done. If she could not be pacified then he would throw her out as he might a soiled rag. A ruined girl, cast out of doors alone, had but a short existence on the London streets. She had no husband, or any family in London, no protector powerful enough to give him cause for concern. Charteris did not know it then but he had made a huge error of judgement, greatly underestimating the girl's character. Anne's modest submissiveness in carrying out her domestic duties came not from a weakness or pliability of nature but from a proper appreciation of her place and rights in society, the same appreciation that now drove her to obtain the justice she knew she deserved. Her sorrowful laments soon gave way to anger, and she found the courage to confront him. Anne dared to threaten her Master that she would tell her friends what he had done, and take every lawful means to obtain justice. He tried to calm her temper and prevail upon her with his usual oily persuasion and worthless bribes, promising to give her a great many fine clothes and other gifts if she would say nothing of what had occurred. Anne flatly refused all these insulting offers, and the Colonel called her a brimstone bitch, and threatened, with many curses, that he would beat her to death. With extraordinary courage, Anne continued to defy him. Though she was still a prisoner in the house and at his mercy, she persisted that she would have redress for the brutal way in which he had used her.

The argument raged for about an hour, and ultimately the Colonel took a horsewhip and lashed her severely about the arms back and head, then beat her with the end of it. The Colonel's bellowing and Anne's screams would have ensured that the other servants, cowering in the hall next door, would have been well aware of what was happening, but none of them made any attempt at entry. Had the cries been heard in the street, it might not have been thought unusual, especially coming from the Colonel's house. Physical chastisement of a servant, within reason, was not then frowned upon. At length, the Colonel unlocked the door, called John Gordon and told him that Anne had robbed him of twenty guineas. Anne may not have known it then but would certainly have found out later that the punishment if she had been found guilty of stealing more than forty shillings from a house was death. The Colonel ordered Gordon to search her and the incriminating snuff-box with a guinea inside was found in her pocket. To recompense him for the supposed theft, the Colonel ordered Gordon to take all Annes possessions, her clothes and her money, and '... throw the Brimstone-Bitch out of Doors.'[204] Faced with the servants who had stood by silently and allowed

---

[204] ibid

113

the rape and beating to happen, Anne complained bitterly. Their reaction is not recorded. It is not known whether she was allowed time to compose herself, wash away the evidence of the rape, or tidy her clothing, whether her wounds received any attention, if she was offered any food or drink, or even afforded some sympathy. It was about two o'clock in the afternoon when she was finally ejected into the street, alone, in pain from the rape and beating and with only the clothes she wore. The Colonel enjoyed his moment of triumph, and thereafter probably did not give Anne another thought. It was the greatest miscalculation of his life.

For some time, Anne wandered distractedly in the streets of London, hardly knowing where she was. Then at last, her courage and resolve returned. She recalled that she had a friend she could go to called Mary Parsons, and hoped that with her advice she might find a way of obtaining justice. Arriving at Mary's house, she was at first too overcome to speak, then she suddenly burst into tears and cried 'Oh! Mrs Parsons, I am ruined and undone for ever.'[205] Mary asked her how, and Anne replied, 'That Monster, Colonel Chartres, has ruin'd me … he has forced me against my Will, and has lain with me; and not content in satisfying his brutal Passion, but he has used me very severely, he has Horsewhipt me in a most barbarous manner…'[206] Anne then unfastened her clothes, and showed Mary the marks of the lash.

Without further delay, Mrs Parsons took Anne to see to a legal gentleman of her acquaintance, Mr Bliss (spelt Biss in some versions of the trial) to whom Anne told her story, and he too was shown the still fresh marks of the whip on Anne's arms, back and neck. Anne asked if she should apply to a

---

[205] 'The Case of Col. Francis Chartres', p. 125
[206] *The Tryal of Colonel Francis Chartres*, p. 6

Justice, and he said that the quarter-sessions were near and he thought that this would be the best way to proceed. Bliss went immediately with Anne to a Justice to apply for a Bill of Indictment. Unfortunately no doctor or midwife was ever asked to examine Anne's injuries or confirm that a rape had taken place. This did happen in some rape cases of the period, often where the victim was a child who had difficulty in describing her ordeal, but it was by no means a standard procedure.

Initially the indictment Mr Bliss sought on Anne's behalf was not for rape but for assault with intent to ravish. The reasons for this were not made clear at the time, but it is very probable that either Bliss or the Justice advised Anne that if she proceeded against Charteris for rape, which was a felony punishable by death, she was very unlikely to succeed. The most probable outcome was that the accused would counter the charge by claiming that she was a loose woman who had consented to sex, and because of his wealth and position it was he who would be believed, and her reputation would be gone forever. There was also the danger of his charging her with the theft of his guineas and snuff-box, for which, if she was found guilty she might at the very least be transported, and possibly hanged. A prosecution for attempted rape, which was a misdemeanour, would be more likely to succeed. With this advice, it seems that Anne consented to proceed as suggested, and the justices readily granted an indictment against the Colonel on a charge of attempted rape.

On the following day, Anne, together with Mary Parsons went to the Colonel's house to demand Annes property back. It was a bold move, since the women were unaccompanied by anyone who might have protected them from violence. Clearly, neither woman was cowed by the Colonel, whom they found in truculent mood. He again claimed that he had been robbed, and raved about his missing twenty guineas, sometimes upping the amount to thirty, and refused to return Anne's property, saying 'Damn the Bitch, she shall have none.'[207] He ordered his servants to turn 'the bitches' out of doors.

As they trudged home, empty handed, and with little hope of obtaining redress suitable to the savagery of the crime committed, the two women cannot have anticipated that before long Anne and her plight would be the talk of London, and she would be called upon to show her mettle before some of the most eminent men in Great Britain.

---

[207] 'The Case of Col. Francis Chartres', p. 126

V: HOW THE LAW MAY TURN AGAINST HIM[208]

It was not long before the Colonels most recent confrontation with the law was common gossip all over London, and the chance of embroidering the tale to make it better suit the prevailing taste was too good for some newsmen to resist.

Fog's Weekly Journal commented:

> It is reported about the Town, that a certain noble Colonel lately attempted to rob a Young Woman, a Servant Maid, of her Honour, and that to frighten her into a Compliance with his filthy Desires, he drew a Pistol upon her. — He is to be sued for the Assault, and it is thought considerable Damages will be given against him, not only for putting a young Woman in Fear of her Maidenhead, but for using a Weapon altogether unlawful upon such an Occasion.[209]

Anne never claimed that her employer threatened her with a pistol, but correctly or not, rape at pistol point was clearly something for which he was known.

The bill of indictment found by the justices of Westminster against the Colonel for assault with intent to ravish, was not something that would have greatly troubled him. If he had consulted his legal advisors, and there is no evidence that he did so at that point, they would have told him that even if the case went to trial and he was found guilty, the penalty was

---

[208] British Library, Additional MSS, Add33054, 'Opinion and Advice for Col Charteris in 1730', f. 94

[209] 'London, *December 6*', in *Fog's Weekly Journal*, 6 December 1729, No. 63, p. 2

unlikely to involve imprisonment and that a fine of no more than £20 would settle the matter. In all probability, his response to the news of the indictment was to ignore it.

In any case, during the last two months of 1729 Francis Charteris had matters on his mind that to him were far more important than the rape of a servant girl. Money, of course, was involved, and this time he had foolishly attempted a substantial and audacious fraud on someone very much cleverer than himself, a respected banker, Alderman of the City of London, Member of Parliament for Middlesex, and future Lord Mayor, Sir Francis Child. This was a more sophisticated version of the Colonel's old 'pretending to be robbed' scenario, which he had combined with another favourite device, that of denying his own handwriting on a document. Although Charteris often bemoaned his lack of reputation this did not stop him trying the same tricks again and again, oblivious to the law of diminishing returns. Typically of the Colonel, the scheme was blatant, shortsighted, relied on a great deal of loud bluster and swearing of oaths, was littered with the usual crop of worthless affidavits, and fooled no-one.

During his recent stay in Aix la Chapelle the Colonel had sent a letter of advice to Alderman Child, stating that he intended to draw a sum of £5,000 from his account at the bank. Not long afterwards, a bill (the equivalent of the modern day cheque) was sent over by messenger to the London bank, which was accepted and paid. When Charteris returned to England he went to see Alderman Child to settle some accounts, and on discovering the charge of £5,000 on his account, pretended to be astonished. He claimed that he had never sent either the letter or the bill, '…and consequently would not allow it, if there was any Law in England.'[210]

---

[210] *Scotch Gallantry*, p. 25

Confronted with his own letter he denied that it was in his handwriting despite the fact that it contained information known only to Alderman Child and himself. As usual, Charteris thought he could bully his way through the problem, but '…both the Banker and his Servants were perfectly well acquainted with his Letters, his Stile, and his Language, to be deceived.'[211] Charteris then claimed that the cheque had been stolen from him and drawn by someone else, and that the letter was a forgery, and declared that he would go through all the courts at Westminster up to the House of Lords to prove it. Ultimately however it was Alderman Child who went to law. Charteris, unable as usual to stop his impudent mouth, believing that the more he ranted, the more likely he was to believed, '…came several times to the *Rainbow* Coffee-House in *Fleetstreet*, and abused the Alderman in his foul Way; upon which he was arrested …'[212] On 12 November the case was to have been presented to a jury of the City of London at the Guildhall, but Charteris managed to get the hearing adjourned to the next term in January 1730 by entering an affidavit stating that there were two material witnesses who were out of the kingdom. While all this was happening, '…another Affair of the like nature was in everyone's mouth…'[213] Someone had recalled the case of the Lancashire oil-man on whom he had pulled a similar trick three years earlier. The story naturally spread, and it was gossiped that '…the Colonel's Character would not stand the Test of an *English* Jury.'[214] 'One might have thought,' said the author of *Don Francisco*, saying what many must have been thinking, 'that he had Affluence of

---

[211] *Don Francisco*, p. 52
[212] *Authentick Memoirs*, p. 51
[213] ibid, p. 52
[214] ibid

Wealth enough to have kept him within the Bounds of Moral Honesty and downright Integrity.'[215]

Unconcerned, the Colonel remained busy with domestic matters, and there was no suggestion that he intended to do anything other than remain in London to see out the latest bout of trouble. He ordered a service of plate from a goldsmith in the Strand, and the bill coming to £257, refused to pay the odd £7. He also commissioned new stabling, presumably for his prized Flanders mares, to be built for his house in George Street, at a cost of £300.

On 5 December 1729, the bill of indictment granted at the petition of Anne Bond was brought before the Middlesex Grand Jury, at Hicks's Hall, a brick and stone sessions house which then stood in the centre of St John Street. The purpose of the hearing was to determine whether there was sufficient evidence to try the defendant at the Old Bailey. This was an event which Francis Charteris regarded as '...scarce worthy his Consideration...',[216] understandably, since he had faced worse situations before. Nevertheless his closest friends took it more seriously, and on the day before the hearing they arranged a meeting which the Colonel attended, presided over by a Justice of the Peace, to discuss the best course to take. The report of this event does not identify either the friends or the justice, but if the gathering did take place then it does suggest that there were some gentlemen at least who had sufficient regard for the Colonel to be concerned about keeping him out of prison. Most of those present took the view that Anne should be offered money to drop the prosecution, and, based no doubt on his ample past experience of such matters, '...the Colonel said, he believ'd the Thing might be made easy for £300. The

215 *Don Francisco*, p. 52
216 *Authentick Memoirs*, p. 52

120

Majority cried, *agree it, agree it, your Character! your Character! Colonel!*[217] The justice, however, disagreed, saying:

> Gentlemen, it is my humble Opinion, that should Mr. Ch—s give a tacit Consent to this Charge, he will find no End of them, and as every one here knows his unhappy Disposition, there will not a Week, nay, I may venture to say, a Day pass, but he may be liable to an Accusation of this nature: My Advice therefore is, that he exhibit his Person before the two Galleries of Ladies at the *Sessions House*, who will rather applaud than condemn the Action. A Verdict of *Non Cul.* [non culpabilis i.e. not guilty] must unavoidably be given for him, and his Household will then be established in Peace, and he never more driven to the necessity of using his *Night-Cap* or *Purse* to stop the Mouth of every Country Hussy he has an Affair with.

This Speech was received with great Applause, and the Colonel declared, he would 'stand or fall by this Gentleman's Opinion.'[218]

The justice's recommendation, which would save the thrifty Colonel £300, had an understandable appeal.

It appears that no representatives of the Colonel attended the hearing at Hicks's Hall on the following day. If they had done so, then they would have been astonished at a wholly unforeseen turn of events. The wise gentlemen of the Grand Jury, with the indictment for attempted rape before them, also examined the facts as sworn to by Anne, and saw that the two did not match. When the foreman and the jury put questions to Anne it became clear that she was accusing Charteris not of a mere assault with intent to ravish but an actual rape, and moreover they knew all too well the reputation of the infamous

---

[217] ibid
[218] ibid, p. 53

Colonel. Then one of the judges commented to his fellows that Charteris had once made an attempt on his sister. It was enough. The Grand Jury ordered that the first bill should be withdrawn and replaced with another, charging the Colonel with rape. Two men were sent to a Mr Lindon to get the new certificate drawn up, but found that it was not possible to get the work done that night. While he waited for the paperwork to be completed, Bliss told a Mr Harrison (presumably a friend or legal acquaintance) of the remarkable developments. It was only some time later that he discovered that immediately after the conversation Harrison had gone to the Colonel and informed him of the court's decision.

When the newspapers reported the Grand Jury findings, they coyly omitted to mention the name of the accused, but such a revelation was unnecessary. There were any number of Colonels residing in London, but the public understanding was that there was only one to whom the story could have referred:

> At the last sessions of the Peace held at Hicks's Hall for the County of Middlesex, a Bill of Indictment was found by the Grand Jury (one having been found before at Westminster, for an Assault with an intent to Ravish, &c) against a *certain noted Colonel* for Felony, in committing a Rape on the body of Anne Bond, Spinster, a Person of good Character.[219]

That Friday was not a good day for the Colonel. On the same evening he was served with a writ by Alderman Child regarding the defamatory words spoken at the Rainbow coffee house. Realising that he was in imminent danger of arrest, Charteris quickly organised an escape. On the following day, the warrant for the Colonel's apprehension on the rape charge was issued

---

[219] 'London December 20', in *The Weekly Journal or the British Gazetteer*, Saturday 20 December, no. 238, p. 3

by Lord Chief Justice Raymond, and delivered to his tipstaff, Mr Chadwick Chambers, but when an officer was despatched to make the arrest, the quarry had gone. The Colonel had left London that same morning '…with a great Retinue…'[220] It was soon leaked to the newspapers that the Colonel had gone to Brussels to bring over two material witnesses in the case between himself and Alderman Child. As *Fog's* dryly put it:

> We hear the noble *Colonel Chartres* is gone Abroad to do Honour to his Country, being set out a second time upon his Travels with a great Equipage.[221]

Charteris also spread a new rumour, in which there were some unsubtle changes to the story he had initially told. He had gone abroad, he claimed, '…in search of one that lived with him, whom he accuses of stealing a Bill of Exchange to the amount of some thousands of Pounds, and leaving a forged Bill of Exchange in his Trunk in lieu of it; which the Colonel knew nothing of, till he went to the Banker's to receive his Money, and found that the true Bill was already paid to some other Person.'[222] '…That frivolous Errand,' as the author of *Don Francisco* described the escapade, 'may be justly compared to a Man's looking for a Needle in a bundle of Hay.'[223] The suspected individual was never named, and the whole story was undoubtedly cooked up by the Colonel in his efforts to defraud Alderman Child of £5,000, or at least to escape

---

[220] 'Wye's letter verbatim', in *The Caledonian Mercury*, 15 December 1729, p.8153

[221] 'London *December 13*', in *Fog's Weekly Journal*, 13 December 1729, No. 64, p.2

[222] 'Brussels, December 29 1729', in *The Brussels Gazette*, quoted in *Authentick Memoirs*, p. 49

[223] *Don Francisco*, p. 53

punishment for the attempt.

The Colonel and his retinue arrived at Dover on 9 December where he at once hired a vessel to take him to Ostend. According to *Authentick Memoirs*, while the master of the ship, Mr Sampson, was busy carrying his baggage on board, the Colonel took the opportunity of going to Sampson's house and persuading Mrs Sampson, who was young and attractive, that he was ill and needed to lie in bed. The lady having shown him to a chamber, the Colonel shut the door on her, and made a violent attempt on her virtue. She was obliged to break the window with her hands and cry out for help, which fortunately arrived in time. Frustrated, Charteris then went to the coffee house and tried to rape a servant maid, but was prevented by some gentleman in the house. Sampson and the girl were later said to have ordered a prosecution against him, but if the story is true, they did not proceed. The entire account of his actions at Dover may be sheer invention as it is hard to imagine Sampson then consenting to take Charteris onto his ship.

Charteris must have been confident that despite the warrant being out for his arrest no-one was going to send an officer to Flanders to get him. He was certainly not in hiding, indeed his actions seemed to be calculated to draw attention to himself. A letter from Brussels dated 28 December reported:

> At Ostend the Colonel rode about the Streets in a strange unaccountable Manner, with a great Mob about him; and did the same there on the Great Market Place.[224]

From Ostend he travelled to Brussels where again, he behaved in the same boisterous way. The *Caledonian Mercury* stated:

---

[224] 'London', in *The Universal Spectator and Weekly Journal*, p. 3, no. LXIV, Saturday 27 December 1729

Touching Colonel Chartris, whom we mentioned in one of our former, to have set out hence for Brussels, arrived there as Letters from thence advise, on Sunday 25th Instant N.S. in a Post-Berlin, making a great Noise in the Streets.[225]

His business there was supposedly to '…confer with Mr *Lenires* the Tapestry-Merchant, the Thing surprized the whole City; Mr *Lenires* having always had the Reputation of a very honest Gentleman.'[226]

Contemporary observers did not attempt to explain why the Colonel rode around Ostend and Brussels as he did. There are no similar reports of such behaviour in London which means that either he did not ride in that way there, or that he did and it was not considered remarkable enough for comment. This racketing-about was possibly an extension of his habitual self-righteous noise-making which he indulged in whenever caught out in some nefarious activity, based on the principle that the louder he was, the righter he appeared to be. It was also a splendid opportunity to show off the new equipage and horses.

In Brussels it was rumoured '…that the Colonel went to visit a certain English Lord, who had resided there many [years]; but was refused Admittance…'[227] This Lord was revealed by the *Echo, or Edinburgh Weekly Journal* to be William North, Lord North and Grey, a Catholic, and Jacobite sympathiser living in exile. Charteris was nominally a Presbyterian, and therefore of the Protestant Church, although his life suggests a complete disregard for the principles of any Christian denomination. He was, however, a known associate of Wharton, an ardent Jacobite, a friendship which may have had more to do with the

---

[225] 'Wye's letter verbatim', in *The Caledonian Mercury*, 1 January, p. 8183

[226] *Authentick Memoirs*, p. 50

[227] *Caledonian Mercury*, op. cit.

younger man's ability to stand a round of drinks than his politics.

Early in January the British newspapers were reporting that Charteris was every day expected back in London, but this was based more on hope than facts. Even in 1730 the newspapers knew how to keep a good story alive. The Colonel remained in Flanders, and, as he anticipated, no attempt was made to bring him home.

The next session of trials at the Justice Hall, Old Bailey was due to commence on 16 January and last for five days. Had Charteris returned to London before that date, he would very possibly have been arrested immediately, and stood trial in the same month. January also saw the dispute with Alderman Child come to court. Charteris cannot have intended to remain exiled on the continent indefinitely. His home and his possessions were in Britain, and he was not going to be parted from them for any longer than he needed. All he required was time to deal with the case brought by Alderman Child and prepare for the felony trial. Not until he was satisfied with his defence would he return.

By mid-January the Colonel was on his way home, carefully timing his movements so as to avoid the Old Bailey sessions but arrive in time to deal with Alderman Child. There was a brief delay in Dunkirk (some reports place this incident in Calais), where he had a dispute with the customs officers who detained his prized berlin and Flanders mares. The reason for this seizure were not described but it should be recalled that these items had been won at cardsharping the last time he had been abroad, and it was most unwise of him to place them once again within easy reach of their original owner, and make a display of them that was so noisy and public it was reported in the newspapers. Somehow, the Colonel smoothed over the customs men, and sailed for England, arriving in Dover late on 18 January. The following morning he set out for London, and most probably arrived on 22nd.

The dispute with Alderman Child had been set down for proceedings at common law at the Guildhall on 23 January. As a last desperate ploy to escape justice, Charteris tried to stop the hearing by going before the Court of Chancery where he was granted an injunction against Child, but Child countered by taking the case before the Lord Chancellor who overturned the injunction. Charteris probably realised by now that in taking on Alderman Child he had gone too far. It must have been with some reluctance that the Colonel finally agreed to a settlement with Child under which he was obliged to pay both the £5,000 and the legal charges of the case, '… besides which, it was left to Arbitration, what farther Satisfaction he should give the Alderman for having so scandalously defam'd him.'[228]

With this matter settled he could now concentrate on the rape trial, which was to take place in the following month. He appointed a Mr Strange as counsel. It is possible, as was widely believed, that Anne was offered substantial sums of money to drop the proceedings, and refused. This may have been mere rumour based on the Colonel's known methods of slithering out of similar difficulties in the past.

Despite the fact that there was a warrant out for his arrest there are no reports of the Colonel being arrested or bailed before the trial, and he probably remained at liberty. The *History* reports that he '…kept himself private…'[229] during that time. He may have been obliged to give an undertaking not to leave London again before the sessions commenced, and to surrender himself voluntarily at the Justice Hall on the day

228 *Scotch Gallantry*, p. 25
229 *History*, p. 44

appointed for his trial. His lengthy absence abroad and freedom on his return gave Charteris an enormous advantage over the other defendants languishing in Newgate in that it afforded him much greater opportunity to organise his defence.

If Charteris' legal advisors had discussed with him the odds of his being convicted of rape, they would have told him that it was almost impossible. Both statistically and culturally it was very unlikely. In the previous ten years there had only been thirty-four trials at the Old Bailey for similar crimes. Omitting the one case where a sexual assault was committed during an armed burglary, in itself a hanging offence, there had been thirty-two rape trials and one for assault with intent. Seventeen of the victims were aged 13 or less. Of these, three were only 5 years old. Where the victim was under the age of ten, the rapist was often acquitted, even in the face of compelling evidence of serious injury, because it was considered that the child was too young to swear to the facts in court. If the victim was an able-bodied adult the usual lines of defence were for the accused to claim that sex had been consensual, or that it was a malicious prosecution. It was easy enough to find witnesses willing to swear that the complainant was of loose morals.

The defendant in the one assault case was found guilty. John Dale had attempted to rape an eight year old girl, and there was medical evidence of severe injury. He was fined ten marks (a mark was 13s 4d) and imprisoned for six months. In the thirty-two cases where there was an initial charge of rape, there were twenty-six acquittals. In three of the remaining six cases there was a verdict of guilty on a reduced charge. Samuel Street was acquitted of raping a severely disabled 17-year-old, but was found guilty of assault, fined 20 marks and imprisoned for six months. William Nichols was, despite evidence of penetration, acquitted of the rape of a 5-year-old, but found guilty of assault. He was fined 40 marks and imprisoned for 3 months. Robert Lander was acquitted of raping a 16-year-old, but found guilty of assault with intent and fined 10 marks.

Only three men were found guilty of rape. Thomas Padget had severely beaten a 5-year-old, leaving her 'lacerated bruised and inflamed.' She had 'not suffer'd a Penetration, but an Injection had been made on the Orifice,' and 'the Parts had received Infection.'[230] The jury, considering the barbarity of the crime, found him guilty but, possibly because there was no actual penetration, he was only fined 20 nobles (a noble was *6s 8d*) and imprisoned for six months. The other two men were sentenced to death by hanging; Christopher Samuel Grass, a married man whose brutally torn victim was aged 12, and James Booty a 15-year-old apprentice who raped a 5-year-old child. Booty later confessed to the crime, and several other rapes also of very young children. He was suffering from venereal disease and had heard he would be cured by having intercourse with a virgin. Grass was reprieved but Booty was hanged in May 1722.

In the ten years prior to the Charteris trial therefore, only one man, Robert Lander, had been found guilty at the Old Bailey of a sexual offence where the victim was an able-bodied adult woman, and he had been punished with a fine of 10 marks, or £6 13s 4d. Every aspect of the case against Charteris gave him ample reason to be sure of an easy acquittal. There were no witnesses to the crime, and no medical evidence, only Anne's unsupported word against his. In a court of law, the evidence of females was given less weight than that of males, and the evidence of servants where they disagreed with their

---

[230] 'Thomas Padget, sexual offences: rape', in *The Proceedings of the Old Bailey*, Ref: t17270222-72

masters, hardly counted at all. Anne could not deny that she had accepted the gift of a valuable snuff-box. It could be argued that she had already received financial compensation for any injury, which, as the law then stood, nullified her right to prosecute. The fact that the initial indictment had been for a misdemeanour called the entire case against Charteris into question, and must have further added to his counsel's confidence that the trial would be a brief formality followed by a celebratory drink. Understandably, '...he still was advised *to see it out* ...'[231]

Anne also appointed counsel, Abel Kettleby. Beyond the assistance of Mary Parsons and Mr Bliss, it is not known what, if any, help Anne had in bringing the case against Charteris. She certainly did not have the financial resources, but may have been helped by sympathetic friends. In addition, many people might have considered it well worth their time and money to help anyone in a case against Charteris, from motives of revenge or pure entertainment. It is not unknown for legal men to give their services free of charge in a case of some magnitude which they think might make their reputation and benefit them far beyond the fee they have waived. In view of Charteris' frequent recourses to litigation, Mr Kettleby was probably well aware that in any case where the Colonel was involved there was a good chance of substantial sums of money changing hands at some point. Even if counsel initially agreed to act for nothing, he might be very well rewarded later on. *The Oxford Dictionary of National Biography* goes much further: 'It is not clear whether, or to what degree, the rape charge may have been engineered by influential parties hostile to Charteris.'[232] Hostile parties, of whom there must have been

---

[231] *Authentick Memoirs*, p. 53

[232] H.G.C. Matthew, and B. Harrison (eds), *Oxford Dictionary of*

legions, hearing of Anne's accusation, might well have helped her, but the word 'engineered' here contains a suggestion that the accusation itself was not genuine. There are two counters to this allegation. First of all, neither Charteris nor any of his legal advisers believed that the case had been instigated by his enemies, as such a defence was never offered. It should be remembered that this was a defence Charteris had used before, notably in the case brought by James Carruthers for the rape of Janet Watson in 1722. More importantly however, if Charteris' enemies had wanted to destroy him the very last ploy they would have chosen was to get a servant girl to charge him with rape, a move so clearly doomed to failure from the very start that it would not have been worth the effort.

The Justice Hall in which the trial of Colonel Charteris was to take place was erected as a part of the massive rebuilding that took place after the Great Fire of 1666. It is usually referred to as the Old Bailey from the street in which it stands, which itself is named after the old fortified wall, or 'bailey', of the City of London. 'A fair and stately building & very commodious…', says the inscription on an early print, 'ye court room being advanced by stone steps from ye ground and inclosed with rails and banisters & having on each side of it large galleries for the reception of spectators.'[233] In an important trial, these galleries, for which an admission fee was charged, would be crowded with the wealthy and titled of both sexes, eager for sensation. Their inferiors, just as greedy for a good show, could cluster for free in nearby courtyards.

There were eight sessions in a year, each lasting four or five days; usually there was one each in January, February, April,

---

National Biography (61 vols, OUP, New York, 2004), vol. 2, p. 210
[233] C. Gordon, *The Old Bailey and Newgate* (London, T. Fisher Unwin, 1902)

May, July, September, October and December. This meant that prisoners waiting for their trials might have been incarcerated for several weeks, depending on when they were arrested. The court was conveniently close to Newgate prison from whence on each day of the sessions the turnkeys delivered their miserable handcuffed charges. The prisoners, shuffling in heavy leg irons, passed via a large gateway through a high wall topped with spikes, to enter an open courtyard with similar high spiked walls on either side. This was the bail-dock, where those due to be tried that day were obliged to wait their turn. In front of them was the courtroom, and they were able to see directly into it, and hear everything that transpired within, since in 1730 it was, on the side facing the bail-dock, open to the elements. Most of the 'gaol delivery' as they were known, stank of the prison, and many may well have carried deadly infections. The layout of the court was therefore designed to protect as far as possible the officers and spectators from unpleasant odours and disease. The courtroom would have been liberally strewn with strong smelling herbs and vinegar, while bouquets of fragrant flowers were placed on the judges' bench which was elevated several feet above the level of the yard. Where the accused persons stood — the picture of Francis Charteris on trial illustrates a square dock surrounded by a wooden rail or bar — there was a particularly heavy litter of vegetation.

On Wednesday 25 February 1730 the sessions opened before Sir Richard Brocas, Lord Mayor of the City of London. On the bench were Mr Justice Price, Mr Baron Thompson, Mr Justice Probyn the Worshipful Mr Sergeant Raby and '…others of His Majesty's Justices of Oyer and Terminer…'[234]

---

[234] *Proceedings of the Old Bailey*, Ref: f17300228 1-71

Mr Strange, the Colonel's counsel, proposed before the court that his client '... might be permitted to surrender himself the Day following, to take his Tryal...'[235] and the motion was duly granted. The news-hungry Mob, jostling about in the yard outside the Justice Hall heard the pronouncement as soon as it was given, and within minutes the news that the Colonel would be tried on Thursday would have spread to every adjacent hostelry. Before the day was out the forthcoming trial would have been the single most talked-about event in London.

VI: I DESERVE TO BE HANG'D[236]

On the morning of Thursday 26 February 1730, Francis Charteris surrendered himself at the Justice Hall to take his trial. He travelled in style, probably by carriage or sedan chair, and was '…gallantly attended…'[237] by his servants and others who were to give evidence on his behalf. So confident was he of a rapid acquittal that he had already arranged for a celebratory supper with friends that evening, '…not in the least suspecting the fatal Consequences that necessarily attend on such illegal Practices. In fine, he stood unconcern'd intirely depending on the strength of his Evidences, who were most of them of his own Family…'[238] The yard next to the court-house and the narrow street must have been packed with crowds eager to get a glimpse of the notorious Colonel; a rabble of journeymen, apprentices, idle youths, old women, and soldiers, many gathered into groups which would throughout the day and long into the evening debate the outcome of the trials. Despite the season, there was no comfortable or sheltered place for even a wealthy defendant to wait. Eighteenth-century newspapers only mention the weather when it was exceptional, so it can be assumed that there were no storms that day, but both prisoners and the common Mob were expected to brave the February air. What Charteris thought of the open bail-dock, its malodorous inhabitants and the noisy crowds is not recorded.

---

[236] *The Tryal of Colonel Francis Chartres*, p. 5

[237] *Don Francisco*, p. 53

[238] ibid, p. 54

The spectacle had also attracted the Quality who crowded into the galleries. 'His Grace the Duke of Argyle, the Duke of Manchester, Sir Robert Clifton, and other of the Nobility and Gentry were at the Sessions House to hear the said Tryal',[239] reported the *Daily Courant* while *The London Journal* added, 'There were present at the Trial two Knights of the Garter, besides other Persons of Distinction.'[240] The Colonel's wife, daughter and son-in-law demonstrated the measure of their support and concern for him by remaining in Scotland. To his rueful family this was yet another of those scrapes from which the Colonel would no doubt emerge soiled but uncowed, and very little poorer.

The Old Bailey records for the sessions which commenced on 25 February 1730 do not list the cases in the order in which they were heard, so it is not known exactly with whom Charteris shared the bail-dock. The newspapers reported that on the first day, four men, Francis Hackabout, Peter Rivers, John Carter and Richard Hanson, were found guilty of the capital offence of highway robbery, while two more highwaymen who had also committed murder, Ferdinando Shrimpton and Robert Drummond were to be tried on the Friday. Charteris' trial was the only one for a capital offence mentioned by the newspapers as taking place on 26 February, so his companions would have been an assortment of petty thieves. Only one other rape case came before the bench that session. George Rowson was indicted for '...Assaulting, Ravishing, and Carnally knowing...'[241] Elizabeth Bickle, who was just ten. He had lured her into Islington fields with the

[239] 'London', in *The Daily Courant*, 27 February 1730, No. 8856, p. 2

[240] 'London', in *The London Journal*, 28 February 1730, p. 2, No. 552

[241] George Rowson, 'Sexual Offences: Rape', *Proceedings of the Old Bailey*, Ref: t17300228-66

promise of a penny and some food. A passer by, Edward Reynolds, had heard the child's cry and saw her lying on her back, with Rowson on top of her, '...his private member drawn...'.[242] Reynolds dragged Rowson off the screaming girl and after a considerable struggle was able to get him to a lockup. A surgeon was in court to state that he had examined the child and found '...a Depression of the interior Parts...'[243] The court felt that the child was too young to give sworn evidence, and ordered that Rowson should remain in gaol and be indicted only for assault at the next sessions. (He was tried at Hicks's Hall on 10 April, found guilty of the misdemeanour, and sentenced to be whipped twice from Islington Turnpike to the church, and then to be kept to hard labour at Clerkenwell-Bridewell for a year.)

The proceedings opened at 8 a.m. The jurymen arrived and were sworn in, kissing the grubby and well-worn black leather binding of a chained Bible, before taking their seats. In 1730 there was not one jury box but two, facing each other across the court, since juries for both the City of London and the County of Middlesex sat at the Old Bailey. Witnesses, not yet permitted in court, clustered about the doors, waiting to give evidence, while counsel fluttered their papers and talked to each other in low voices. At length the robed judges arrived, with the Lord Mayor, aldermen, sheriffs and the Chief Justice of the Court of Common Pleas. Bowing to counsel, they took their seats. Although his name is not mentioned, Alderman Child may well have been present. It is hard to imagine him missing the opportunity. When the justices indicated that they were ready to proceed, the clerk to the court read out the first indictment. The prisoner named was brought to the bar which

---

[242] ibid
[243] ibid

136

separated the accused from officials, and he or she stood facing the judges and the witness box. Above the bar was a mirrored reflector, placed so that light from the windows could fall onto the faces of the accused, to allow the court to judge their truthfulness from facial expression. A sounding board was suspended overhead to amplify their voices. Common prisoners, as most were, confined for up to several weeks in filthy and crowded conditions, brought with them the stink of the gaol, which rolled about the court like an invisible miasma, enveloping the barristers and clerks and even reaching the bench. Court officials nervously sniffed at bottles of vinegar, pomander pots, or lumps of camphor, their only protection against the dreaded gaol fever (nowadays known as typhus), which had been known to carry off innocent and guilty alike.

Trials of the period were usually very short. The sessions record for February 1730 listed seventy-two cases for hearing in four days, and they were usually heard in batches of about six. When one jury had heard its first group of cases it would consider its verdicts while the other jury heard the next batch. Few trials could have taken as much as an hour, and most would have been dealt with in minutes. There must have been time to dispose of ten or twelve before the Charteris trial commenced. Since it was anticipated that the Colonel's trial would last longer than most the justices may well have decided to break for lunch first, and they would have been handsomely regaled in the dining room which lay directly above the court. In some good humour, and possibly a little relaxed from good wine, they would have re-assembled between noon and 1 p.m. to hear the case against the Colonel. According to *The Daily Courant*, the trial of Colonel Francis Charteris lasted an extraordinary four hours.

A mezzotint published shortly after the trial shows the Colonel standing at the bar of the Justice Hall, surveying the court with an attitude of perfect composure. His thumbs are tied together with cord. *The Grub Street Journal* referred satirically after the trial to '…a man of honour … brought to the Bar, and placed among common Felons, with his thumbs tied in a most scandalous manner…',[244] which suggests that this was an accurate depiction. The majority of those being tried having been brought directly from Newgate or other prisons, would have worn the wrist and leg irons which had been loaded onto them immediately on admission to gaol, but Charteris, who had avoided imprisonment thus far, was not in irons. The cord tied about the thumbs was a method of torture recently introduced into the British legal system with the object of ensuring that the prisoner entered a plea. Those convicted of a felony automatically forfeited all their property to the Crown, so to save their families from impoverishment, some prisoners tried to avoid conviction by refusing to enter a plea, without which the trial could not take place. This was an act of fatal desperation. In Newgate there was a room dedicated to the purpose of extracting a plea. It was called the Press-Room. There, prisoners were shackled spread-eagled to the floor and heaped with increasingly heavy weights until they either entered a plea or died. Although this practice was still legal in 1730, it had recently fallen into disuse and been replaced by tying the thumbs with whipcord which was tightened until the desired result was obtained, a procedure carried out in open court. Charteris had a great fortune to lose if he was convicted, and so the cords were in place. In the event, torture was not required. The clerk of the court read over the indictment:

---

[244] *The Grub Street Journal*, 12 March 1730, p. 1

...That you, the said Francis Chartres, not having the Fear of God before your Eyes, but being moved by the Instigation of the Devil, did on Monday the 10th Day of November, in the Year of Our Lord 1729, violently and feloniously assault Anne Bond, Spinster, and by Compulsion and against the Will and Consent of the said Anne Bond, did force the said Anne Bond, so that you had carnal Knowledge of her Body ... that you forcibly enter'd her Body, and satisfied your lustful Desires...[245]

The Colonel entered a plea of not guilty.

The jury which Charteris faced would have been composed entirely of men drawn from the County of Middlesex.[246] They had to meet a property qualification — a freehold worth £10 a year — and would mainly have been in wholesale, retail and manufacturing trades, or wealthier artisans. Some of them may have held prominent civic offices. They were expected to be knowledgeable about their community, and were most unlikely to know nothing of the venal and close-fisted Colonel. The jurors' findings often expressed the personal concerns they brought into the courtroom, and the character of the prisoner was an important factor in their decision. Charteris, blithely anticipating an easy acquittal, appeared to see no irony in a man notorious for not paying his bills unless actually prosecuted expecting a favourable verdict from a jury largely composed of tradesmen.

Whether Charteris made an attempt to bribe the jurymen is unknown. 'The prosecutions of rich or great men are frequently the occasion of much bribery, forgery and perjury'[247]

---

[245] *The Tryal of Colonel Francis Chartres*, pp. 3-4

[246] Appendix 3

[247] *The Grub Street Journal*, op. cit.

commented the *Grub Street Journal* in an editorial written shortly after the trial. He may well have felt himself so secure that he did not trouble to do so, relying instead on his other favourites, forgery and perjury. Perjury was common in the period. The penalty for this offence was to stand in the pillory, but in practice the laws were rarely enforced. The purchase of suitable witnesses on both sides was easy, inexpensive and risk-free.

Unlike today, counsel of the period made no formal address to the jury or cross-examination of witnesses. The trial was in effect a direct confrontation between the defendant and his accuser. It would be almost unthinkable now, but Anne would be subject to questioning by the man indicted for raping her. She must have known what she was facing, and throughout the trial her courage never faltered, and her story remained unshaken.

Anne's counsel, Abel Kettleby, opened the case, with '…a very eloquent and learned Oration…'[248] to the bench, observing that '…though Facts of this Nature were now-a-days made little Account of by too many Persons of Levity, yet they had always been, by all civiliz'd Nations, nay, even by many barbarous ones, rank'd among Crimes of the most heinous Nature.'[249] He proceeded by calling the evidence for the King. First to appear was Anne who began by describing all the events leading up to the rape. 'The Evidence that the Woman gave was very plain and full',[250] it was observed.

As Anne told the court how she had refused to go to bed with her Master, the Colonel interrupted her testimony, asking her if she knew nothing of a letter she had brought to him. Anne replied she knew of no letter, whereupon he pulled a

---

[248] *The Tryal of Colonel Francis Chartres*, p. 4
[249] Applebee, p. 196
[250] *Don Francisco*, p. 54

document from his pocket exclaiming, 'Well, if I do not prove that you sent this Letter I deserve to be hang'd.'[251] Anne was asked to go on with her statement, and when the Colonel tried to interrupt her a second time the bench ordered him to hold his tongue. It was an astounding moment, but the reaction of the Colonel and spectators is unrecorded. For a man of substance peremptorily to be told to keep quiet so his former maidservant could say her piece was a very clear indication of where the sympathies of the court lay.

When Anne testified that the Colonel had had carnal knowledge of her, Mr Strange interrupted asking how she was sure of this, and if she knew the meaning of the words. This question must have been aimed at showing that Anne had been mistaken about what had occurred, but it was not necessarily a wise thing to ask. It assumed that she was innocent of sexual matters, whereas his client and witnesses were claiming the contrary. It may, alternatively, have been a question designed to entrap her into showing more knowledge than she professed. If it was, it misfired. Anne, as befitted a modest girl who had been asked to describe the sex act in front of a crowd of mostly male strangers, '…seemed a little confused and at a Stand…',[252] unsure of a suitable reply. The judges told her that she must '…speak plain and tell the naked Truth, that the Law required it…'[253] and Mr Kettleby kindly helped her out by asking if the prisoner had entered her body. She replied that she was sure he had. Asked if she had her petticoats on, she said that she did, but the Colonel took them up, and held her down on the couch. None of his servants had come to her assistance, '…for they were so much under his Command, and

---

[251] *The Tryal of Colonel Francis Chartres*, p. 5
[252] *Case of Col. Francis Chartres*, p. 123
[253] Applebee, p. 198

frequently addicted to his Pleasures, that they durst not interpose.'[254] The court wanted to know what followed next. Anne was again silent, but when the question was repeated she replied (and the reaction of the tittering gentry in the gallery and the coarse Mob outside can only be imagined), 'A great deal of Wet.'[255]

The Court asked Anne if she had complained of the Colonel's usage, and she replied that she had done so that very same day.

Once Anne had completed her evidence, Charteris was informed that he was now at liberty to ask her what questions he pleased. He began rapidly to fire questions at her, but if he was hoping to bully her into confusion he was to be disappointed. He first suggested to Anne that she had lived at Cockerham, had seen him in Lancashire, that her sister lived on his estate and that she knew the Lordship was his, all of which she firmly and unhesitatingly denied.

The letter was a vital part of the Colonel's defence, since Anne had claimed that she had not known who he was when she came to work for him. If he could prove that she had arrived with a letter addressed to him, she would have been shown to be a liar and her case would have collapsed.

'Did you not bring me a letter?' he demanded

'No; I brought no Letter,' she replied.

'If I don't prove it I'll be hang'd' he exclaimed in exasperation.[256] It was now very clear to the spectators that so far from imposing his personality on a meek and helpless maidservant, the Colonel was getting by far the worst of the exchange.

---

[254] 'The Case of Col. Francis Chartres', p. 124
[255] ibid
[256] Applebee, p. 199

'Did you never lie in Bed with your Master?' he persisted.

'No' Anne fired back. 'I was in the Truckle-bed one Night, when she, who was my bed-fellow lay with you, and you called me to come to Bed to you; you said you *Lancashire* Bitch, come to Bed to me, and lie on the other side of me, that I might lie in State; this was the fifth Night; and I slipt on my Gown, and went down Stairs, and sat their all Night; and I was told, you had ordered I should have no bed; I was not willing to lie there at all; but was told, you was ill, and I must…'

How was it, asked the Colonel, that she had lain in the truckle bed in the same room as him after he had offered to lie with her, something she said was so disagreeable to her that she resolved to get away from the house if it was in her power? Anne replied that this was because another servant had lain in the truckle bed with her.

Under a fresh torrent of questions, Anne, who was getting more confident by the minute, denied that she had brought him his breeches with the guineas in the pockets (he was now talking about fifty guineas), and denied that she had hidden the snuff-box with the guinea in it behind the grate. In case the court should be in any doubt as to where the guinea had come from, she volunteered the explanation that she had been given the money by his two gentlemen visitors.

'Did you tell my Servants that you had met with bad Usage?' asked the Colonel.

'I complained to every Servant that I had bad Usage,' Anne replied.

'What was the bad Usage?' he asked, unwisely.

'In being ravish'd and horsewhipped,' was the terse response.

'Did you not accept of a snuff-box?' he insinuated.

'That was given me the second Day after I came: I said I did not want it. I would not have it: you said I should have it; keep it in your Pocket, if it be lost, you shall be answerable for it,' said Anne, stingingly.

The Colonel's next two questions did not dignify a longer reply.

'Did not you bring the Chamber-Pot, and hold it and take my Member out of my Breeches?'

'No.'

'Did you not tell some of the Family, that since I had so much Silver, I should have my instrument tipp'd, for it would not please a Woman?'

'No.'[257]

One can imagine the relief of Mr Strange when his client declined to question Anne further.

Mary Parsons then gave evidence of Anne coming to her saying that she had been ravished and whipped, and accused of stealing twenty guineas, and her clothes kept from her. She described the attempt to recover the clothes and how she had taken the girl to Mr Bliss.

Bliss told the court that Anne had been brought to him by Mary Parsons, and how, after hearing her story, he had helped get a Bill of Indictment found. He also mentioned that Anne had told him she had been whipped both before the rape and afterwards.

The last witness for the prosecution was Sarah Colley, who testified that she did the washing for one of the prisoner's servants (presumably an upper servant). The Colonel had asked her if she knew of any likely country girls that she could send to him. He ordered her to go to the Crown and Wheatsheaf on Ludgate Hill, and '… bring one Mrs Betty to him; but not to mention his Name, and he would give her a guinea.'[258] No

---

[257] ibid, p. 200
[258] ibid, p. 201

144

further details cast any light on this evidence and the identity of Mrs Betty remains a mystery, but Sarah Colley may well have been the woman who spotted Anne at the door of her lodgings and decided to complete her errand there and then.

The prosecution witnesses having given their statements, the court asked the prisoner what he had to say in his defence. Charteris claimed that Anne had frequently granted him her sexual favours, and sent him letters, and he had one such letter to produce in court. He asserted that the prosecution was only brought to extort money from him. The gentlemen on the judges' bench were stern, and may have known something of the Colonel's penchant for forged documents. They said that letters alone were not sufficient unless he could show that they were in Anne's writing.

The Colonel now brought his witnesses, the first of whom was John Gordon, the clerk to the kitchen. Again, it was Charteris who did the questioning. Gordon told the court that a woman he identified as Anne Bond had come to his Master's house and given him a letter for the Colonel which he delivered. He had later come into the parlour where the letter was being read by a visitor to the house, Mr Irving.

Gordon said that on 10 November the Colonel had been ill, and had got up at two o'clock in the morning and sat in the parlour. Anne, said Gordon, had then got up and brought the Colonel his breeches and held them while he put his legs in them. Such a personal and intimate task was normally the duty of the Master's manservant, but this evidence suggested to the court both a familiar relationship between Anne and her Master and an opportunity to steal the guineas that were supposed to be in his pockets. Gordon described the breeches as being made of brown cloth. Some tea was brought, and soon afterwards the Colonel returned to his chamber and lay down on the bed. Gordon said that his Master got up again at four, went out at six, and did not return until ten, which suggested that Charteris was absent from the house at the time Anne said she had been raped. It was after his return that the Colonel was said to have missed the money in his pockets and ordered Gordon to fetch Anne, '...the Woman that had lain with him that Night...',[259] to ask her about his guineas. Gordon said that when he ordered Anne to go up to her Master, she did not follow him, but backed away and ran to the 'House of Office' (the privy) pretending that she needed to go there, but '...she did not stay there to do anything, no longer than she could go to it, and come back again...'[260] When she returned he observed that she did not go directly to her Master's room, but first ran to the bed-chamber and put something under the fireplace. After she had gone he searched to see what was there and found a snuff-box with a guinea in it. Gordon said that he followed Anne into the Colonel's room where his Master ordered him to search the girl, which he did, but found nothing. His Master then charged Anne with stealing twenty guineas from his breeches pocket. Gordon told the court that Anne '...was very easy all the time she was in her Master's Service...'[261] and had never made any complaint of ill treatment until after she had been charged with theft.

Gordon denied that he had called Anne upstairs to the Colonel earlier on the morning of 10 November. He said that the room where Anne said the Colonel had raped her was

---

[259] ibid, p. 202

[260] ibid

[261] Anon, *The Tryal of Colonel Francis Charteris for a RAPE Committed on the Body Of ANNE BOND, Who was tried & found Guilty at* Justice-Hall *in the* Old Bailey, on Fryday the 27th of *February* 1729-30 (London, Sylvanus Pepyat, 1730), p. 9

towards the street, beside the servants' hall where all the servants were in the morning and none of them had heard any noise or crying out. He had been in that hall with the others and had heard nothing. He added that Anne had lain in the truckle bed the very first night she came to the house, and every night afterwards, alone, except for only two nights when Mary (in some versions Margaret) White another servant, lay with her. Anne had stayed out late on the Sunday night, so the Colonel had called for Mary, and she lay in the truckle bed as well as Anne that night. On the night before the alleged rape, Gordon said that Anne had spoken to the other servants saying that as her Master was a man of money he ought to have his instrument silvered, for he was not able to please a woman. She had said this 'In the Kitchen, among all the Men and Women Servants, and they laugh'd at it.'[262]

Mr Irving was a gentleman and a friend of the Colonel. He said that he had been visiting the Colonel on the Sunday before the King's birthday (26 October, since the birthday was celebrated with peals of bells four days later), when John Gordon came in with a letter saying that a woman had brought it, and was waiting below for an answer. Irving said the Colonel bid him open the letter and read it, which he did. The letter was signed 'Anne Bond'. It was Irving's belief at the time that the letter came from a whore, as he knew the Colonel made no secret of those matters.

At last, the Colonel was able to produce his letter in evidence, and Irving swore it was the same one he had seen on the day of his visit. The Colonel, said Irving, had sent for the woman whose letter it was, and Anne was brought before him, wearing a riding-hood. The Colonel called for tea, and spoke to Anne as if she was an acquaintance, saying 'Nanny, How do

---

[262] Applebee, p. 203

you do? How long have you been in Town?'[263] and enquired after friends in the country. According to Irving, Anne told the Colonel that she had been in town three weeks. This was of course untrue, though whether Irving knew it is unknown. His host then asked him to leave the room, which he did, leaving the Colonel and Anne alone together for a time. When he returned he found Anne sitting in the chair, another indication of the familiarity of the relationship. Another gentleman was expected on a visit, so the Colonel said 'Nanny, go down into the Kitchen among the servants, and when I want you, I will call for you.'[264] Anne obeyed, and according to Irving the Colonel then told him that he had known Anne at Cockerham, '…that she pretended to be a very modest Girl, but one of the Servants, where she had liv'd had lain with her.'[265]

The judge asked Anne whether Mr Irving was in the room when she went to the Colonel's to be hired. She replied, 'No, he was not in the Room.'[266] Irving was then asked if he had heard any conversation between the prosecutor and the prisoner concerning the letter. This question may well have put Irving on the spot. It would have been strange if there had been no such conversation, but having already had his account of events denied by Anne, he may have decided not to risk adding any further detail. Sensibly, he answered 'No'.[267] Irving may well have visited the Colonel on the Sunday in question but the entire story about his being a witness to Anne's arrival was probably a fabrication.

---

[263] Pepyat, p. 10
[264] Applebee, p. 203
[265] ibid
[266] ibid
[267] ibid

Questioned from the bench Anne again denied that she had ever sent or brought a letter.

The next witness was John Gourlay, described as the Colonel's valet-de-chambre, but under his nickname of Trusty Jack, almost as notorious a figure as his master. He said that he had been in the room with his master and Mr Irving when a servant brought a letter. He went down and saw Anne Bond standing at the door, '…and she said to him, I know you very well, I have seen you at my Sister's House at Cockeram.'[268] Like Irving, Gourlay confirmed that the date of this event was the Sunday before the King's birthday. The next day he had gone out with Anne with money to fetch her clothes out of pawn, and had questioned her about several people in the country, in order to verify her story, and found that she knew them as she had claimed.

Asked where Anne had slept he said that every night she had lain in his Master's room, and that his Master used to bid him send the girl in to him. There was, he said '…a great Harmony betwixt them, and she commended her Master for his Kindness to her.'[269]

The judges now asked Anne if she had come to the Colonel's house on a Sunday and she replied that it was on a Monday. Presumably, as she believed it to be towards the end of October, this was Monday 27th, the day after Mr Irving's visit.

Gourlay was shown the letter, and told the court that he had seen it lying open on the table and had picked it up and read it. He had then put it in his pocket, and later took it out and put it among his other papers before going to Flanders.

Mr Irving was now shown the letter, and asked if it was the one he read at the Colonel's. He said it was, and pointing to

---

[268] ibid, p. 204
[269] ibid

Anne, declared, 'This is the woman that was brought in by the Servant, upon reading the Letter.'[270]

Again, Anne was asked if Irving was present when she first came to the Colonel's house. She said he was not. Asked if she knew him she replied, 'Yes, I have seen him frequently.'[271]

A Mr Coon was brought forward to state that he knew Anne very well and was familiar with her handwriting. He examined the letter and said that he believed it to be in her hand. The letter was now shown to Anne and she was asked if she did not bring it to the Colonel's. She studied it for some time and eventually said she could not read it (whether this was due to lack of reading skill or unfamiliarity with the handwriting was not clear, but later evidence confirmed that Anne could read the printed word). She was asked if she could write, and said, 'Yes, a little'.[272] A paper and the pen of the court writer were handed up to her; she wrote her name, and the paper was passed to the bench. Comparing it with the letter, the judges declared that the writing of the letter and Anne's writing were not the same.

By now, the Bench was getting the measure of the Colonel's witnesses, but since both Irving and Gourlay had said that Anne had brought the letter it was ordered that it be read out in court.

Addressed to Colonel Charteris it said:

Hon. Sir
   I Understand you are in Town, if your Honour pleases, I should be glad to wait on you, I come from Cockeram in Lancashire; I came the next Door to Mr Jones, and should be proud to wait on you; if your Honour pleases to give me the

---

[270] ibid
[271] ibid
[272] ibid

Liberty: pray pardon this Freedom, I am with Submission, and the greatest Respect, your humble Servant to command.

Ann Bond

I wait at your Door for an Answer.
Wednesday Night
Three o' Clock.[273]

The contents of the letter explained the Colonel's eagerness to show that Anne came from Cockerham. Had she indeed lived in that village, proof would have been readily available in the form of witnesses who knew her there, and the Colonel had had ample time to find and bring them to London, but none ever appeared either at the trial or later. The identity of Mr Jones remains unknown.

The next witness was another of the Colonel's servants, James (in some versions Thomas) Davis. The Colonel requested that Davis should be asked if he had not seen the prosecutor '...in the naked Bed with him?'[274] Davis said he had, and that Anne lay every night in her Master's room. He claimed that afterwards he had asked her if she was not ashamed to go to bed with her Master and she had replied that she was not, for she was used to it. Questioned from the bench, Davis said that he had come as servant to the Colonel on 4 November, and had first seen Anne and his Master naked in bed together the following morning. The gentlemen of the bench had very strong views on the correct behaviour for a manservant. Asked how he had come to see what he reported Davis replied that on hearing the bell ring, he opened the door and went in without knocking. This was too much for their lordships who asked '...what Business he had to go into his Master's Chamber, without knocking, and being but just come,

---

[273] ibid, p. 205
[274] ibid

was a Stranger? And whether, or not, it was saucy and impudent in him to do so?'[275] Davis paused to think for a while before replying that he went into his Master's bed-chamber under pretence of drawing the curtains after the Colonel was in bed, but it was really to see if Anne was in bed with him, as he had a mind to lie with her himself. The court enquired whether his Master had called him into the room and he said no, whereupon he was told by a sceptical bench that he was probably the first servant that ever presumed to take that liberty.

When the housekeeper, Hannah Lipscomb, was called, the Colonel said he wanted her to be asked how many times she had seen Anne in bed with him. Hannah obligingly testified that Anne had lain in the truckle bed on the first night she came to the house, and thereafter with the Colonel. She said she had seen Anne in bed with the Colonel in the morning on several occasions when she came into the room to light the fire. The bench failed to point out that lighting the fire was a menial task carried out by one of the lower servants and well beneath the dignity of a housekeeper. Her coming into the room unbidden was not challenged. Hannah said that she had never heard Anne make the least complaint of any ill-usage until the last day when she was charged with stealing money. Charteris requested that the housekeeper be asked about the comments Anne had made about his private member. Hannah said that she had heard Anne say that her Master's instrument was worn out, and as he had a great deal of money it should be tipped with silver. Asked from the bench if she knew the meaning of the expression 'lying in state' as used by the Colonel, she at first declined to answer, then being pressed to

---

[275] ibid

do so, said that she had heard from vulgar people that it referred to a man lying with three women at once.

The Colonel's next witness, Thomas Vaux (he is confused with Thomas Cooper in some accounts) was a saddler who told the court that at 5 a.m. on 1 November, one of the Colonel's servants came and fetched him, saying that some horses had broken loose, and needed fitting with halters. He said he had gone into the Colonel's bed-chamber to speak to him, and seen Anne Bond in bed with her Master. When she saw Vaux, she rose from the bed wearing only a shift, took up her clothes, and went into the next room to dress, making him a curtsey as she went by. Once again, the court was being asked to believe that anyone might and indeed did march in and out of the Colonels bedroom in the early hours of the morning at will. The bench interrupted, asking Vaux if he could not halter a horse in a stable without going up at five o'clock in the morning into the Colonel's chamber. Vaux said that he wanted to get his orders from the Colonel, as the Colonel often struck out items from his bills and did not pay them if he had not given specific orders about them. Those tradesmen observing the trial would have detected a ring of truth in this part, at least, of Vaux's evidence. Vaux claimed that the servants had permitted him to go up to the Colonel's room unannounced, '…which being very improbable, his Evidence was not credited.'[276] Vaux added that the next morning when he brought round some items for the horses, he had spoken to Anne and '…being her Countryman and familiar with her…',[277] he had asked her about the Colonel's ability, and she had replied, '…he was quite unable, for his Affair was no better than a Piece of Pudding.'[278]

---

[276] *The Tryal of Colonel Francis Chartres*, p. 7
[277] *Pepyat*, p. 13

Thomas Cooper, the master of a ship said he had been in Flanders, and on his arrival at Dover had received a message to come to the Colonel. Arriving early in the morning he was called up to the Colonel's bedchamber, which by this point in the trial appeared to be one of the most popular thoroughfares in London, and naturally found Anne Bond in bed with her Master. Questioned about the date, Cooper said he could not be positive about this as he did not have his journal with him but it eventually transpired that the event could have taken place no later than the first week of October. Mr Kettleby quickly pointed out that this was some eighteen or nineteen days before Anne came to the Colonel's house, and the court drew its own conclusions about the mariner's evidence.

Mary White, the servant who had shared the truckle bed with Anne, said she had often seen Anne in bed with her Master. She had never heard Anne complain of any violence or barbarous treatment until she had been charged with the robbery. On 10 November Anne had brought the Colonel's breeches to him. He had gone out at six and returned at ten, and it was then he had missed his money. A gentleman had come on business, and the Colonel had put his hands in his pockets and said he had been robbed. He had then ordered Mr Gordon to bring Anne to him, saying that it had to be either Anne or herself who had taken the money, there being no-one else in the room. When Anne arrived he demanded that she own up to the theft, saying that if she did, he would not tell her family. Anne had replied that she could not own what she knew nothing of. Soon afterwards, Anne was turned out of the house. Mary said she had been in the servants' hall that morning and had not heard Anne cry out. The breeches, she said, had been black.

---

[278] ibid

The next witness was the man who had called on business, Mr Hamilton, an upholsterer who had come to put up some curtains. He said he had been with the Colonel between eight and nine in the morning on 10 November. The Colonel had been sitting on the couch and put his hand in his pocket to take some money out. He then said he had had fifty guineas in his pocket the previous night but had lost twenty of them. No doubt this well-practised act was extremely convincing.

Charteris asked if the court would enquire into the character of the prosecutor, and this was done, but not to her detriment. All her past employers had nothing but good to say of her, and whatever efforts the Colonel had made to find evidence of a bad character had come to nothing.

Mr Bell said that Anne had lived with him for about a year and '…said she was … as honest, modest a young Woman, as ever came into a Family… She behaved herself very religiously, and when at any Time she could not go to Church, she had always some good Book in her hand.'[279] His wife added that she had known Anne in the country, and '…she was always very modest, and honest: that she never perceived the least immodesty by her…' Asked if she thought Anne would '…forswear herself, to take a Man's Life away?' she answered 'No.'[280]

Mr Harwood said that Anne '…behaved herself very modestly and soberly, and kept her Church very constantly, and he did believe her to be a very modest sober young woman, that would by no means forswear herself…'[281] At Mr Allen's she had also behaved modestly and honestly and her departure was not because of any misbehaviour.

---

[279] Applebee, p. 208
[280] ibid
[281] ibid

All the evidence was now in.

The jurymen retired to consider their verdict during which time the Colonel was obliged to return to the bail-dock to stand among the other felons. Eighteenth century juries usually arrived at a verdict very quickly, often within a few minutes. Contemporary accounts of how long they were absent in the Charteris case vary from fifteen to forty-five minutes. Since Juries in rape trials often acquitted the prisoner of the felony but found him guilty of the misdemeanour of attempted rape, Charteris and his counsel may have deduced that this was what was being mooted. Such a result would not have disturbed the supper plans. As he waited, however, a friend, who must have heard a rumour of the likely result, approached him and told him that he would certainly be found guilty of rape, and that it would be advisable to remove the most valuable of his effects from his house and place them in hiding. Trusty Jack was ordered back to George Street where plate and jewels were speedily carried off.

On their return, the foreman of the jury announced the verdict of 'guilty', a popular decision greeted by '…loud Acclamations at the Sessions-House…'[282] The court at once gave orders that the keeper of Newgate take the prisoner into safe custody and that especial care should be taken that he did not escape. Charteris, who despite the warning, must have been stunned at this turn of events, was immediately secured by the keeper's men, and removed from court. Onlookers stated that he '…seem'd greatly dispirited',[283] which to a man of his boundless self-importance and arrogance was a very

---

[282] *Authentick Memoirs*, p. 57
[283] 'London', in *Fog's Weekly Journal*, 28 February 1730, No. 75, p. 2

substantial change in demeanour. '…Some Noblemen going away, said to one another, *Frank will certainly be hang'd.*'[284]

---

[284] *Authentick Memoirs*, p. 57

VII: EVERYBODY THAT KNEW HIM HAD A FLING AT HIM[285]

As the Colonel was conducted from the Justice Hall by the gaoler's men, it must have seemed to him that the unthinkable had just happened. In fact, every turn of events had been to Francis Charteris, unthinkable. When he threw Anne Bond out of his house he had never imagined he would see her again, and yet she had marched back to his door demanding her property the very next day. Shutting his door against her with a curse for the second time, he had not believed that an unprotected servant girl would take him to law, yet she had. If the reports of his offering her £300 to forget the whole thing were true that ought to have made the entire affair disappear — after all, it had worked for him before — but he had found to his astonishment that she preferred justice to money. He had regarded the trial as a mere formality, but suddenly the doors of Newgate were opening to receive him. There was another shadow, another unthinkable, which, judging by past events, he should not dismiss as a possibility — Tyburn and the noose. More immediately, however, there was another consequence which chilled his avaricious soul and which he knew even as he was being taken away was already being put into motion. As a convicted felon, all his goods, chattels, lands and tenements were forfeit to the Crown; and the Sheriffs of the City of London and County of Middlesex and the High Bailiff of Westminster were taking possession of his effects. Only the constraints of distance would delay the loss of his

---

[285] *Don Francisco*, p. 8

country estates.

As soon as the verdict was announced, the officers of William Morice, High Bailiff of Westminster under the command of his deputy Samuel Baldwin, were ordered to George Street to seize the property of the newly convicted felon, not realising that the occupants had been forewarned. When the posse of constables, beadles and their assistants, numbering about forty men in all, arrived, they found the Colonel's house locked against all-comers and the servants, '...three lusty young Wenches...',[286] prepared for a vigorous defence of the property.

Baldwin at once demanded that the women surrender and allow his men to enter the house, but they shouted defiance out of the windows, refusing to admit him, saying, '...they were amply provided with all sorts of Necessaries, and would abide the last Extremity, rather than give their Master's House up to be plundered by a Parcel of Robbers.'[287]

As the neighbours crowded into the street to watch developments, Baldwin deployed siege tactics, ordering that a 'Line of Circumvallation' be drawn about the house — presumably, since he had enough men, this would have consisted of a human rather than a fortified barrier. Then, since he knew they might be there for some while, he arranged for his men '...to be refresh'd with Beer, Ale, and Brandy, which was brought into the Camp in great plenty, from the Neighbouring Ale-Houses.'[288] The brandy might have been unwise under the circumstances, and one of the beadles, '...animated and fir'd with the Liquor...',[289] attempted to climb

---

[286] *Authentick Memoirs*, p. 55

[287] ibid

[288] ibid

[289] ibid

up to the chamber window, whereupon one of the women fired a pistol at him, wounding him in the chest. Some of the officers quickly departed with their injured comrade, while others retaliated with a battery of brickbats hurled at the windows and walls. The servants held firm, but Baldwin was able to take over the stabling next to the house where entry was not opposed, and found sixteen coach horses, including the Flanders mares, and eight saddle horses together with the Colonel's berlin and chariot. These were seized and removed to a property in Ormond Mews, and to the Fleece Tavern in Tothill Street.

By midnight, Baldwin had still not been able to gain entry to the house, and a rumour was whispered about that the three women who had defied him were preparing to sally forth with their pistols, upon which half of his forty men deserted him. It later transpired that this report had been spread by the Colonels friends, to intimidate the officers and provide a better opportunity for the servants to carry away the household effects under cover of darkness.

The house remained under blockade all night and most of the following morning, but at eleven o'clock, the women hung out a white smock as a signal for capitulation. Perhaps the Colonel's legal advisors had prevailed upon him to order his staff to cooperate with the Bailiff's men. Mr Morice who had arrived at the scene, said that he would grant no other terms than that the 'Girls of the Garrison'[290] should march out with only their own apparel and whatever goods belonged to them. The women demanded that they should be allowed to depart in a hackney coach with the windows drawn up in the manner of a covered wagon, and to this Morice agreed, but instead of leaving by the front door they managed instead to get into a

---

[290] ibid, p. 56

neighbour's house and make their escape that way. As soon as Morice's officers knew the house was unattended, they entered through the windows.

For two days carts went back and forth carrying furniture, plate and linens, with fifty dozen bottles of fine wines, to be stored in an empty house in Old Bond Street. Cash was lodged with a Mr Drummond, a Charing Cross goldsmith. The total value of these items was estimated as £7,000 to £8,000.

In addition to these measures, the Sheriffs of London and Middlesex had issued orders forbidding all transfers of the convict's money or shares at South Sea House and the offices of any other companies in which he held investments. They then proceeded to seize all the Colonel's stock and cash held at those offices. Orders were also despatched to the Sheriff of Lancashire, authorising him to seize the Colonel's three Lordships in that county. The trustees of the estate of the Duke of Wharton presumably needed no instructions, and immediately seized the Manor of Wooburn, which the Colonel had purchased from the Duke, and which was still subject to a substantial mortgage.

Morice, suspecting that the servants had removed some of the Colonel's goods to nearby hiding places before the arrival of his men, obtained a warrant and had '…the House of Plaisterer…'[291] in the parish of St George searched for the Colonel's plate and jewels, but found nothing. Another gentleman in New Bond Street had his house entered 'in a violent and riotous manner' by Samuel Baldwin, 'on pretence of seizing the goods and effects of Colonel Charteris.'[292] The

[291] *The Echo or Edinburgh Weekly Journal*, Wednesday 18 March, Number LXIII, p. 240
[292] 'Thursday Nov. 12', in *The Grub Street Journal*, 19 November 1730, p. 2

occupier later took legal action against Baldwin for the disturbance.

News of the Colonel's conviction took London by storm. 'When the News was first spread about the Town, Mankind was amaz'd; People stood aghast, looking at one another like Statues…' 'All gossip on the other burning news items of the day ceased:

> The Demolition of *Ch—s*, and the *Opening* of his Maid's *Port* and *Harbour*, and in what Manner he had raz'd the fortifications of her Vertue was the Subject on which all Conversation turn'd.[293]

'We had several extraordinary Cases which have diverted the Town this Month, in the Course of judicial Process, and whose Conclusion have been very Extraordinary,' commented the compiler of *The Political State of Great Britain*, adding that 'The Famous Col. *Charters*, eminent on many publick Occasions; and particularly for being immensely Rich,' had received a 'long, full and fair Tryal.'[294]

The almost universal reaction was rejoicing in the verdict, for Francis Charteris was one of the few men of his time equally hated by all classes. The Mob revelled in the conviction of a wealthy rogue for a crime against a servant, while the Quality loathed him for the utter contempt he showed for every principle of honour and fair dealing. The legal profession saw the outcome as a valuable boost to the public perception of the effectiveness of the criminal justice system.

---

[293] *Authentick Memoirs*, pp. 1-2

[294] Anon, *The Political State of Great-Britain* (60 vols, London, Printed for the Executors of Mr Boyer, and sold by T. Warner, 1730), vol. 39, p. 217

Rumour quickly dredged up and circulated stories of the Colonel's real and supposed former misdeeds, although even the popular scribblers knew where to draw the line. '…Of all the Reports now reigning against him, we must in Justice acquit him of attempting a Rape upon the Body of his own Grandmother in *Scotland*, for we are assur'd it is without all manner of Foundation…'[295]

The newspapers were unequivocal about the justice of the verdict. '…He had several Evidences to invalidate the Charges in the Indictment, but their Depositions being full of Inconsistencies and Contradictions, he was capitally convicted, and thereupon carried up to Newgate',[296] observed the *Daily Courant*, while the *London Journal* stated that 'His chief Defence was a sham Letter sworn to by his Footman to come from her, which was proved to be a forgery.'[297]

The pamphlets published anonymously soon after the trial also had no doubts about the correctness of the verdict. 'The Evidence for the King being very positive and clear, and of good Credit, and the Colonel's Witnesses being full of Inconsistencies and Contradictions…'[298]

Viscount Percival, who described Charteris in his diary as '…one of the greatest and most known rogues in England…', observed, 'At his trial he made a mean defence, the main of it consisting in a letter his footman swore to as of her writing, which was disproved…'[299]

A poem published anonymously later that year read:

---

[295] *Authentick Memoirs*, p. 3

[296] 'London', in *The Daily Courant*, 27 February 1730, no. 8856, p. 2

[297] 'London', in *The London Journal*, 28 February, no. 552, p. 2

[298] *Authentick Memoirs*, p. 54

[299] Percival, vol. 1, p. 75

No thinking Jury cou'd espouse your Cause,
So strong her Evidence, so plain our Laws;
Your Witnesses their Parts did over-act,
Their Honour, like your vigour, we suspect.[300]

Opponents of Robert Walpole took particular delight in the downfall of his crony, *The Grub Street Journal* quoting lines from Sir Samuel Garth's satirical 1699 poem, *The Dispensary*:

...Little Villains must submit to fate,
That Great Ones may enjoy the world in state.[301]

However villainous the Colonel was believed to be, Anne was not seen as an innocent by all. The London rumour-mill was busy grinding, and stories were current that '...he lay with [Anne] twelve nights, before she swore the rape on him...',[302] and that she had been offered and refused two hundred guineas to '...let the matter drop ...'[303]

Newgate Prison, which Francis Charteris so unexpectedly entered on 26 February 1730, was a handsome stone-built edifice which, like the Justice Hall was built after its predecessor had been burned to the ground in 1666. It is not known how many prisoners it was intended to hold, but there were no limits on admissions, and by 1730 it would have been severely overcrowded, to the extent that by 1770 it had to be rebuilt.

One of the first things Charteris would have noticed about Newgate was that it operated as a business whose main object

---

[300] Anon, *The Reprieve: An Epistle from J—ck K—ch to C—l C—s* (London, A. Moore, 1730), p. 4

[301] *The Grub Street Journal*, 12 March 1730, no. X, p. 1

[302] Percival, vol. 1, p. 75

[303] ibid

was to extract as much money from its inmates as possible, something which under different circumstances he would have applauded. So lucrative was the office of Keeper that it could not be purchased for under £5,000, just the kind of investment that attracted him. Every prisoner entering the jail was obliged to pay the sum of 3s to the keeper, and there were charges to be paid both to the keeper and the turnkey on discharge. The prison was divided into two main sections, called the 'common side' and the 'master side', within which felons and debtors were kept separate. Where and how well the prisoner was lodged depended entirely on his or her ability to pay for accommodation and upkeep. On the common side, poor prisoners did not pay for rooms but were expected to find their own beds and bedding, and if unable to do so, went without. In practice this meant that they were crowded together in dark, unheated and unsanitary conditions. The stench was appalling, and those confined without hope did not trouble to clean their apartments, preferring instead to spend their final days on a last riot of debauchery. The most basic food was provided, and anything else they had to buy or have brought in. Many prisoners on the common side starved for lack of money or friends, or died of gaol fever, their bodies taken out in carts and thrown into a pit at the nearby churchyard of Christ Church Newgate. Others went mad and had to be heavily chained. Some were already mad when they were admitted. The master side was cleaner and less crowded and there was a fire in cold weather. Two prisoners could share a room and a bed with bedding at a cost of 1s 3d a week apiece. Those who preferred to sleep alone paid 2s 6d.

For the wealthiest prisoners who desired a measure of luxury and refinement, there was always the Press-Yard (not to be confused with the Press-Room) where they could stay in spacious, clean and airy private rooms with comfortable beds. There was a yard 54 feet in length and 7 wide, paved with Purbeck stone, where the privileged few could walk in the open air. While the Mob languished in unwashed squalor, the Quality held levées, and receptions, entertained friends of both sexes and had the best food, drink and entertainment. These luxuries came at a premium. For admission to the Press-Yard apartments there was a sliding scale of fees from £20 to £500 depending on what the keeper thought the prisoner could afford. In addition to this, the weekly rent of a room was 11s 6d, of which 1s was paid to a woman to make the fires and clean the rooms, and the rest went to the gaoler. The prisoner had to provide his own fire, candles, food, drink and bed linen. For an additional fee, the gaoler would bring in prostitutes.

As soon as Francis Charteris entered Newgate he was marked out as a man who could be milked of money. On arrival he would have been conducted to a chamber close by the main gate known as the 'condemned hold'. It was a bleak, dark unheated room about 15ft by 20ft, with a plank floor, and one tiny window. Ring-bolts were fastened into the walls to which unruly prisoners could be chained. It served both as the place where condemned felons waited to be taken for execution and as the reception room for new prisoners, where they were first placed in irons. There, the Colonel would have been loaded with the heaviest shackles available and left alone to contemplate his fate. After a passage of time, carefully calculated to allow the prisoner to drive himself into a frenzy of despair, the gaoler would reappear and if the Colonel complained bitterly of this unwarranted treatment of a man of quality, it would be intimated that on the payment of a certain fee he might be privileged to wear a lighter set of shackles. In a friendly yet firm manner the financial arrangements under which he would be accommodated would have been made clear, and eventually the Colonel was conducted to his new apartments.

Charteris was said to have been lodged in a room in the Press-Yard once occupied by Major Oneby, a gambler who had killed a man in a quarrel and was, against his every expectation condemned to hang. On 3 July 1727, the day before he was due to be executed, 53-year-old Oneby cut his wrist with a pen-knife and bled to death. Contemplation of his predecessor's fate cannot have improved the Colonel's mood.

On the top floor of the prison was a chapel which both debtors and felons were obliged to attend on Sundays. It was divided into solidly constructed pens, and there was a separate compartment for those under sentence of death. Condemned prisoners were taken to the chapel twice a day, '...where they receive such Admonitions as are necessary to prepare them for future Happiness...'[304] On the morning of an execution, the Blessed Sacrament was administered to those who were about to suffer, and a special sermon was preached, an event for which the public pews were always filled to capacity by an attentive audience. The Colonel was disinclined to fit in with the requirements of the prison, and refused to attend the religious services. His reported behaviour suggests a brooding sulk.

> The *Ordinary* of Newgate, in his Account of the Behaviour of the Malefactors, says, That one Fr—s Ch—ris would not come to Chapel, nor hear Prayers in private, but said he was a *bigoted* Presbyterian, and that if he wanted Prayers, he would call for a Presbyterian Divine. — Who this bigotted

---

[304] B. Langley, *An Accurate Description of Newgate* (London, T. Warner, 1724), p. 47

Presbyterian Fr—s Ch—ris is, I can't tell, nor has the
Ordinary given us any Instance of his Bigottry to Religion.[305]

On the evening of Saturday 28 February, the fifty-one
prisoners who had been found guilty during the four days of
hearings, were all brought to the Sessions House to be
sentenced. Thirty-two were sentenced to transportation, three
were to be whipped, and six were branded. Ten, including
Francis Charteris were due to be sentenced to death, and were
placed in the dock together. The Colonel appeared in a
'…Horseman's Coat, with two Footmen waiting without the
Bar.'[306] His companions that day were mainly thieves. Richard
Hanson had committed an assault after robbing a man of his
hat, William Newcomb had been discovered in the act of
burglary, John Carter and Peter Rivers had, at pistol point,
robbed a man of a pair of silver buckles, a corkscrew and 3s 4d,
Francis Hackabout had committed highway robbery and
assault, Stephen Dowdle had stolen a gold watch, and
Elizabeth Doyle, a pickpocket, had returned from
transportation. Only two men had committed murder, the
highwaymen Ferdinando Shrimpton and Robert Drummond.
While robbing a coach they had shot a man in the arm, an
injury from which he died eight days later.

There was a last gamble on the Colonel's behalf. His counsel
demanded that the indictment against him should be read in
Latin. There was no precedent for this, but he was indulged
and the request complied with. It was probably a ploy to
provoke some error in the proceedings with which to obtain an
arrest of judgement, under which counsel could move that
judgement be withheld on the grounds that there had been a

---

[305] 'London *April 25*', in *Fog's Weekly Journal*, 25 April, no. 83, p. 2
[306] *Authentick Memoirs*, p, 57

miscarriage of justice. Failing that, a mistake at this stage could form the basis of a later application for a Writ of Error which could overturn the verdict. In the event, the indictment was read without error, and counsel, who seemed to have run out of ideas, offered nothing more on his clients behalf.

The justice, Mr Serjeant Raby, Deputy Recorder of the City of London, donned his black cap, and after warning the prisoners to prepare for death, he pronounced sentence. When he came to the words, 'That you be hanged by the neck until you are dead — dead — dead', the turnkey slipped a loop of string over the prisoner's thumb, and tightened it to show how the noose would be tightened around his neck at Tyburn.[307] The next hanging day was Friday 17 April.

It was later rumoured that once sentencing was over, Shrimpton, '…a merry Malefactor…',[308] turned to the Colonel and asked on behalf of himself and the other condemned prisoners for a guinea for drink, saying it was the custom among felons for he who had most money to treat the rest at such a time. The Colonel was said to have replied, '…Deel d— mn him if he would part with a Guinea since there was but one condemn'd Wh—re among Nine Men.'[309] Whether or not the story is true it is certainly in character.

Immediately after sentencing Charteris was conveyed back to the prison by sedan chair, the chair being '…followed by vast Crowds of People, all highly approving of this remarkable Instance of Divine vengeance and Human Justice, by their loud and repeated Acclamations.'[310]

---

[307] W. Besant, *London in the Eighteenth Century* (London, Adam and Charles Black, 1902), p. 531

[308] *Authentick Memoirs*, p. 57

[309] ibid, p. 58

[310] ibid

And so Colonel Charteris disappeared into what was now his condemned cell, where, depending on which rumour the public chose to believe, he spent his time campaigning for a pardon, disporting himself with prostitutes, or lying on a bed of sickness close to death. Nothing could be done for him immediately since he could not petition for a pardon until the Judges had made their report to the King, and they had departed London on circuit as soon as the sessions ended. The delay in the report was thought to be deliberate, so that '…every one might get the firmer impression & information of what was forfeit to them.'[311]

There was, of course, precedent for the execution of a Charteris. Contemplating his possible doom, the Colonel must have gloomily recalled the fate of his cousin Alexander some eighty years previously. Tyburn, the principal place of execution in London, was then an open grove which lay near what is today's Marble Arch. The gallows — the famous triple tree — consisted of three stout posts each eighteen feet in height in a triangular formation connected by crossbeams nine feet long, and was capable of hanging up to twenty-four prisoners simultaneously. On hanging days, of which there were five or six a year, the condemned felons, after having their shackles struck off, and the hempen rope placed around their necks, climbed into a horse drawn cart to which they were securely tied, and were brought from Newgate along streets lined with turbulent crowds. Public executions were seen by the Mob as an opportunity for riotous behaviour, drunkenness, dancing, swearing, fighting, lewdness, crime and profit. The atmosphere was of a large, noisy and uncontrolled

---

[311] National Archives of Scotland, Legal correspondence addressed to Archibald Stuart, WS, Letter from George Skene of that ilk, 7 April 1730, GD237/20/8

street party. Upstairs rooms in the houses along the way were rented to wealthy onlookers, who entertained themselves while they were waiting for the main event with cards, music, champagne and sex, and at Tyburn itself, seats were sold at premium prices on a specially-constructed stand. In the streets, and milling about the gallows, vendors and pickpockets made the most of the celebrating throng. A popular hero, such as a highwayman, a handsome well-dressed young man with a reputation for daring, who made a show of bravery on his way to die, might be offered drinks and nosegays along the way. A reviled figure would be jeered and pelted with stones and filth. The Colonel would have had no doubts as to his likely reception, and the best he could hope for was being permitted to travel in a closed carriage rather than the open wagon with the common felons. At the gallows, however, he would have had to mount the wagon, and have the noose placed about his neck. There was no drop, as such — no hope of a swift and merciful breaking of the spine. When the moment came, the horse would be urged forward leaving the occupants of the wagon dangling by their necks to die in a slow agony of strangulation. Sometimes relatives hung onto the prisoner's feet to speed up the process, or the hangman would accept a fee to perform this service. Poor prisoners would have had the additional horror that their unclaimed bodies would be given to hospitals for dissection. The Colonel knew that his family and friends would want to recover his body and remove it for proper burial, but there had been instances where the angry Mob had intervened, seized upon the body of someone they especially disliked and tossed it from person to person like a stuffed doll. Sometimes a body had been handed over in good faith to a 'grieving widow' who turned out to be an agent for an anatomist. The public dissection of the corpse of Colonel

Francis Charteris would have been one of the great celebrity events of the decade.

The first evening after sentence of death Charteris was reported to be '...in great Confusion and Disorder...'[312] It was said that he was visited in his cell by another prisoner, the 'famous Roger Johnson', who cheered him up by singing a merry catch of his own composing with the chorus '...when a hanging we do go...'[313] — with which the Colonel was reported to be 'wonderfully delighted.'[314] This was later angrily denied by Johnson, a thief and counterfeiter well-known in his own right.

The next morning being a Sunday, the Minister of the prison, Mr Guthrie, having conducted the service in the chapel in the presence of the other condemned, and noticing that Charteris had not been present, knocked on the door of the Colonel's cell and was admitted. It was reported that as soon as he entered the room, the Colonel jumped up, put his hand in his pocket, and pulled out some money saying, 'What's your Fee, what's your Fee?'[315] Guthrie replied that '...he demanded no fee but only came to wait on him, and to be Assistant to him, as it was his Duty to all gentlemen in his unfortunate Circumstances.'[316] This only threw the Colonel into one of his rages. 'Then ... if you don't want a Fee I don't want you; so pray go about your Business.'[317] Guthrie retreated, and the prisoner commented, '...The Man was in a confounded hurry, sure; 'twas time enough to talk with him when his Friends

---

312 *Authentick Memoirs*, p. 58
313 ibid, p. 59
314 ibid, p. 60
315 *History*, p. 45
316 ibid
317 ibid

Endeavours had fail'd, and he was included in the Dead-Warrant.'[318] The main thing occupying Charteris' mind was the seizure of his goods, especially his prized horses, and he wrote a polite letter to Mr Morice asking him to come and see him. Morice duly arrived and allegedly finding the Colonel dining on fish said he was '...glad to see him so well disposed to the *Lent* season...',[319] to which the Colonel was said to have replied, '...indeed it was the veryest *Lent* he had ever kept in his Life; for that he had not touch'd nor scarce seen a Woman for several Days past.'[320]

Charteris begged the bailiff not to sell his horses, for he hoped before long to be '...*in Statu quo*...'[321] and able to purchase them back himself. Morice kindly assured him that he should have first refusal. The Colonel may have been placing his confidence in a letter he had written to '...a certain great Lord in Power...'[322] but on the following day, to his great dismay, he received news that the letter '...was torn in pieces, with all the tokens of Contempt, the Moment it was delivered... He sigh'd and wept, and there appear'd a great Alteration in his Temper, and some of the soberest of his Friends expected a happy Disposition towards a repentance...'[323] He is said to have called for a bible and read it with great attention, until some army officers came to visit him. After a conversation mainly consisting of '...the most extravagant Complaints...'[324] against the prosecutor and jury, the '...fit of

---

[318] *Authentick Memoirs*, p. 60

[319] ibid

[320] ibid

[321] ibid, p. 61

[322] ibid

[323] ibid

[324] ibid

seeming Repentance soon left him.'[325] In low spirits once more, a turnkey was said to have tried to cheer him up by singing him 'The Condemn'd Minuet' — a composition, it was claimed, that was normally sung by prisoners the night before their execution. If true (and the author of *Scotch Gallantry* poured scorn on the story), it was no more than the Colonel deserved.

Apart from Morice, Charteris received other visitors who were not identified, and was also in time, permitted to leave his own room to visit his fellow prisoners. He is known to have visited a Mr Castle whose room lay on the same floor. Castle was a co-conspirator with Sir John Fenwick, whose plans to assassinate King William III had been exposed in 1696.

The news of the Colonel's condemnation had been rapidly succeeded by a general buzz on the prospects of his being pardoned, which was the subject of wagers. 'We hear great Intercession has been made to save the Colonel's life, but as yet without effect',[326] observed *The Grub Street Journal*, adding what the editor knew to be a vital factor in the Colonel's chances of a reprieve, 'He is reckon'd worth 200,000 l.'[327] In Edinburgh it was rumoured that the odds being offered on the Colonel escaping execution were ten guineas to one in favour, and no-one was in much doubt as to how such a pardon might be obtained. Shortly after the trial, *The Grub Street Journal* published a carefully worded editorial which named no names:

> To condemnation succeeds an application for a pardon; which can seldom be obtained, without false representations of the character of the person convicted, and of the circumstance of

---

[325] ibid
[326] 'Saturday Feb 28' in *The Grub Street Journal*, 5 March 1730, p. 2
[327] ibid

his conviction... But since it seldom happens, that any Great man is capitally convicted, who has not before been guilty of the like, or of some other crime of equal magnitude; how can such a Person be represented to a Prince, as a proper object of his mercy, but by a complication of falsities?... This opens a large scene of bribery and corruption.[328]

This was undoubtedly a satirical linking of Charteris with Walpole, popularly referred to as 'The Great Man'.

'We hear of no Rapes to have been committed for three Weeks past', observed *Fog's Weekly Journal*, pointedly. 'Colonel *Francis Chartres* is still in Newgate, notwithstanding the Reports of his being pardon'd.'[329]

No sympathy was expressed for the loss of the Colonel's properties. '...The Havock made of his Immense Wealth, meerly upon the Advantage of a Verdict, by which they tell us, above 100,000 l. of his Estate has been seiz'd by the Sheriffs, High Bailiffs, and such like Officers, to whom such Perquisites belong; but which was certainly not intended, to extend to such sums, has entertained the Town for at least this whole Month, and the whole of his Fate is not yet determined.'[330]

A Charteris execution would have been an enormously popular diversion for every level of society, but it was never thought to be a serious possibility. The press of that period when reporting on prisoners condemned to death, often commented that certain individuals were sure to be pardoned because they had powerful friends. *The Grub Street Journal* observed:

---

[328] *The Grub Street Journal*, 12 March 1730, p. 1

[329] 'London, *March* 14', in *Fog's Weekly Journal*, 14 March, no. 77, p. 2

[330] *Political State*, vol. 39, p. 321

> That Persons of considerable fortune or quality, tho' liable to
> the same capital penalties with those in a lower station, yet
> should not have those penalties inflicted on them, has been
> thought seasonable in all nations ... tho' this is looked upon
> by their inferiors as too great a privilege...[331]

The editor was being satirical, but revealed what was then considered common practice. '...It is expected he will be pardoned', wrote Viscount Percival in his diary on the day of sentencing. 'The late King, as likewise Queen Elizabeth, would never suffer a man condemned for a rape to be executed, as not believing it possible for to commit the crime unless the woman in some sort consented.'[332] Nevertheless the whole course of events since the crime had gone so counter to prevailing practice that the Colonel can hardly have felt secure. He may well have contemplated the last resort of bribing his guards to allow him to escape, a supplementary service often provided to wealthy prisoners.

Even statements made in his favour revealed a thorough public appreciation of the kind of man he was. Those who said he should not hang, believed this not because of his character, and history, for which it was felt he should have been hanged many times over, but because of a prevailing opinion, among men especially, that hanging was not an appropriate punishment for rape when the victim was by far the social inferior of the criminal.

> BLOOD! —— must a Colonel, with a Lord's Estate,
> Be thus obnoxious to a Scoundrel's Fate?
> Brought to the Bar, and sentenc'd from the Bench,
> Only for ravishing a Country Wench? ——

---

[331] *The Grub Street Journal*, 12 March 1730, p. 1
[332] Percival, vol. 1, p. 75

Shall Men of Honour meet no more Respect?
Shall their Diversions thus by Law be check'd?
Shall they b'accountable to fancy Juries
For this or t'other Pleasure? —— Hell and Furies!
What Man thro' Villainy would run a Course,
And ruin Families without Remorse,
To heap up Riches. —— if, when all is done,
An ignominious Death he cannot shun?[333]

The Grub Street Journal declared with undisguised sarcasm that rapes were '…one of those diversions which are proper only for Gentlemen…' and thus unfit to place before a jury of common tradesmen:

> In a Case of this kind, the Jury ought to consist of officers, or other Men of honour, who would be able to judge whether the accused person was qualified to ravish or not. And if it should appear, that the supposed criminal is a person duly qualified, either by Birth, Education or Fortune, for such Entertainments; and that the person pretending to be ravished is much inferior to him in Condition; then it might be thought proper to acquit the Gentleman honourably, and oblige the Woman to live with him, as long as he should please. But if he should desire to have no further Conversation with her, she might be sent to some house of Correction. These Methods, if well pursued, would soon put an entire stop to these troublesome Indictments, and Gentlemen would be able to enjoy their proper Diversions unmolested.[334]

This article was attributed to 'Timothy Noodle', a name then associated satirically with Walpole.

---

[333] Applebee, p. 209
[334] *The Grub Street Journal*, 9 April 1730, p. 1

The Colonel's mood cannot have been improved by the news that on 4 March, Elizabeth Doyle — sentenced to death on the same day as he — had, without any great ceremony, been pardoned and discharged. Francis Charteris, confined with the dangers and extortioners of Newgate, with public opinion very much against him, the media plunging their knives into what shreds of reputation he may have had left, and the wheels of the law turning slowly, might have felt he had only one hope of saving his life and property — his estranged family. This meant an appeal to someone he disliked intensely, his fortune-hunting son-in-law, the Earl of Wemyss.

VIII: THE OBJECT OF REGAL PITY AND COMPASSION[335]

Soon after the Old Bailey verdict, Trusty Jack was dispatched express to Scotland carrying the news of his master's conviction. It was later reported that on hearing of her father's plight the Countess of Wemyss, by now the mother of seven children, '… fell extremely ill.'[336] Janet was unable to accompany her husband who set out for London almost immediately. Although some newspapers claimed that the Earl of Wemyss arrived in London on 2 March, it was actually at 4 p.m. on the 14th when the Earl arrived together with a companion, James Bruce, '…a young Gentleman who is going to travel.'[337] After dining at the King's Arms Tavern in New Bond Street, Wemyss went to see the Colonel in Newgate.

From the moment of his arrival in London, Wemyss was tireless in his efforts to assist Charteris, both to save him from the gallows, and reverse the order for the seizure of his property. He took lodgings at a Mr Russell's on Ludgate Hill, '…for the conveniency of attending his father in-law…',[338] and visited him regularly, coordinating the campaign with such drive and efficiency that the newspapers were soon reporting it to be a foregone conclusion that the Colonel would be free.

'Does not Chartres' misfortunes grieve you?', wrote playwright John Gay to Jonathan Swift on 31 March, 'for that

---

[335] *Don Francisco*, p. 53
[336] 'London', in *The Daily Post*, 21 March, no. 3277, p. 1
[337] 'London, *March 21*', in *Fog's Weekly Journal*, 21 March, no. 78, p. 2
[338] 'London', in *The Daily Journal*, no. 2873, Saturday 28 March, p. 2

179

great man is like to save his life and lose some of his money, a very hard case!'[339]

There is no record of what Wemyss actually thought of his father-in-law, and his actions were probably solely motivated by the fortune that was at stake. It was probably no secret that Charteris intended to make his grandson Francis his principal heir, and the Earl may have anticipated that the boy being a minor, he would have control of the Colonel's estate in the event of his son inheriting. In the ensuing months he left no avenue unexplored to save the Colonel and his property. One of his first actions was to present a petition to the King for the Colonel's release, but he was quickly advised that nothing could be done until the King had met in Council to discuss the fate of the felons convicted at the February sessions.

On 23 March, *The Edinburgh Evening Courant* stated, 'We hear that the Report of Colonel Charters will not be made to his Majesty in Council till some time after, because several Witnesses are to be re-examined relating to the said Colonel's Trial, before the Twelve Judges, as soon as they return from their respective Circuits.'[340] If true, there is no record of such examinations.

While Helen Charteris was not expected to play a prominent part in the campaign to save her husband, it was recognised that her support could be a powerful bargaining tool. She would be seen as a steadying influence on the old goat, her presence by his side proof that even the incorrigible Colonel could be tamed into behaving himself. Soon after the Earl departed for London it was announced that she too was on her way. At first it was thought that the Countess had accompanied

---

[339] *The Correspondence of Jonathan Swift*, vol. 3, p. 385
[340] 'London March 17', in *The Edinburgh Evening Courant*, 23 March 1730, p.2037

her, but for the time being, Janet Wemyss remained in Scotland, indisposed. Helen Charteris arrived in London on 2 April, and took lodgings in Warwick Lane near Newgate, the better to conduct her own campaign for the Colonel's pardon. 'His Wife…', it was observed, '(tho' he no Ways deserved it) was indefatigable in her Solicitations.'[341] Nevertheless she may have had a few strong words to say to her husband in private. 'She is a Gentlewoman of a great many personal Endowments, who being sensible that all his Calamity and Distress are principally owing to that debauched Life to which he has been too frequently addicted, she could not forbear complaining against his Conduct in giving such a Creature an opportunity to Ruin him…'[342]

The next point of attack was the Colonel's victim. Depositions were soon in preparation regarding Anne Bond, and Charteris wrote to Mr Gibson, the Recorder of Lancaster asking him to make enquiries into Anne's character, obtain affidavits and return them to the judges of assize to be transmitted to London and laid before his Majesty in Council. Given his efforts in the 1711 case, it is reasonable to suppose that had Charteris found nothing to suggest that Anne was of bad character he could easily have found suitable people who, for a price, would put their signatures to whatever lies he required. It was rumoured that he had been visited in prison by '…several Persons of Distinction…'[343] and that '…several Depositions are taken in relation to the Character of *Anne Bond*, tending to discredit some things that were sworn by her at his Tryal … and these Depositions coming, some of them, from Persons of Credit and Reputation, a Minister, a Physician,

---

[341] *Don Francisco*, p. 54

[342] ibid, pp. 54-5

[343] *Scotch Gallantry*, p. 36

a 'Squire, and others where *Bond* Lodg'd ...'[344] If they existed (and journalistic invention should not be dismissed as the basis of this report), none of these papers has ever come to light or their contents made known. It was part of the Colonel's usual procedure in such situations to have his cronies spread lies to assist his case, and it was inevitable that some of his stories about Anne's character would be believed. On 4 March, Viscount Percival wrote in his diary:

> I heard the king intends to pardon Colonel Chartres, it being found out that the woman he would have ravished was a common strumpet, at least it is so related at Court. All the world agree he deserved to be hanged long ago, but they differ whether on this occasion.[345]

The Viscount also reported a visit to court on 11 March where among other things the King and Queen talked to him '...of the irreligious ends of Sir Godfrey Kneller [the portrait painter] and Colonel Chartres...'[346]

One great advantage for Charteris was his ability to call upon the assistance of an old friend who was now in a powerful position. By mid-March he had committed the care of his affairs relating to his estates to the Edinburgh drinking companion of his youth, Duncan Forbes, who had by then risen to be the Attorney-General of Scotland. Forbes, whose loyalty had never wavered through all the Colonels misadventures, kept a low profile during negotiations, but was undoubtedly a major influence.

Wemyss soon decided that the best way of protecting his father-in-law's property in the short term was to buy it back,

---

[344] ibid, p. 26
[345] Percival, p. 76
[346] ibid, p. 235

and he proceeded to acquire the most important items. By 18 March he had taken possession of the chariot and berlin. On 28 March, some of the Colonel's household goods were carried back to the house in George Street, the Earl of Wemyss having recovered them from the High Bailiff at the cost of £1,000. Wemyss had also purchased the Colonel's horses for £700. Some of the property was returned without charge. It was reported in April that 'The high Bailiff has restored the Col. All his Linnens.'[347]

When the transactions were completed the newspapers estimated that Wemyss had spent a total of £3,000 buying back goods and chattels seized by Morice's men, although some furniture and valuables still remained in the Bailiff's hands. How the normally impecunious Earl came by such funds is unknown, but it is possible he may have been able to issue promissory notes on the security of the value of the estate.

The sheer extent of the Charteris estate was causing unusual headaches for William Morice. In the scramble to seize the Colonel's effects some unscrupulous individuals had seen an opportunity to enrich themselves.

> A Suit, we hear, is going to be commenc'd by Order of the Treasury, against the High Bailiff of Westminster, touching his seizure of the Col. Chartres' Goods and Chattels in the Liberty of Westminster, John Edwin Esq; laying Claim to them by Vertue of a Grant of King Charles II to his Father and his Heirs &c. Of the Office of Proprietor of the Waste and Spoil in the said Liberty of Westminster.[348]

---

[347] 'London March 28', in *The Echo and Edinburgh Weekly Journal*, 8 April, no. LXVI, p. 243
[348] 'London March 21', in *The Edinburgh Evening Courant*, Tuesday 24 March to Thursday 26 March, p. 2075

This claim was soon dismissed.

> We hear the Pretensions of John and Thomas Edwin, Esqrs:
> to the Effects of Col. Chartres seiz'd in George Street
> Hanover Square, are wav'd; Mr Morice appearing to act under
> the just and legal Title of Lessee to the Dean and Chapter of
> Westminster, of the Soil and Water thereof, for which he
> pays, pursuant to the Lease made at his first Entrance on his
> Post 100 l. Per Annum, and that their Claim, as by Charter
> from K. Charles I, extends only to the Districts of the Palace.[349]

The seizure of the Colonel's South Sea stock and cash by the
Sheriffs of London and Middlesex had led to their squabbling
with Morice since he had also laid claim to the property, and at
the end of March the matter was referred to the Attorney
General and lawyer Thomas Lutwyche for determination. It is
not known how, or indeed whether, this was resolved.

While all this activity was going on, the Press was making the
most of the fall of this most hated celebrity, and unauthorised
biographies were being issued as fast as they could be written
and printed. All the authors preferred to remain anonymous,
although Alexander Pope believed that Benjamin Norton de
Foe, said to be the natural offspring of Daniel Defoe, was
writing a life of the Colonel. The authors of these rival
publications were understandably scathing about the accuracy
of the others. 'A Grubstreet Edition of the Life of Col.
Chartres has been sold about the Streets for this Day or two,
but is most wretched Stuff', commented *The Universal Spectator
and Weekly Journal*, probably referring to *Don Francisco*, 'tho'
next Monday the Publick will be oblig'd with *Memoirs of the Life
of that Great Man*, by an authentick Hand, which will be very

---

[349] 'London March 24', in *The Edinburgh Evening Courant*, p. 2072,
Thurs 26 March to Mon 30 March.

much worth the Perusal of the Publick.'[350] A week later its pages advertised *The Authentick Memoirs* in which the compilers of the newspaper must undoubtedly have had a hand. The author of *Scotch Gallantry* denounced both *Don Francisco* and *Authentick Memoirs* as stuffed with'…improbable Accounts … barefac'd Obscenity … known Falsehoods…' designed to '…swell their Pamphlets to a twelve-penny Size.'[351] *The History of Col. Francis Ch-rtr-s* commented, 'It is a misfortune common to all Great Men, that upon any Casualty that befals them, they are constantly murder'd by a Pack of Scriblers, who write themselves into a Dinner at their Cost, without any Regard to Truth, or even common Decency…'[352] and criticises *Don Francisco* and *Authentick Memoirs*, in both of which, especially the latter, '… abundance of Stories are father'd on him, wherein he had no more Concern than the *Grand Turk*…'[353] Only *Don Francisco* makes no comment on rival publications which suggests that it was the first to be distributed.

The compiler of *The Political State of Great Britain* turned his anger upon these rag-tag biographers, accusing them of '…heaping Scandal and Slander upon him in Print; Publishing Fabulous and Romantick Relations of things said to be done by him, and which indeed are not only scandalous but false; I might say all of them false, because as those infamous Libellers, far from tying themselves down to strict Justice and Truth of Fact, have published meer Fictions and Romances as real Matters of Fact: So have they, even where any thing has been true in Fact, loaded it with Circumstances which could

---

[350] 'London', in *The Universal Spectator and Weekly Journal*, Saturday 7 March, no. LXXIV, p. 2

[351] *Scotch Gallantry*, p. 3

[352] *History*, p. 1

[353] ibid, p. 2 (incorrectly numbered 42 in 4th edition)

have no foundation in truth. And this has been so Notorious, that some who have been charged with being concerned with this Gentleman in such and such Affairs, have publickly vindicated both him and themselves, and declared to the World that they knew nothing at all of it.'[354] Such publications were '...loading the Afflicted, worrying and perplexing a Man that is already more than sufficiently perplex'd and disorder'd... Whoever he is that has the Hand of publick Justice upon him, is sure to have Weight and Affliction enough to grapple with, and had not need to have his Load made heavier; and to load such with Falsehood and Calumny, with Slanders, Satyrs, Banters, and Rallery, is a Treatment that I thinks wants a name, and such as no Man of good Principles can think of with Patience.' The writer may have been echoing the thoughts of other sympathetic souls when he added '...he seems already to have paid very dear for his Diversion.'[355] Unfortunately none of the critics of the pamphlets describe which stories they know to be false and which are embroidered but with a basis of truth.

Libellous pamphlets were then a commonplace entertainment especially where the subject was widely considered to be a scoundrel and therefore fair game. An anonymous letter to *The Grub Street Journal* protesting about this practice observed, 'I know a second [scribbler] who went to a person of honour in the *Tower* with a virulent Libel, by which he proposed, to his face, to ruin him under such a sum of money to suppress it. And a third, who did the same to the worthy Colonel Charteris.'[356] The use of the word 'worthy' is undoubtedly satirical. If someone did try to extort money from

---

[354] *Political State*, vol. 39, p. 322
[355] ibid
[356] 'To Mr Gilliver', *The Grub Street Journal*, 5 November 1730, p. 2

the Colonel, offering in return to suppress a libellous pamphlet, he cannot have known his subject very well. The author of *Scotch Gallantry* refers to a '…Political Bookseller, famous for publishing Obscene books…' who visited the Colonel in prison, '…thinking to get more of him for suppressing his Piece than he should of the Town by publishing it, propos'd to him the stifling of the Scandalous part of it, which otherwise would come abroad.' The Colonel's reply was, 'D—mn the World! I care not for what it says or knows of me; and troth Sir, if you pretend to be of another Opinion, no body will believe you.'[357]

The case was also the subject of popular ballads, one of which tells of '…a rich rascal.'

> Who would ravish, forswear, and pick Pockets and cheat,
> And by Men was oft beaten, and Women did beat:
> A favourite worthy of BOBBY the Great!
> > *Which no body can deny.*

> For a rape he once fled from his own native Clime,
> And with Pistols but lately attempted the Crime;
> Sure he ought to be hang'd that is caught a third time,
> > *Which no body can deny.*

Despite the subject of the ballad enjoying the protection of 'BOBBY the Screen', the author hoped for justice to take its course:

> If his majesty's Grace will let Villainy swing,
> O then all honest Hearts they will cheerfully sing,
> Boys, hang up the Col'nel, and God bless the King,
> > *Which no body can deny.*[358]

---

[357] *Scotch Gallantry*, p. 36

One part of Charteris' campaign for a pardon was a much belated attempt to curry sympathy by spreading reports that he was desperately ill. On 10 March he was visited in Newgate by a Dr Pringle, '…being greatly indisposed',[359] according to the *Daily Post*. The poor state of his health in recent years and the known hazards of Newgate easily enabled him to convince medical men that imprisonment was detrimental to his condition. Despite these reports there was no great outpouring of public sympathy or demands for his release.

The newspapers next recorded an uncharacteristically charitable act. 'Robert Drummond and Ferdinando Shrimpton are so ill in Newgate of the Gaol Distemper that they are hourly expected to expire; and Yesterday Col. Charteris (who likewise is dangerously ill) ordered them a Guinea for their Relief.'[360] If the story was true, it was a guinea very calculatingly spent.

On 2 April when the burgesses of the City of Westminster were due to entertain William Morice to a dinner and entertainment at the Bell Tavern, the bailiff was obliged to decline their hospitality, being called away to Newgate on account of Charteris' supposed affliction. This cannot have improved his mood. Morice's young wife had died after a serious illness the previous November and his father-in-law was dangerously ill. He was unlikely to have had much patience with someone trying to wring sympathy out of a mostly feigned indisposition.

---

[358] From a manuscript in the Harvard Library quoted in M.O. Percival (ed), *Political Ballads Illustrating the Administration of Sir Robert Walpole*, Volume 8 of *Oxford Historical and Literary Studies* (Oxford, Clarendon Press, 1916), pp. 35-6

[359] 'London', in *The Daily Post*, p. 1, no. 3267, 13 March 1730

[360] 'London', in *The Daily Journal*, Saturday 4 April, no. 2884, p. 1

On 3 April Charteris was visited in Newgate by Dr Mead of Ormond Street, who was persuaded to write a letter to the Duke of Newcastle, a Whig minister, and one of Walpole's inner circle, suggesting that the Colonel was very ill. It was a blatant attempt to gain sympathy, and almost certainly overstates the prisoner's case, but it does give an interesting insight into Charteris' general state of health at that time.

> My Lord
>   I do myself the honour to acquaint Your Grace that I visited Coll Chartres last night, and found him very ill; he has a continual fever, and as his Constitution is much broken with former frequent returns of an Asthma and Dropsy, I do really think him to be in very great danger. Gaol Distempers are always very bad, and reckoned of a malignant nature, and without doubt, close Confinement, uneasiness of mind, etc make the Case more hazardous. I am of opinion, that nothing would contribute so much to his recovery as the removing him out of such a dismal Place.[361]

Newcastle took this seriously enough to visit the Earl of Wemyss to discuss the Colonels situation on the following day. It is interesting that the letter was addressed to one of Walpole's associates and not the Great Man himself. It is apparent from later events that Walpole had not washed his hands of the Colonel, but the minister may have insisted that no approaches were made to him directly in writing, or destroyed any that were.

The newspapers obligingly reported that Charteris was so ill with asthma and fever that it was thought he could not recover. When this did not produce a public clamour for his freedom another, more affecting report was prepared. 'Col.

---

[361] *The Complete Hanoverian State Papers*, SP36/18 part 1, p. 5

Chartres is so ill in Newgate of a Fever, that he hath four Blisters on, and is attended by three eminent Physicians.'[362] A blister was a poultice spread with an irritant mixture applied to the skin with the object of improving circulation. One can only speculate on the reaction of his many victims to the thought of the Colonel lying on a bed of sickness in a gaol cell, his body plastered with these painful applications.

On 7 April George Skene of that ilk wrote to Archibald Stuart a Writer to the Signet of Edinburgh:

> ...He is just now so bad in prison that the Judges were [s]ent for express from the Country Seats after their Return from the Circuit to make their Report to the King ... for before the Report no dead warrant is sign'd or pardon granted so his friends might get him out before he should die, whether or not he is really at the point of death time will trye.[363]

Whatever the actual state of his health, the prospect of a long and possibly fatal stay in Newgate was a very real one. Charteris cannot have forgotten the fate of his mistress Sally Salisbury, a young woman dead after nine months of imprisonment. One of the men condemned on the same day as the Colonel, Stephen Dowdle (or Dowdale) aged 44, had received his Majesty's pardon, only to fall ill of gaol fever. He died in Newgate on 5 April. It must therefore have been with some alarm that the Colonel discovered that as the law then stood, the length of his stay in Newgate — assuming he was not executed — was a decision that lay in the hands of one person — Anne Bond, the woman he had raped and whose

---

[362] 'London', in *The Daily Post*, 6 April, no. 3290, p. 1

[363] National Archives of Scotland, Legal correspondence addressed to Archibald Stuart, WS, Letter from George Skene of that ilk, GD237/20/8, 7 April 1730

character he was now attempting to defame. While the King, as the initial prosecutor of the case, was entitled to pardon the convicted man, it remained open to Anne to turn prosecutor herself, enter an appeal against the pardon, and have the whole case tried again. If she elected to do this, the Colonel would have to remain in prison until the appeal was heard, which Anne could delay for up to a year. There was only one way out of the situation — a personal meeting with Anne, and a deal. 'Charters and his friends', wrote George Skene of that ilk, 'finding that he might certainly Remain in prison (tho' he had no earthly evidence to condemn him) and probably would have Rotten and died there, they thought fitt to compound the matter…'[364]

On 4 April the Colonel's advisors, one of whom was almost certainly Duncan Forbes, prepared a formal document of legal opinion and advice. The primary concern of this unsigned paper was saving the Colonel's life.

> I will take the freedom of communicating my thoughts upon the whole matter of the Colonel's unfortunate Case and Condition, as well as the method of his proceedings, as how the Law may turn against him, either with, or without His Majesty's Pardon.
>
> 1st
> It is, I think, absolutely necessary, that the Woman should be agreed with, that the Release and Bond that have been resolved upon should be executed, and the Question of the Col's not being capable of taking any benefit of the Release, by reason of his Conviction, is a nicety which at this time, ought not to be regarded.

---

[364] ibid, 2 May 1730

2d

Let the Petition to the King be presented without loss of time, even before the Judges can make their Report, and let the Petition suggest the Fact as it stands upon Record. That the Indictment was found against him at the General Sessions held at Hicks's Hall on such a day, that he was tryed, and convicted at the Old Bayley on such a day, and had Judgement of condemnation passed on accordingly in the same Sessions. He may in his Petition suggest his Zeal for his Majesty's Person and Government, and more especially his Behaviour in the Preston Rebellion, but by no means to meddle with any thing that concerns the Conviction, and he may conclude with imploring His Majesty's most gracious favour and indulgence in giving him such relief as in his great goodness and Royal Wisdom he shall think fit, and concluding specially either for his Life or Estate or for both together.

3.

The Woman to sign the Petition under words to this or the like Effect. That for her part, she has nothing to say, to hinder or interrupt, any favour that His Majesty shall be graciously pleased to bestow upon the Petitioner...

4.

If the King shall pardon his Life only, and not give way to a Writ of Error to reverse his attainder, I think all his estate, both real and personal, in England, is gone...

5.

But if His Majesty shall so far indulge him as to grant him leave for bringing a Writ of Error, and that a Judgement of reversall shall be obtained upon it. Then all the forfeiture accrewed to the Crown will cease, and he will be in Statu quo...

After some opinions on property matters the writer adds the

sound advice:

12.
Let the Col. confide in two or three of his Friends that are
best acquainted with proceedings of this kind, for in multitude
of advisers there are variety of opinions, which lend greatly to
uncertainty and Confusion.

4th April 1730.[365]

As Charteris read these words, the mocking spectre of his
cousin Alexander, pleading for his life in similar terms just
prior to his execution, must have risen before his eyes. After all
his efforts to destroy Anne's character it must have been
frustrating for the Colonel to read that he was not to 'meddle'
in any of the circumstances of the conviction. As he
considered this he received two pieces of welcome news. His
daughter had at last recovered her health and was on her way
to London, and thus far no action had been taken to seize his
possessions in Lancashire.

On 6 April a meeting was arranged between Anne Bond and
'…several Persons of Distinction and eminent Lawyers at the
Horn Tavern in the New Palace Yard, Westminster.'[366]

Those persons were the Earl of Wemyss, '…also a Great
Advocate for Scotland', and Mr Bernard, '…an eminent
Attorney of this City…'[367] The 'Great Advocate' must have
been Duncan Forbes.

---

[365] British Library, Additional MSS, Add33054, 'Opinion and Advice
for Col Charteris in 1730', ff. 94-6
[366] 'London', in *The Daily Post*, Wednesday 8 April, p. 1, no. 3292
[367] 'London April 9', in *The Echo or Edinburgh Weekly Journal*,
Wednesday 15 April, no. LXVII, p. 247

There is no record of what took place at this crucially important meeting. It is not known if Anne was represented by a lawyer or even a friend, or whether she faced these eminent gentlemen alone.

Newspapers speculated that Anne:

> …made several extraordinary Discoveries touching the Rape which Col. Chartres was convicted of having committed on her the said Ann Bond who is now kept in an Apartment not far from Surgeons Hall. — We don't think proper as yet to give the Particulars of her Discovery; meantime, 'tis discoursed by some, as if the Colonel will be very soon bailed out. — 'Tis said that before he went to Flanders, he made a Will, by which he left 10000 l. to the Lord Elcho, eldest Son to the Earl of Wemyss, 7000 l. per Annum, to Francis Wemyss his Lordship's second Son, and 5000 l. to each of his Lordship's Daughters, 5 in Number, also 50 l. to the Earl for a Ring, and 1000 l. to his poor relations.[368]

This was not so very far from the truth.

The public waited eagerly for revelations, but nothing was forthcoming, and it is probable that this account of the meeting was merely a guess by the newspaper. The main tenor of the discussion was undoubtedly to ask Anne's agreement that she would not raise any objections to the Colonel being pardoned. In return for that assurance, she would be paid the sum of £800, more money than a girl of her station was ever likely to see in several lifetimes, and easily enough to establish her in a business that would ensure her and her family a comfortable future. The little we know about Anne suggests that she was a level headed, practical girl. She had made her

---

[368] 'London April 9', in *The Echo or Edinburgh Weekly Journal*, Wednesday 15 April, no. LXVII, p. 247

point publicly that she was an innocent outraged, and she knew that the Colonel had suffered for his crime. There was nothing to be gained from standing on principle. She signed the agreement. Mr Kettleby had judged the value of his involvement well, as he was awarded £100. Whatever depositions and affidavits the Colonel had had prepared in his defence in which he claimed that Anne was of bad character never saw the light of day. Perhaps this was one of the conditions of the agreement. It did not, however, stop him from declaring that they existed. The Colonel never could keep his mouth shut.

The news of the agreement had a miraculous effect on Charteris' health, and it was reported that the Colonel, '…who has been very ill, was last Night much better.'[369]

On 10 April the King met in Council to decide on the fate of the prisoners condemned to hang at the February sessions, and the Colonel's personal petition was read out. In this document Charteris, referred to in the third person throughout as 'the Petitioner', ignored his counsellors' advice not to comment on the conviction and obstinately continued to rely on the letter he had produced at the trial despite the fact that it was considered to be a forgery, and the evidence of his witnesses who were believed to be liars. He stated that he had been condemned '…upon the single evidence…'[370] of Anne Bond, who had claimed she did not know his name when she was first in his service, offering in contradiction the evidence of his witnesses and the letter addressed to him by name. He also said that it had been 'proved'[371] at the trial that Anne had slept in a

---

[369] 'London', in *The Daily Courant*, 10 April, no. 8893, p. 2

[370] Public Record Office, Petition of Francis Charteris read to the King in Council PRO/30/29/3/1/4, p. 1

[371] ibid

truckle bed in his chamber on the first night of her service with him and had been '…frequently seen in the same Bed as your Petitioner…'[372] Anne, he went on, was dismissed from his service on 10 November, '…on suspicion of having Privately taken money out of your Petitioners Pocket but without complaining of any Rape…'[373] and he '…had several other Witnesses who could have proved Criminal familiarity between the said Ann Bond and Several other Persons and that the said prosecution was set on foot with a Design to extort a sum of Money …'[374]

Charteris then typically claimed to be older and more infirm than he actually was. '…Your Petitioner is three score years of age and upwards has been for Twelve months past and was on the said day 10th of November, afflicted with Dropsy Asthma and many other infirmities and under the Care of Physicians which makes it altogether impossible that your Petitioner could be guilty of the fact laid to his Charge.' Assuring his devotion to his Majesty's person and service he claimed, inaccurately, to have '…appeared in Arms at his own Expense against the Rebels at Preston.'[375] The mention of expense is a nice touch.

It should be noted here that despite Charteris' counter-accusations against Anne of both perjury, and theft, there was never, even before the agreement was signed, any suggestion of Anne being charged with any crime.

Whatever the King's personal opinion of the Colonel, the pardon was probably a formality.

---

[372] ibid
[373] ibid, p. 2
[374] ibid
[375] ibid, p. 3

This Day Mr Justice Price, Mr Justice Probyn, Mr Baron
Thomson, Recorder of the City of London, who sat upon the
Trial of the Criminals at the last Sessions at the Old Baily,
attended his Majesty in Council (at which were present his
Royal Highness the Prince, the Lord Privy Seal, Lord Steward,
Lord Chamberlain, Duke of Bolton, Duke of Rutland, Duke
of Argyll, Duke of Montrose, Duke of Ancaster, Earl of
Westmoreland, Earl of Chesterfield, Earl of Burlington, Earl
of Abingdon, Earl of Scarborough, Earl of Loudon, Earl of
Findlater, Earl of Marchmount, Earl of Stair, Earl of Hay,
Earl of Sussex, Viscount Townshend, Viscount Lonsdale,
Viscount Cobham, Viscount Falmouth, Viscount Torrington,
Lord Wilmington, Mr Chancellor of the Exchequer, Lord
Chief Justice Eyre, the Lieutenant-general of the Ordnance,
and Henry Pelham Esq;), to make Report of the Trials of such
as were capitally convicted at the said Sessions; and among
others, the Case of Colonel Francis Charteris, condemned for
a Rape committed on the body of Ann Bond; And his Majesty
having heard severally of the opinions of the said Judges upon
the said Case, who all agreed in their Report, was pleased, by
the unanimous Advice of his Privy-Council, to order the said
Francis Charteris should be pardoned, and forthwith admitted
to Bail.[376]

Two of the other condemned prisoners were also granted the
King's mercy. Richard Hanson was reprieved and John Carter's
sentence was commuted to transportation.

Charteris was not entirely without friends. ''Tis talk'd that
when the Report was made Yesterday to the King in Council,
touching his Case, a certain great Lord said, That a Seizure had
been made of the Colonel's Effects by some Persons, that was
neither legal nor justifyable.'[377]

---

[376] 'London, *St James's April 10*', in *The London Journal*, 18 April, no.
559, p. 2

On the same day Charteris was granted a bailable warrant and appeared in court at the Old Bailey. '…It is the second Time he has had the good Fortune to find Favour for the same Offence',[378] *Fog's Weekly Journal* reminded its readers. The Earl of Wemyss and his friend James Bruce stood surety for him in the sum of £500 each, and he provided his own surety of £1,000, in order to plead his pardon at the next sessions. Two other sureties were, reportedly, Colonel Edward Ridley, Captain of a Company in the third Regiment of Foot Guards, and Colonel Richard Ellis, both these gentlemen being Justices of the Peace. Nothing further is known about their involvement, except that Ridley was said to have visited Charteris in Newgate. Charteris was formally discharged from Newgate, and at eight o'clock that evening he was carried in his sedan chair to his wife's lodgings in Warwick Lane.

Even before Charteris was released, *The Grub Street Journal* had anticipated the popular reaction, in an editorial written shortly after his conviction, a satirical defence of the rapist of quality and fortune. Protesting against the unfortunate practice of squandering a gentleman's money on bribing villains, and the reduction of the deference due from the common people to their superiors, editor Richard Russel proposed that men of consequence should be exempted from prosecution for murder, sodomy and rape. This, he suggested, should be regulated after the manner of the Game Act, which restricted possession of firearms to the nobility. The following passage can only have referred to Charteris:

---

[377] 'Wye's Letter Verbatim, 11 April', in *The Caledonian Mercury* 16 April, p. 8367

[378] 'London, *April* 18', in *Fog's Weekly Journal*, 18 April, no. 82, p. 2

But by whatever means, and upon whatever considerations … a wealthy, but notorious Criminal is pardoned; the common People … generally exclaim against it… Their clamours will run much higher, if ever it should happen, that such a Person should obtain a pardon for a crime of which he has been capitally convicted, after having committed the like several times, and by means of his wealth saved himself from former convictions: one who, perhaps, from the meanest circumstances shall have raised himself to immense wealth by the vilest and basest methods, who by his sleight of hand shall have conveyed to himself the estates, and by his debaucheries corrupted the morals of great numbers of Gentlemen: in short, one whose whole life shall have not only been one continued scene of intemperance, profaneness, lewdness, and villainy, but who shall have continually boasted and gloried in the most flagrant instances of his wickedness. If ever such a case as this should happen, the People, who will look upon such a wretch as a common nuisance, will be apt to censure the compassion showed towards him, as cruelty to the Public.[379]

Jonathan Swift — who believed the Colonel to be much older than he was — wrote in *An Excellent Ballad* concerning Dean Thomas Sawbridge, tried for rape in June 1730:

Ah! dost thou not envy the brave Colonel Chartres,
Condemn'd for thy crime at threescore and ten?
To hang him, all England would lend him their garters,
Yet he lives, and is ready to ravish again.[380]

Walpole's opponents were quick to accuse him of using undue influence in procuring the Colonel's release. Pulteney, referring

---

[379] *The Grub Street Journal*, 12 March 1730, p. 1
[380] 'An Excellent New Ballad', in W.E. Browning (ed), *The Poems of Jonathan Swift, D.D.* (2 vols, London, G. Bell and Sons, Ltd., 1910), vol. 1, p. 191

to the minister's well-known penchant for bribery, and freedom with public funds, stated 'I know but *one other estate in England*, which hath been *scraped* together by such means; and I make it a question whether all Mankind will not allow the Proprietor of it to be the honester Man; *Him* I mean, whom you lately saved from the Gallows; and it is the only Thing you ever did in your life for nothing, when you had an opportunity of making a Penny; but perhaps, you might think the Similitude of your Characters and Circumstances made it impolitick to let Him suffer the Punishment, which He deserved.'[381]

In Scotland, the news of the Colonel's freedom was greeted with some relief, not least because his family was still held in respect. In reporting the pardon the *Edinburgh Evening Courant* referred to '…the Affair with his Serving Maid; the particulars of which we forbear to insert, out of Regards to the Noble and Honourable Persons his Relatives.'[382]

On the 11 April the Earl of Wemyss went to the Royal Court to express his humble thanks for the release of his father-in-law, but this was far from being the end of the legal struggle. The Colonel's ageing body was worthless without his estates. If Charteris succumbed to his increasingly suspect health, there was nothing to stop his fortunes from vanishing into the public coffers.

---

[381] Pulteney, pp. 43-4

[382] *The Edinburgh Evening Courant*, Tuesday 3 March to Friday 6 March, p. 2047

IX: THE STALLION WHEN GROWN OLD[383]

From the moment of the Colonel's release there were frequent reports in the newspapers that he was imminently about to leave London, his destination variously given as Bath, Bristol, Hornby Castle, Roehampton — '…for the benefit of the Air'[384] — Scotland, or Aix la Chapelle. These tales of impending departure may have been deliberately leaked to the news-gatherers, to give Charteris the freedom of movement he needed for the campaign to recover his property. Despite his pardon, he was still officially guilty of a felony: saving his jowly neck from the hangman's noose had only preserved his life, not his fortune. A return to Lancashire was not, in any case, an option since his properties there were still forfeit to the Crown, and he was unlikely to meet a warm welcome when seeking lodgings. There was further bad news from the country. According to *Fog's Weekly Journal*, 'Col. Chartres has been struck out of the Commission of the Peace for the County Palatine of Lancaster.'[385]

He remained in London, where he was busy with meetings and petitions. One of the first things he is said to have done on his release was send for his grandson, '… Francis Chartris Weems, 2nd Son to the Earl of Weems, from Scotland, in order to send him to one of the Universities for the

---

[383] *The Reprieve*, p. 7

[384] 'Wye's Letter Verbatim 11 April', in *The Caledonian Mercury*, 16 April 1730, p. 8367

[385] 'London, *April* 18', in *Fog's Weekly Journal*, 18 April, 1730, no. 82, p. 2

Improvement of his Education'.[386] This may just have been a rumour spread to improve the Colonel's standing since there is no later report of the boy arriving in London.

If he indulged in his customary debauchery it was not reported, however there is good reason to believe that he had severely curtailed or even ended that part of his life, at least while he remained in the capital. Everything that is known about the Colonel's activities after his release suggests that someone had had a very serious word with him. He would be pardoned, and if he went through the correct processes he would eventually get his property back, but there was a condition. He must give up his house in George Street, discharge his servants and toadies, keep company with his wife, and behave himself. Any return to his old ways would not be tolerated.

On 13 April he was rumoured to have found lodgings in Leicester Fields (later known as Leicester Square) and the effects he had had with him in Newgate were carried there by hackney coach. This was either a false report designed to confuse the scribblers, or he moved again very quickly, for only days later he was living in an area then known as Kensington Gravel Pits near fashionable Shepherd's Bush. The district was noted for its salubrious country air and had long been favoured by invalids. *The Grub Street Journal* could not resist mentioning that this was '…not far from Tyburn…'[387] He must have been a recognisable figure as he travelled about London. On 18 April he was in a hackney coach on his way to Chelsea when he was spotted by the Mob, who, outraged that he was sharing a carriage with two women, '…(thinking he had had enough of

---

[386] 'From the Evening Posts, April 11', in *The Caledonian Mercury*, 16 April 1730, p. 8365

[387] 'Saturday April 18', in *The Grub Street Journal*, 23 April 1730, p. 3

one)…',[388] commented *Fog's Weekly Journal*, stopped the vehicle, dragged the Colonel out into the street and delivered a sound and no doubt satisfying beating. '*Had the Col had his deserts, [i.e. been hanged] he had avoided this ill usage*',[389] commented *The Grub Street Journal* sympathetically. 'This Adventure puts me in Mind of a Story of a Fellow that was found in Bed with two Women,' added *Fog's*, 'and being carried before a Justice, the Magistrate ask'd the Meaning of his having two Women in Bed with him at once; the Fellow answer'd gravely, he could not help it; *It was owing to the Richness of his Constitution*; upon which the Justice discharg'd him. — Methinks the Mob should have heard the Colonel's Defence, before they treated him so ill.'[390]

The Colonel's female companions (who might have been his wife and daughter, their faces unknown in London) were never identified. At least he fared better than his two Newgate chums, Shrimpton and Drummond who, together with Francis Hackabout, William Newcomb and Peter Rivers, had been executed the day before.

Although there is no evidence that Charteris ever contracted that most dreaded consequence of confinement in Newgate — gaol fever — Colonel Edward Ridley, one of his sureties, who had visited him in prison, fell ill. Both Charteris, and Colonel Richard Ellis, Ridley's fellow surety, together with a third, unnamed gentleman, visited the invalid at his home on Soho Square but on 23 April, Ridley died. It was reported that Ellis contracted gaol fever during this visit to his friend, and before April was out he too succumbed. His companion was also

[388] 'London *April* 25', in *Fog's Weekly Journal*, 25 April 1730, no. 83, p. 2

[389] 'Saturday April 18', in *The Grub Street Journal*, 23 April 1730, p. 3

[390] 'London *April* 25', in *Fog's Weekly Journal*, 25 April 1730, no. 83, p. 2

taken dangerously ill but recovered. Only Charteris seems to have escaped unscathed. *'The friendship of some persons is frequently more fatal than their enmity'*,[391] observed *The Grub Street Journal*.

Helen Charteris had moved to new lodgings near Burlington House on Piccadilly, and in early May the newspapers reported that the couple was cohabiting there. Her husband was soon sighted riding about town in a berlin drawn by six fine Flanders mares, presumably the same ones that Wemyss had brought back from Morice.

There was one more formality before he could finally consider himself free. On 15 May it was reported that 'Col. Charteris appeared in court; and pleaded his majesty's most gracious pardon, for the rape he committed on the body of Anne Bond.'[392]

On 19 May the Colonel met with Mr Morice at the Bailiff's lodgings at Holland House to try and agree ways in which his estate and effects could be restored to him. Morice was kind enough to return some valuable curiosities without charge, and was rewarded for his generosity by Charteris commencing a suit against him for recovery of the rest of his property. Morice was clearly not a man to be rattled by idle threats, and when this action came to nothing, Charteris eventually reached the sad conclusion that getting his property back would cost him money.

One aspect of the Colonel would never change. On 2 June he was arrested in Fleet Street as the suit of a runner at Newgate for a debt of £50 for services performed during his confinement. This was not the kind of behaviour he was expected to indulge in while on bail, and presumably he was persuaded to pay what was due, since nothing more is heard of

---

[391] 'Thursday April 30', in *The Grub Street Journal*, 7 May 1730, pp. 1-2
[392] 'Friday May 15', in *The Grub Street Journal*, 21 May 1730, p. 3

the action. Later that month he was on the road to Wooburn Green to settle his affairs regarding the estate purchased from the Duke of Wharton. On his conviction the estate, on which he had a mortgage of £26,000 had been seized by the late Duke's trustees, Lord Bingley and Thomas Gibson and a meeting had been arranged to negotiate its return.

Charteris made one last desperate attempt to nullify his conviction. He petitioned the King for leave to bring a Writ of Error to reverse the judgement given at the Old Bailey. In this rather pathetically-worded document Charteris whines that because of the conviction, '…his Blood is become corrupted so that no person can take any descent from Your Petitioner nor can Your Petitioner inherit from any other besides many inconveniences of a different kind…'[393] He also claimed that '…there are several Errors in the Proceedings and Record of the said Conviction and Attainder',[394] but did not indicate what these were.

On 28 May the petition was referred to Sir Phillip Yorke, the Attorney General, and Charles Talbot, the Solicitor General for their report and this was presented to his Majesty in Court at Windsor on 18 June. No grounds were found for admitting that there had been an error, and the Colonel soon learned that his application had been refused. While it would not have pleased the King and Court to see a member of the gentry fall victim to the common hangman for raping a servant, there had never been any doubt of Charteris' guilt. The verdict would stand, and the Colonel's personal effects remained in the hands of the High Bailiff.

Sir Robert Walpole was no stranger to attacks by his political enemies but the downfall of his crony was a gift which they

---

[393] British Library Additional MSS. Add.36138, p. 260
[394] ibid

exploited to the full. In May a satirical print appeared, a pastiche of one issued earlier that year glorifying Walpole, who was depicted ascending a rock where Minerva sat offering him a duke's coronet. The new publication, entitled *To the Glory of Colonel Don Francisco upon his delivery out of Gaol*, showed Charteris emerging from Newgate, climbing steps carpeted with purses of gold towards the seated figure of Plutus, Greek God of wealth, who deflects the sword of Justice with one hand while leading the Colonel from his prison with the other. A many-headed leviathan represents the Mob, with a Latin motto which translates as 'They speak what they think'. Below is a Latin poem, which translates:

> Though yet, most noble Sir, 'tis not your Charter,
> Who have deserv'd a Rope, to wear a Garter;
> Yet have you gain'd the great Man's chief Affection,
> And scap'd the Gallows Twice by his Protection...

An anti-Walpole satire, published in *The Craftsman* and attributed to Henry Fielding, suggests that the Colonel's print was the original later transformed into '...a Panegyrick on his *Friend, Confident*, and *Patron*...'[395]

During the Colonel's protracted negotiations, there were minor irritations, as his servants were regarded as fair game for street robbery. On Monday 13 July between 2 and 3 a.m. his footman was robbed in New Bond Street of his watch, snuffbox and money. '*If this* Footman *procured these unnecessary ornaments by cogging of dice, there was no harm done, Rob-thief being a lawful game*',[396] commented *The Grub Street Journal*.

On 14 July both Charteris and Wemyss were at Windsor. The newspapers optimistically reported that they were taking

---

[395] 'Measure for Measure', in *The Craftsman*, 8 August 1730, p. 1
[396] 'Tuesday July 14', in *The Grub Street Journal*, 16 July 1730, p. 2

leave of the court prior to journeying north, but London had not yet seen the last of the Colonel.

The pair was at Windsor again the following week. On 20 July, 'Round about 3 in the morn, the E. Of Weems and Col. Charteris, being dressed to go to Windsor, the Col. Sent Mr Leslie, his Gentlemen, cross the way to his stables, whom 4 Foot-robbers attacked, and robbed of his money, and a bunch of keys belonging to his master.'[397]

On the following day Wemyss, who must have felt that he had done all that was required, returned to Scotland, accompanied by a Captain Johnston and a Mr Pringle, but his father-in-law remained in London, still oppressed by a maze of technicalities.

While there was every prospect that Charteris would eventually have his properties outside London restored to him, it was not going to be straightforward. He could not halt the machinery of forfeiture, which had to run its course, and this must have left him with the uncomfortable suspicion that if he put a foot wrong the King's generosity would suddenly evaporate. In July documents were prepared appointing commissioners to make enquiries into the extent of his estates in Middlesex Westmoreland and Lancashire, '…his Majesty being willing to assert the Rights of the Crown though he should be graciously pleased to restore them to him again.'[398] In due course the commissioners reported that the estates in Lancashire had an annual value of £4,050. The contract with the late Duke of Wharton for the purchase of his manor in Buckinghamshire was valued at £25,500. The two houses in George Street, his home and the property he rented, were listed as worth £200 and £135 per annum respectively.

---

[397] 'Monday July 20', in *The Grub Street Journal*, 23 July 1730
[398] 'Aug. 13', in *The Monthly Journal*, August 1730, vol. III, p. 153

Charteris had by now thrown himself on the hospitality of the friend and correspondent of Duncan Forbes, John Scrope, Secretary to the Treasury, who wrote to Forbes on 28 July:

> Your friend Colonel C. hath found the way to my house & makes me believe he is well satisfied with the care I take of him: everybody is pulling a feather from him which is what I detest, notwithstanding he can spare them as well as any of his neighbours. His unskilfulness in business astonishes me, when I consider the estates he hath got.[399]

It was vital that the Colonel and his lady make a formal public display of their new found amity, and the *Caledonian Mercury* stated in a report dated 4 August: 'Col. Chartris and his Lady being perfectly reconciled, and having made proper Dispositions for cohabiting together, he having cashiered his Man *Trusty Jack*, and other evil Agents, they are to be presented to their Majesty's this Week…'[400]

Charteris must have been in regular correspondence with Duncan Forbes who wrote to Scrope on 11 August:

> I am frequently entertained with the strongest panegyrics imaginable of you by my worthy friend Colonel Charteris: he swears nothing less than a divinity can forgive injuries so readily, and delight so much in doing good. He flatters me with imputing some part of your good nature to him to my intercession, and insists I should return you thanks.[401]

Only Forbes could describe Charteris as 'worthy' without a

---

[399] *More Culloden Papers*, vol. 3, p. 40

[400] 'London Aug 4', in *The Caledonian Mercury*, 10 August 1730, p. 8563

[401] Anon, *Culloden Papers, Comprising an extensive and interesting correspondence from the year 1625 to 1748* (London, Printed for T. Cadell and W. Davies, Strand, 1815), letter 150, pp. 114-15

hint of sarcasm.

On 13 August the documents authorising the enquiries into the Colonel's country estates were approved, and later that month Charteris presented '...an humble Petition to his Majesty, praying to be restored to the said Estates.'[402] At the same time — and if true this can scarcely have been a coincidence — 'We hear Col. Charteris has presented the Rt Hon. Sir Robert Walpole, a Horse Furniture of Green Velvet, curiously embroider'd with Gold of great Value.'[403]

Shortly afterwards, a financial compromise was reached on the return of the Colonel's London properties whereby the sum of £5,000 (£4,800 in some newspapers) was payable to William Morice, £1,650 to Mr Barber, the Sheriff of London, and £1,650 to Sir John Williams, Sheriff of Middlesex, each of those three gentlemen signing a document releasing the effects. On 24 August Mr Morice departed for France on urgent family business but before he left he gave orders that several of the Colonel's valuables should be immediately returned to him. This included the notorious couch.

On 29 August, Helen Charteris, presumably feeling that her husband no longer needed her support, started the long journey home. Two days later:

> ...Col. Charteris had deliver'd to him ... his famous Machine or Couch, on which the Rape of Anne Bond was sworn to be committed, together with the several Wheels, Stretchers, Pillows, &c. belonging thereunto, a Piece of Workmanship scarce to be equall'd in the Kingdom. He had also at the same Time five pieces of rich Chints, with other Things, deliver'd back to him gratis, by Order of the said Mr Morice.[404]

---

[402] 'Aug. 13', in *The Monthly Chronicle*, August 1730, vol. III, p. 153
[403] 'London September 5', in *The Echo or Edinburgh Weekly Journal*, 16 September 1730, no. LXXXIX, p. 2

Barber and Williams took no chances that Colonel might evade making the payment due under the agreement. At the beginning of September, they escorted their slippery debtor to South Sea House in Threadneedle Street where he was obliged to sell his remaining holdings of company stock (then valued at £103 for 100 shares, and estimated to be worth five or six thousand pounds), and hand over the money.

On 3 October he was ill, and was reported to be back at his house in George Street. 'Sat last Col. Charteris was taken very dangerously ill, and still continues so at his house near Hanover-square, where he is attended by Dr Pringle, and other Physicians.' *The Grub Street Journal* observed, '*Had the Col. put on the* infallible Anodyne Necklace *some time ago, as was generally desired*, this dangerous illness *had been prevented*.'[405] There was at the time a widely advertised quack remedy known as the anodyne necklace, but the editor was undoubtedly referring to the hempen healer of all the world's ills, the hangman's noose.

Given his known poor state of health, this may well have been a genuine indisposition. Papers were being drawn up to restore Charteris to his estates in Middlesex, Lancashire and Westmoreland, so there was no need for him to feign illness. His spirits must have recovered somewhat when on 12 October the King in Court at Windsor gave orders for a Bill to be prepared for his signature granting restitution to Francis Charteris of all his estates and goods. One of the signatories to this document was Robert Walpole. By 5 November the Colonel was sufficiently recovered to go and stay with Sir Robert at his country seat in Norfolk.

---

[404] 'London', in *The Universal Spectator and Weekly Journal*, 5 September 1730, no. C, p. 2

[405] 'Thursday Oct. 8', in *The Grub Street Journal*, 15 October 1730, p. 2

The legal processes were not finalised until 7 December, almost thirteen months after the crime. 'His Majesty,' announced *The Daily Courant*, 'has been pleased to make a Grant to Col. Charteris for all his Estate and Effects forfeited to the Crown by his late Conviction for a Rape, and last Monday a Patent passed the proper Seals for that Purpose.'[406]

Fog's Weekly Journal was more pointed:

> Colonel *Francis Charteris* has had all his Estate, forfeited by his *last* Conviction of a Rape, restored to him; so that we may say he is now as good a Man as he was before.[407]

It has been estimated that the crime against Anne Bond, for which Charteris thought he might have to pay £300, cost him more nearly £15,000, in the region of £2million today. He was still a rich man, but to a miser who grudged every guinea, it must have stung.

It had never been in question that once his business was completed Charteris would leave the capital. London did not want him, and he could never again live the life he had known. At the end of December, Charteris was said to be setting out for the North of England, but this was almost certainly another false report. On 4 March 1731 he executed a deed settling his English estates on his grandson Francis and appointing trustees.

The Grub Street Journal, in a report dated 11 March 1731, stated that on the previous day the Colonel '...set out with a great retinue for Lancashire...'[408] One can imagine the wearied

---

[406] 'London', in *The Daily Courant*, Wednesday 9 December 1730, no. 3097, p. 1

[407] 'London, *December* 12', in *Fog's Weekly Journal*, Saturday 12 December 1730, no. 116, p. 2

[408] 'Thursday March 11', in *The Grub Street Journal*, 18 March 1731, p.

Colonel with his carriages, horses, servants and baggage, leaving London, never to return. Did he stare wistfully from his windows at the teeming streets of the capital that had both silvered his fame and destroyed him, at the fashionable World which now turned its back on him and the women, the thousands of women, young and strong and healthy, forever denied to him? Or did he closely curtain the windows of his carriage in case he was recognised by the hated Mob, his body too old and too tired to stand another beating. Did he ever give a moment's thought to Anne Bond?

On 13 April 1730 Anne Bond had been paid £800 '…by a Gentleman of St Margarets in Westminster…'[409] as a final settlement.

Shortly afterwards, the newspapers, who still regarded her as a celebrity announced in a burst of excitement worthy of a twenty-first century tabloid:

> We hear that the famous Anne Bond, who prosecuted Colonel Charters for a Rape, was married at Gray's Inn Chapel to Charles Heather, a Drawer at a Tavern in Westminster, and that they have since taken a Tavern in Bloomsbury, and design to set up a well painted Head of Colonel Chartres for their Sign.[410]

The story was untrue, its origins unknown, however Anne did have wedding plans.

On 20 April 1730 Anne Bond married Major Smith at the church of St Michael Crooked Lane, on the corner of St

---

1
[409] 'London, *April* 18', in *Fog's Weekly Journal*, 18 April 1730, no. 82, p. 2
[410] 'From the Post-Boys, &c: London April 16', in *The Edinburgh Evening Courant*, Monday 20 April to Tuesday 21 April 1730, p. 2219

Michael's Lane. 'Major' was not a military rank but the groom's Christian name. The marriage 'allegation' or application for the license which took place on the same day shows that on that date the bride was 'upwards of twenty-one years'[411] and resident in the parish of Christ Church in the County of Middlesex, which was in the area now known as Spitalfields. Anne had been lodging near Surgeon's Hall, in the parish of Christ Church Newgate. Either she had moved prior to her marriage, or the record is in error. The groom was one year older and resident in the parish of St Leonard Foster Lane, less than half a mile from the Old Bailey. Unfortunately the application does not give his profession. In August the newspapers reported that Anne and her new husband had taken over Daniel's Coffee House in Lombard Street.

Charteris was not content to let the couple live unmolested. His vindictive streak showed itself again in an unpleasant and unnecessary prosecution. *The Grub Street Journal* revealed — quoting reports in other popular newspapers — 'Some days ago Mr Major Smith, who marry'd Mrs Anne Bond, who cast Col. Charteris, was arrested in some sort of actions by persons employed in that affair, viz. One action for 18 l. another for 1600 l. but the young man says, he owes them nothing, and hath given bail to the actions, being resolved to see them out. We are well assured', added the reports without giving the source of this information, 'that the Col. hath no hand in this affair.' Charteris' litigious and spiteful nature was too well known to let that pass, and the editor of *The Grub Street Journal* could not resist commenting:

---

[411] Marriage Licence Allegations, Faculty Office 1701-1850, 20 April 1730

I wonder at the assurance of my Brethren in vindicating, the Colonels reputation by such an Innuendo.[412]

On 11 November 1731 Anne gave birth to a son, who was baptised Major Smith at the parish church of St Mary Woolnoth in Lombard Street on 30 November. Nothing further is known about the later career of the couple and their son, and the parish registers do not record the baptisms of any more children of Major and Ann Smith. There was a tradition of naming the firstborn son after his father, and the name 'Major Smith' continues to appear in birth records well into the nineteenth century.

The parish registers of St Michael Crooked Lane do contain an entry which should be mentioned here. 'Mrs Ann Smith' was buried there on 23 January 1732. No more details are given. Anne may have fallen victim to fever and infection just two and a half months after the birth of her child, or the record may relate to another person. Anne, the memory of her courage and determination undimmed, disappears from the paper records of history.

Following Charteris' condemnation, Mother Needham may have felt that it was best for her to avoid the law by pretending to be dead. It was a tactic she had tried four years previously with some brief success, but having been exposed once, it was extremely foolish to expect to be believed a second time. In October 1730 a false report was given out that she had died at her home in Park Place. The flimsy lie was soon revealed, and later that month a bill of indictment was found against 'a certain noted Matron for keeping a common Bawdy-house, in the Parish of St James's, Westminster.'[413]

---

[412] 'Saturday Sept 19', in *The Grub Street Journal*, 24 Sept, p. 2
[413] 'London, *October, 17*', in *Fog's Weekly Journal*, 17 October 1730, no.

On 19 March 1731, she was committed to the Gate House prison near Westminster Abbey. Three days later she was at the Westminster quarter-sessions where '...the infamous Mother Needham, who has been reported to have been dead for some time, to skreen her from several prosecutions, was brought from the Gate-house, and pleaded not guilty to an indictment found against her for keeping a lewd and disorderly house, but for want of sureties was remanded back to prison.'[414]

On 26 April she was convicted for keeping a disorderly house, fined 1s, ordered to stand in the pillory twice, and to find sureties for her good behaviour for three years. This may sound like a lenient sentence, but the pillory was never a trivial matter. To the rowdy Mob, hungry for entertainment, a celebrity in the pillory was fair game to be pelted with rubbish, dead dogs and whatever filth the streets of London abundantly provided. An unpopular personality might be bombarded with stones.

On 30 April 1731 Mother Needham was taken to stand in the pillory in Park Place. She hired some men to screen her from missiles, and, though it was a requirement of the law that her face be exposed, laid herself face down on the ground under the pillory. No-one made any attempt to pull her upright. Despite these precautions she was severely pelted, and suffered heavy injuries. The attraction of seeing the punishment of such a notorious woman was too much for one boy who climbed up a nearby lamp post for a better view, slipped, and fell upon some iron spikes '...and tore his belly in so violent a manner, that his bowels came out, and he expired in a few hours in great agonies.'[415] Mother Needham's second

---

108 p. 2
[414] 'Tuesday March 23', in *The Grub Street Journal*, 25 March 1731, p. 3
[415] 'Saturday May 1', in *The Grub Street Journal*, 4 May 1731, p. 2

ordeal was to have been five days later, but after her first experience, she languished, badly injured and in constant terror of having to face the Mob again. She died on 4 May.

Nothing is known for certain about Charteris' activities during 1731. He probably spent time at Hornby Castle, though according to Musselborough legend, he '…lived chiefly at Stony hill, where, it is said, he indulged in all licentiousness…'[416] If he did, it was in the face of continually declining health.

Despite later speculation about the Colonel's final illness, there is no evidence that he was suffering from any venereal disease, neither does he appear to have contracted typhus while in Newgate. The symptoms most often mentioned in accounts of his condition in 1730 are asthma and dropsy, or in today's terms, breathlessness and oedema. Together they suggest congestive heart failure. His father's early death may point to a hereditary weakness. The stress of his condemnation and imprisonment followed by months of campaigning to restore his properties can only have aggravated his condition.

Nevertheless, he outlived the man who had sentenced him to death. If the Colonel had been following the London news, he would have learned that Mr Serjeant Raby had been taken ill in court on 26 January 1732. Placed in a carriage, he died before reaching home.

By February 1732 the Colonel was living in Hornby Castle, and was so ill that private letters sent to London sparked off a spate of premature newspaper announcements of his death. Charteris knew his time was fast approaching, and determined to die in Scotland, he ordered that he should be carried to Stoneyhill. Messengers were sent on ahead, and on 11 February it was known in Edinburgh that he was on his way.

---

[416] *History of the Regality of Musselburgh*, p. 188

In great discomfort, and against the advice of his doctor, he made the journey, arriving on 16 February. On the following day *The Caledonian Mercury* reported: 'Yesterday Colonel Francis Chartris arrived at his fine Country Seat of Stonniehill. We hear he is much indisposed.'[417] For once, this was not an exaggeration. Despite a later report that the Colonel was 'in the way of Recovery'[418] Colonel Charteris was dying. A few days later he was said to be 'relapsed and dangerously ill',[419] and '…in a very languishing Condition …' using 'opiates in great Quantities.'[420]

He was attended by Edinburgh doctor John Clark who wrote to Duncan Forbes on 22 February:

> …The terriblest patient I ever had in my life is your monster of a Landlord. I was obliged to go 16 miles out of town to meet him on the road from Hornby, where they thought [he wou]ld have expired. I lived two days in hell upon earth and [brought] him with much difficulty (on Wednesday last) to Stonyhill, [where he i]s dying exactly as he has lived, only I think since he was [told that he i]s dying he swears little or none at all. He can[not] sl[eep] nor eat & has no other complaint either of pain or sickness, so that he seems to be dying of a d[ecline] of nature, his blood being exhausted. I understand he h[as re]membered you in his testament, he having left you the lif[e rent] of Stonyhill with some acres about it, and 1000lbs. ster. [to your] son. I should think the legacy is not a dishonest purchase [for] you, but what you will

[417] 'Edinburgh', in *The Caledonian Mercury*, 17 February 1732, no. 1851, p.9519
[418] 'Edinburgh', in *The Caledonian Mercury*, 21 February 1732, no. 1852, p. 9523
[419] 'Edinburgh, Feb. 24', in *The Daily Courant*, 2 March 1732, p. 2
[420] 'London, March 4', in *The Country Journal or, The Craftsman*, Saturday 4 March 1731-2, no. 296, p. 2

think of it since it comes out of a [letter torn] heap is more than I can tell, for he told me (in tal[king about] another affair) that your honesty was so whimsical that it was 45 per cent. Above Don Quixote. As for his own, the only sign he shews of it was one day when he thought he was going off he ordered with a great roar that all his just debts should be paid.[421]

In his more lucid moments, his customary meanness surfaced. A minister, Mr Cumine, attended the Colonel on his death bed and conducted prayers for him. The Colonel '…asked at his daughter, who is exceedingly narrow, what he should give him; she replied "that it was unusual to give any thing on such occasions;" — "well then," says Charters, "let us have another flourish from him," so calling his prayers. So you see he has dyed as he lived.'[422]

On 20 February he was still able to consider the future of his grandson. In 1729 he had appointed Helen as the boy's tutrix, but he had since learned that Helen was suffering from breast cancer, and he executed another deed appointing the Countess of Wemyss as Francis' tutrix in the event of his wife's death. The dying Charteris was in little doubt about his eventual destination, 'Upon deathbed he was exceedingly anxious to know if there was any such thing as hell, and said that were he assured there was no such place, being easie as to heaven, he would give thirty thousand.'[423] There were no takers. On the night of 24 February a terrible storm raged over Edinburgh and its environs, with heavy rain and hurricane force winds.

---

[421] *More Culloden Papers*, vol. 3, pp. 49-50. The gaps are due to the decay of the document.

[422] *Private Letters now first Printed*, Letter LIII, Honourable John Crawfurd to the Honourable Miss Peggy Crawfurd, Edinburgh, 27 February 1732, p. 81

[423] ibid, pp. 80-1

Attended by these howling harbingers, Francis Charteris breathed his last. Some of his neighbours said that the dreadful noise was the sound of the gates of Hell rumbling open to receive the Colonel's soul, some claimed that his passing had caused the unrest in nature, and '...other more sharp-sighted folks saw a great deal of men on horseback, I suppose divels...'[424]

The notice of his death, dated 28 February, which appeared in many newspapers was, judging by its respectful wording, and the details supplied of the proposed burial, issued by his family:

> On Thursday the 24th instant died Francis Charteris of Ampsfield, Esq; at his House of Stonnihill, near this City, in the 57th Year of his Age, descended of an ancient and honourable Family in this Country. He was married to Mrs Helen Swinton, Daughter of Sir Alexander Swinton of Mersington, one of the Senators of the College of Justice; by whom he has only one Daughter, married to the Right Hon. James Earl of Weems: To whose Second Son he has left the Bulk of his plentiful Estate, and great Portions to all the other Children, with several Legacies to his Friends and Relations. Tomorrow his Corps will be transported to this City, and interred in the Grey Fryers at Two o' Clock after Noon.[425]

On 29 February the funeral cortège left Stoneyhill and headed towards Edinburgh where the Colonel was to be buried in Greyfriars Kirkyard. Charteris was not well-liked in Stoneyhill, whose inhabitants must have despised to a man the libidinous lifestyle of their most notorious resident. Once the news of his death had passed around the little town, they began to prepare

---

[424] ibid, p. 81

[425] '*Edinburgh, Feb 28*', in *The London Journal*, Saturday 11 March 1732, no. 663, p. 2

for the event. As the funeral procession left the house it was obliged to pass along the main avenue. Crowds lined the street, bringing with them an accumulation of rubbish with which to pelt the coffin. Mud, ordure, entrails and dead animals were the popular missiles of the day. '...It is traditionally recorded here, that the populace assembled in the avenue down which the funeral procession of that wretched person had to pass, and bespattered the hearse with filth and garbage.'[426]

By the time the cortège had reached Edinburgh, the demonstrations were more muted. 'On Tuesday the Corpse of Col. Francis Chartres of Ampsfield, was interred in the Gray Fryars Church-Yard, with Great Pomp and Solemnity.'[427] Perhaps this was another family announcement as *Fog's* heard the story differently, and couldn't resist its usual dig at Walpole:

> They tell us from Edinburgh, that when Colonel Francis Charteris was buried, a great Number of People attended the Corps, and, when it was laid into the Ground, they gave a loud Huzza. —— —— This Honour has scarce been done to any Man before him, nor, perhaps will to any other after him, except a Gentleman, who is known to have been long a dear Friend of his and who stood by him in the worst of Times.[428]

There is no grave-marker showing where the Colonel is buried. The records of Greyfriars Kirkyard show that the Colonel's last resting place was 'Close to the South Syd of Kinlochs Tomb...',[429] a large monument dedicated to his mother's

---

[426] *History of the Regality of Musselborough*, pp. 188-9

[427] 'Edinburgh, Mar 3', in *The Daily Journal*, Saturday 11 March 1730, no. 3490, p. 1

[428] 'London *March* 11 1732', in *Fog's Weekly Journal*, 11 March 1732, no. 175, p.2

family on the north boundary of the burial ground.

Contrary to popular rumour, there does not appear to have been any great demonstration against the Colonel in Edinburgh. Had there been it is hard to imagine that the newspapers of the day would have failed to report it. It seems, however, that over the years, the demonstration in Musselborough was amplified in the telling and the location transferred to Greyfriars. 'The populace at his funeral raised a great riot, almost tore the body out of the coffin, and cast dead dogs, &c. into the grave along with it',[430] stated John Arbuthnot, the physician and satirist who was to compose the Colonel's most scathing epitaph. London-based Arbuthnot was almost certainly not present at the event.

Francis Charteris had made his will in June 1729, long before he had any reason to be grateful to the Earl of Wemyss. The most important aspect of this document was its detailed provisions to ensure that none of his fortune fell into the hands of his son-in-law. Although he had had ample opportunity to make amendments, he must have felt that intervening events had given him no reason to do so. The bulk of his estate was left to his grandson and favourite Francis. Had Francis died without issue before the Colonel's death, the fortune would have gone to Francis' younger brother James or his male heirs, failing that, to any younger male child of Janet Wemyss as yet unborn, or failing that, to Janet and the male heirs of any subsequent marriage, and if all these avenues failed, to the female heirs. Clearly, the Colonel only felt safe

---

[429] Family History Centre, Burial records Greyfriars Kirkyard, 29 February 1732, film 1066746

[430] T. Caldwall (ed), *A Select Collection of Ancient and Modern Epitaphs, and Inscriptions: to Which are Added Some on the Decease of Eminent Personages* (London, T. Caldwall, 1796), p. 7

leaving his fortune to Janet if her first husband was dead. It was a condition of the inheritance that male heirs took the name and arms of Charteris, and if the heir was female, she should either marry a man of the surname Charteris or her children and heirs should take that surname. If anyone inheriting failed in that duty they were to lose all rights to their inheritance which was to pass to the next heir in line 'as if the person so failing to assume use & bear the Surname and Arms of Charteris had never existed.'[431] The arrangement thus ensured that the Colonel's fortune never became the property of anyone with the surname of Wemyss. One might charitably suggest that the Colonel's motives were pride in his family name. Either that or a hatred of his son-in-law he meant to extend beyond the grave.

The people to whom he gave authority to administer his estate were his wife, Helen; his daughter Janet; John Campbell, 2nd Duke of Argyle and Greenwich, and his brother Archibald Campbell, Earl of Hay, both of whom had fought against the Jacobites in 1715; Sir Robert Walpole; Duncan Forbes; his old school-friend and cousin, Sir Francis Kinloch, and three senators of the college of Justice.

If Francis Wemyss, only five when the will was made, inherited as a minor, the trustees of his inheritance would have had the duty to administer the estate in the boy's best interests, and the Colonel must have feared that if James got hold of the money it would be frittered away. The example of John Charteris the prodigal 11th Laird of Amisfield must still have been fresh in his mind. Another consideration may well have been political. Insofar as Charteris was political he sided with

---

[431] Public Record Office, Will of Francis Charteris PROB 11/650 f. 366

the Whigs, in support of the Hanoverian reign, and suspected James of Jacobite tendencies.

To Helen he left an annuity of £600, his house in Parliament Close, Edinburgh, and its furniture, plate and moveables. To David Lord Elcho he left the sum of £10,000, to enable him to pay off any debts he inherited from his father when he acceded to the Earldom.

Janet received a lifetime annuity of £1,000, the money being for 'her own receipt and discharge ... and without the subscription or consent of her said husband...' and not to be assigned to '...any debt or deed of ... her husband nor be at all at his disposal or under his administration...'[432] The same stipulation was to apply to the sum of £6,000 for Francis' younger sister, Frances and the £5,000 each for his brother James and the other sisters to be paid on marriage or reaching the age of twenty-one.

The Colonel also left funds for the maintenance of the younger children until they reached the age of twenty-one, stipulating that the money was not to be used for any other purpose. The only persons to have any power over deciding on the education, residence or travelling of Francis or the other heirs were Helen, John and Archibald Campbell and Sir Robert Walpole. If 'James Earl of Wemyss or any other of their tutors and curators or any other person or persons whatsoever' claimed any power over those decisions or 'interpose or hinder the same',[433] then David Lord Elcho and any other representatives of the house of Wemyss would lose all right to the sum of £10,000 and Francis and the younger children would lose the money appointed for their maintenance during

---

[432] ibid, f. 372
[433] ibid, f. 371

their minority, the money to go into a fund for provision for the younger children of his heirs.

He also left 'the free and full use'[434] of the mansion with either the gardens or any eight acres of land of his estate at Stoneyhill to Duncan Forbes. According to other documents he also left Forbes the sum of £1,000, and his stable of horses to Sir Robert Walpole.[435] After the Colonel's death the teetering marriage of Janet and James Wemyss finally collapsed. The terms of the Colonel's will, which gave rise to considerable litigation, may well have been a precipitating factor. The couple quarrelled, and eventually separated. The children were placed under the guardianship of the Duke of Argyll, and the Earl made his home in Durham, while Janet and the children went to live with Helen Charteris at her house in Parliament Close, Edinburgh. The Countess of Wemyss may have become a patroness of the arts, since two works are dedicated to her. *Instructions for the Use of a Young Lady of Quality or, the Idea of a Woman of Merit* by Trotti de la Chéterdie was translated from the original French and published in Edinburgh in 1734. The dedication naturally loads the Countess with praise for her '…Perfections of Mind, and Graces of Person…' and '…the Humanity of Your Disposition, and that happy Benevolence, that equally promotes Your own Peace, and the Happiness of those who are honour'd with Your Acquaintance…'[436] Janet was evidently regarded as a model of respectability and receptive to literature with a moral message. The book emphasises the importance of piety to young women anxious to maintain their spotless

---

[434] ibid, f. 373

[435] *Private Letters*, p. 79

[436] T. De La Chéterdie, *Instructions for the Use of a Young Lady of Quality or, the Idea of a Woman of Merit* (Edinburgh, W. Cheyne, 1734), p. iv

reputations in the world, and advises avoiding coquettish behaviour, vanity, pride, jealousy and the vice of gaming.

Janet revealed her less serious side by bestowing her favour on *The Disappointed Gallant, or Buckram in Armour*, by Adam Thomson, a ballad opera, published in Edinburgh in 1738 and performed at the New Edinburgh Theatre. This comedy of manners, with its romantic intrigues, secret letters, quarrels, disguises, a mock wedding, songs and a happy ending, was well received by the public.

James continued to spend money at a wholly unwarranted rate, and set about what he had always intended to do — getting his hands on the Colonels fortune. He commenced a legal action against Francis and his tutors, claiming that he was in law the administrator of the bequest to his son, but the wording of the deeds left very little doubt as to the Colonel's intentions. The boy's advisors stated bluntly, '…the Colonel has showed the utmost Anxiety to exclude the earl from having any Interest in his heir Mr *Francis's* education…'[437] Since the Colonel's principal heir was a minor at the time of his grandfather's death, James eventually managed to get control of the money the Colonel had left his second son, and made substantial inroads into it. Later, he borrowed his eldest son's £10,000 and never paid him back. No sum was too small to escape his depredations. When Helen Charteris died in Edinburgh (she was buried on 10 November 1733), James appropriated the family silver she left for the use of her grandchildren.

Janet Wemyss spent much of her old age in France where, as a wealthy widow she again became plagued by fortune hunters.

---

[437] National Archives of Scotland, GD1/867/2. Printed information by Robert Dundas, advocate for Mr Francis Charteris and his tutors against James, Earl of Wemyss, p. 19

She returned to England, but quarrelled with her children over the disposition of her finances. Legal proceedings were still in progress when she died at her home in Taplow on 1 March 1778.

David, Lord Elcho took part in the 1745 rebellion, was attainted of treason and fled to France, where he died without issue. James Wemyss died in 1756, and it was ultimately the Colonel's heir, Francis who succeeded to the earldom. Thus it is that the Earls of Wemyss to the present day bear the surname Charteris.

X: THINK NOT HIS LIFE USELESS TO MANKIND![438]

If the Charteris case had no discernible influence on the outcome of later eighteenth-century rape trials, its celebrity status ensured that the issue of rape and how it was treated in courts was the subject of intense public debate over the course of several months. Its true impact was political, a demonstration that the protection of the most powerful man in Great Britain could not screen a rogue from the process of the law in the face of public opinion. Even Walpole must have been left with the uncomfortable feeling that he was not unassailable. His political decline and fall lay not many years in the future.

No-one publicly lamented the Colonel's death though his friends may have felt regret for a colourful companion gone, and his career of possibilities unrealised and talents misused. His life was seen as at best a valuable example to others of those sins and depravities to avoid. The most generous thing said about him was that he was not a hypocrite.

> All Charter's crimes were open done,
> In face of men and skyes…[439]

The best known satirical epitaph was written by the polymath and author Dr John Arbuthnot:

---

[438] 'Epitaph attributed to John Arbuthnot', J. Butt (ed), *The Twickenham Edition of the Poems of Alexander Pope* (10 vols., London, Methuen and Co Ltd, 1939-67), vol. III ii, p. 86

[439] 'An Answer, by a Lover of Truth', in *Private Letters*, p. 83

Here continueth to rot
The Body of FRANCIS CHARTRES,
Who with an INFLEXIBLE CONSTANCY,
And INIMITABLE UNIFORMITY of LIFE,
PERSISTED,
In spite of AGE and INFIRMITIES,
In the practice of EVERY HUMAN VICE;
Excepting PRODIGALITY and HYPOCRISY:
His insatiable AVARICE exempted him from the first,
His matchless IMPUDENCE from the second.
Nor was he more singular
in the undeviating PRAVITY of his MANNERS
Than successful
in ACCUMULATING WEALTH.
For, without TRADE or PROFESSION,
Without TRUST of PUBLIC MONEY,
And without BRIBE-WORTHY SERVICE,
He acquired, or more properly created,
A MINISTERIAL ESTATE.
He was the only Person of his Time,
Who cou'd CHEAT without the Mask of HONESTY,
Retain his Primeval MEANNESS
When possess'd of TEN THOUSAND a YEAR,
And having daily deserved the GIBBET for what he DID,
Was at last condemn'd to it for what he COULD not DO.
Oh, Indignant Reader!
Think not his Life useless to Mankind!
PROVIDENCE conniv'd at his execrable designs,
To give to After-ages
A conspicuous PROOF and EXAMPLE,
Of how small Estimation is EXORBITANT WEALTH in
the Sight of GOD,
By his bestowing it on the most UNWORTHY of ALL
MORTALS.[440]

---

[440] *The Poems of Alexander Pope*, vol. III, ii, p. 86

This epiter, with minor variations was reprinted in other contemporary collections.

Arbuthnot's friend, poet Alexander Pope, was more succinct.

Here *Francis Ch—s* lies — Be civil!
The rest God knows — perhaps the Devil.[441]

Poems, books and plays published immediately after the trial mainly took the view that Charteris was innocent of rape, though not of assault with intent. This was almost certainly not a personal comment on the veracity of Anne Bond. Love of irony led the authors to conclude that Charteris, while well worthy of a hanging for all his previous offences, had on this one occasion been wrongly convicted, because he was impotent. The idea of the notorious rake, who had undoubtedly ruined by seduction and raped large numbers of women, being incapable of an erection, was far too good to dismiss as just a ploy of his trial defence. They wanted to believe it.

Impotence in life can presumably be cured in the afterlife, according to *Don Francisco's Descent to the Infernal Regions.* This twelve page drama was published almost immediately after Charteris' death, being advertised in the Daily Journal of 28 February 1732. The rapidity with which it was produced suggests that it may have been in preparation from the first incorrect reports of his death about ten days before it actually occurred. It is not known if the piece, scarcely more than an interlude, was ever performed.

The setting is Hell, and Mother Needham's ghost enters, wanting to know what the 'dreadful Bustle' and 'noisy shout'[442]

---

[441] 'Applied to F.C.', *The Poems of Alexander Pope*, vol. III, p. 297
[442] Anon, *Don Francisco's Descent to the Infernal Regions, an Interlude*

is all about on the shores of the river Styx. Even Pluto, King of the underworld, has left his throne and come in person to escort the new arrival. Mother Needham is delighted to see the approach of her old lover.

> Thanks to the Fates, who've cut his Thread in twain,
> And brought the *Goat* unto my arms again.[443]

Francisco arrives, heralded by Charon:

> Fame's Trumpet long has sounded all your Deeds,
> Your Rapes, your Murders, shook our shores and Reeds.[444]

This is the only suggestion anywhere that Charteris may ever have committed murder.

Francisco is initially happy with his reception, but when Pluto reveals that he is about to be tried by the 'infernal Judges',[445] he is understandably taken aback:

> And am I doom'd then to be try'd again?
> That very Thought creates a tort'ring Pain.
> My last dread Trial to my Mind appears,
> Shocks my unconquer'd soul, creates new Fears.

Mother Needham quickly reassures him.

> Here Perjury's a Trade, and you so skill'd
> In that deep Art…
> So raise your Courage, and dismiss your Fear.[446]

(London: Printed for S. Slow, 1732), p. 3
[443] ibid, p. 4
[444] ibid, p. 5
[445] ibid, p. 6
[446] ibid, p. 7

Cheered by this news, he buckles down to his usual business:

> Trusty Procuress! Ransack all your Stores,
> And fetch FRANCISCO a young Brace of Whores.[447]

But his old friend has some bad news for him. Disembodied souls who have tasted of the waters of Lethe have no further thoughts of '…Gay Delights and youthful Scenes of Joy.'[448] Francisco is having none of this, and points out that Pluto got where he was because of a rape.

Mother Needham, while powerless to bring him the wenches he craves, has another plan to please him:

> Let you and I, like wand'ring Turtles wooe,
> Renew past Pleasures, and in Raptures cooe,…
> In Dreams I often thought you near my Side,
> Oft pleas'd you, too, as should a *duteous* Bride.
> Then let's no longer the fond Bliss delay,
> But name the Time shall be our Wedding-Day.[449]

Francisco views the prospect of a middle-aged bride with all the enthusiasm one might anticipate, preferring to be tried for his crimes instead:

> I'll hear my Doom, and stand to their Decree:
> Be what it will, it is from Wedlock; free.[450]

Away he goes to stand trial, with the scorned Needham predicting:

---

[447] ibid
[448] ibid
[449] ibid, p. 11
[450] ibid, p. 12

If Woman he avoids, he'll meet the Devil's Claws.[451]

A chorus of three furies arrives, bringing the 'forked Crow, and massy Prong', with which to torture Francisco, while the 'fiery Brake' is prepared to receive a 'greater Ravisher than *Tarquin* … th'envenom'd Snake.'[452]

In vain the convict appeals to Hell's judges to repeal their condemnation:

> Away, away, the Time is come,
> That Ch—s must receive his Doom:
> The mighty Ravisher at length submits to Fate.[453]

The Reprieve published on 16 April 1730, is a poem written as if by Jack Ketch (a generic name given to the public hangman) to Colonel Charteris. The writer wonders how Charteris can have so lost the cunning of his native land:

> That thus you dar'd to stand the fiery Test,
> To save your Gold, — and turn a publick jest?[454]

Doubting the truthfulness of the Colonel's witnesses he advises:

> Had you resolv'd to make your Virtue clear,
> Your Incapacity should first appear;
> Your shapeless, sapless Carcass there been shewn,
> With all the lifeless Trumpery of a Drone;
> Undoubted proofs of Impotence alone.
> Grizly Threescore in form had you display'd,

---

[451] ibid
[452] ibid, p. 13
[453] ibid, p. 14
[454] *The Reprieve*, p. 4

> What Jury could believe you forc'd a Maid?
> Some Things the Law demands she soon might feign,
> But never make your penetration plain;
> For when you bravely storm'd the Petticoat,
> You only thrust your — *Night Cap* in her Throat.[455]

The writer, ignoring the fact that Charteris did claim in court to be impotent, suggests that the Colonel only risked proceeding with the case to maintain his reputation as a despoiler of women.

> Proud of the rampant Ravisher's bright Name,
> Bravely you ventur'd all to fix a fame;
> How Strange your Fate! — such Vengeance is your Due,
> Stripp'd and condemn'd — for what you could not do.[456]

The poem then comes to the contrived conclusion that Anne only swore a rape because the Colonel had been unable to satisfy her in bed. These lines do show that one part of her evidence at least had made it into the popular culture. Perhaps Anne's 'a great deal of wet' had become the catch-phrase of 1730.

> O Ch—s! — Ch—s! had you serv'd her better,
> You long might live from Halter free and Fetter;
> *Nan* swore the Rape, — because you cou'd not — *wet her.*
> She ne'er had prov'd you such a vig'rous Sinner,
> But that you did not — put — the Matter in her.
> Cou'd youthful Ardour from your Eye-balls start,
> And God-like Vigour nerve each feeble Part,
> No Rape had stunn'd our Ears, or froze your heart.

> Trust me, who knows the Inwards of that Sex,

---

[455] ibid, pp 4-5
[456] ibid, p. 5

And scorn with trifling Doubts your Soul to vex;
Fearless you still may meet each injur'd Dame,
Cou'd you but lay, as well as raise their Flame,
And sprinkle Drops of Pleasure with the Shame.
The Man that ravishes they can forgive,
But grieve to let the fumbling Letcher live.[457]

After these dubious comments the writer finishes with some good advice.

Then don't affect the Stallion, when grown Old,
But as you've lost your teeth, let go your Hold;
Lay your *Seraglio* down, thou very *Turk*,
And do not teaze your Maids, but let them work.

He even suggests Charteris returns to his wife:

Take your neglected Dearest to your Arms,
And sup at least on Matrimonial Charms;
Too much for such a thankless Wretch she wrought,
She sure may have you, — now you're good for nought.[458]

On 27 March 1730 the *Grub Street Journal* reported that a play called *Calista* which it compared, with undeserved flattery, to *The Beggars Opera* had been forbidden by authority. It was published anonymously later that year. *Calista* is a coarse satire on the adulterous relationship between Lady Catherine Abergavenny and Richard Lyddel. Lumbering across its pages as a gross comic relief, is the gambling, whoring Colonel Francisco, described as '...an extravagant *Debauchée*',[459] cursing

---

[457] ibid, pp. 6-7

[458] ibid, p. 7

[459] Anon, *Calista. An Opera* (London, C. Davies, 1731), Dramatis Personae, p. xi (unnumbered in printed copy)

in broad, almost impenetrable Scots. He is accompanied by gamester Beau Nation, an unkind and inaccurate portrayal of Beau Nash, then a leader of fashion and Master of Ceremonies in elegant Bath, whose main source of income was gambling.

> Too wild, but it will please the Age,
> To see such Actions on the Stage.[460]

Francisco and Nation have very little to do with the main plot which involves the tedious adulterous affairs of bored gentry. Their main concerns are gambling, whoring and drinking. Nation, who has no fortune is obliged to 'cringe and sneer for Six Months'[461] to win a lady's favour, but Francisco is more direct, saying '…if you wou'd hafe a Lawdy sacrifice her Body, you mun furst get her Monies, and thon if yaw or the muccle Dee'l ya might have her Saul, and all that belongs to her, if ya'd refund the Spankey.'[462] We next see these two gallants drunk and dirty, dragging with them Francisco's concubine, a dairy-maid called Olimpia (revealed by a contemporary pamphlet to be a representation of Anne Bond), and a cinder wench, Francisco declaring he will knock down the first constable he meets and swear that the next jade he sees picked his pocket. After knocking down a bellman they break some windows and go off to look for more trouble. This naturally attracts the attention of the law, and they seize hold of the two watchmen pursuing them. Francisco suggests that he, Nation and Olimpia form a bench of justices, and try one of the men for a rape alleged by Olimpia and the other for selling mackerel on a

---

[460] P. Chamberlen (attr.), *The Perspective, or Calista Dissected. To which are prefixed, A Lock and Key to the late Opera of Calista* (London, J. Dicks, 1731), Canto 1, p.2
[461] *Calista*, p. 7
[462] ibid, p. 6

Sunday. The watchmen are ordered to be tied up and rolled into a kennel — the open sewer running down the centre of the street.

After a night of debauchery, Francisco lurches drunkenly into the house of the Countess de Ulto, a notable serial adulteress to whom he has taken a fancy.

'Are you a man or Monster?'[463] she demands.

'Modam,' he boasts, 'that I am a Mon I cu'd prove without speaking ain Word, and tho' my Face is like the Moon at full, my Ports are proportionable…'[464]

Even the lecherous Countess has the good taste to throw him out. Both he and Nation then mount an inept attempt to extort money from the Count de Ulto who recognises them as a pair of scoundrels and orders them from the house. The scene has no other function than to distract the Count so the Countess's new lover can slip past him into her apartment. Francisco and Nation are next found in a bawdy house, with two whores. The Colonel's woman demands a close examination of her customer before any business can be transacted, '…for by that firy Phiz, which is like a blazing Star, I'm afraid it portends some Devastations in the lower Regions…'[465] They withdraw to another room, but he soon hauls her back in, her cap off and petticoats torn, bawling '…this Bitch of a Damnable Woore wo'd have Siller before she had work'd for it and has the impudence to call my HONOUR in question.'[466] The Madam of the establishment comes to see what the noise is, saying 'What, Bully, do you think your self in *Newgate*?'[467] a line calculated to raise a knowing laugh in 1730.

---

[463] ibid, p. 28
[464] ibid
[465] ibid, p. 35
[466] ibid, p. 36

236

Even Nation turns against him, saying 'There's nothing but Hell and Fury, Destruction, Desolation, Damnation and *Bellum Rancum* [Ballum rancum is a dance attended by thieves and prostitutes] in your Company…'[468] Matters are soon made up with an application of money. By the end of the play the Colonel's debauchery has led to fiery consequences, though he has no regrets as he plans to use his infection to revenge himself on a whore who he feels overcharged him. Seeing Nation going after a wench he predicts bitterly that the woman will '…swaur a Raupe agen him, thot he ma pay as deur for it as I'se done'[469] — a comment demonstrating the public's belief that the Colonel had not wholly escaped just punishment for his crime in 1730.

Unperformed when its subject matter was current, it seems unlikely that this play has had a modern revival. Its loss to the theatre-going public remains unlamented.

It was not long before the Charteris case received its first mention on the public stage.

Then, as now, established plays were often given subtle tweaks to reference current events. On 1 May 1730, the scholars of the Charterhouse Foundation performed *Phormio*, by Terence, in which an old philanderer is duped of money. The epilogue on that occasion, spoken by the wily Phormio, included the lines:

> Could at so cheap a Rate *Francisco* 'scape
> His bare intention to commit a Rape,
> Still would *Anne Bond* have been a Name unknown,
> Nor Sheriffs nick'd *the Man* who nick'd the Town.[470]

---

[467] ibid

[468] ibid, p. 37

[469] ibid, p. 53

[470] 'London', in *The Universal Spectator and Weekly Journal*, 2 May 1730,

On 23 June 1730, Henry Fielding's *Rape upon Rape* was first performed at the Haymarket Theatre London. There is no character in it who is a direct representation of Colonel Charteris, but the play's convoluted plot revolves around accusations of rape which must have been the subject of conversation at gatherings of every kind from the moment the Colonel's indictment was made public. The play illustrates the double standards of behaviour then prevalent, and the facility with which a woman's reputation could be ruined by false witnesses. Fielding's main concern, however, was political. In the prologue he laments the corruption in public life which places wealthy individuals, especially those with influential friends, beyond the reach of the law.

> For Vice hath grown too great to be abus'd;
> By Pow'r, defended from the Piercing Dart.[471]

This reference to Walpole's screening his friends from punishment cannot have escaped the audience. When Justice Worthy comments '...Golden Sands too often clog the Wheels of Justice, and obstruct her Course: The very riches, which were the greatest Evidence of his Villainy, have too often declared the Guilty innocent; and Gold hath been found to cut a Halter surer than the sharpest Steel',[472] the allusion to the Charteris case must have been obvious.

Fielding refers to Charteris more explicitly in *The Lottery*, published in 1732. Lovemore, having pursued his adored Chloe to town, is afraid that when he finds her she will already

---

no. LXXXII, p. 2

[471] H. Fielding, *Rape upon Rape; or the Justice Caught in his Own Trap* (London, J. Watts, 1730), prologue p. A2

[472] *Rape Upon Rape*, p. 67

have been ruined, exclaiming 'While she has been flying from my Arms she has fallen into the Colonel's.'[473]

Fielding did not permit Walpole to forget how his part in saving the Colonel from the gallows was viewed by the thinkers of the day, and wrote a satirical essay for *The Craftsman* on the subject of 'screens'. 'A *Prime-Minister*, who conducts the whole Machine of Government, is certainly the best Judge who are fit objects of *Favour*; and if a Man, who hath done him eminent Service, either of a publick or private Nature, should happen to be detected in any *little Irregularities* or *Breach of Trust*, and is violently pursued with the Cry of Justice, it is certainly in his interest, as well as his Duty, to stem the Torrent of popular Resentment…'[474]

The first actual appearance of a Charteris-inspired character on stage was both perfunctory and short-lived. *The Fall of Mortimer* was based on a fragment by Ben Jonson, and completed by the actor and writer William Mountfort. The portrait of the scheming Earl of March, who conspired with his mistress Queen Isabella to depose Edward II, was too good to leave unembellished, and an altered version, laced with references to Walpole, opened at the Little Theatre Haymarket (now the Theatre Royal) on 12 May 1730. In one scene, Mortimer, after reviewing his income from bribes and the grant of lucrative posts (a mere 24,000 marks), on '…a very indifferent day…'[475] commands an entertainment in which no cost is spared, the kind of lavish affair for which Walpole was renowned, '…for those I have to do with are great Belly-

---

[473] H. Fielding, *The Lottery. A Farce* (London, J. Watts, 1732), p. 9

[474] *The Country Journal, or the Craftsman*, 23 March 1734, p. 1

[475] W. Hatchett, *The Fall of Mortimer. An Historical Play. Reviv'd from Mountfort, with Alterations. As it is now acted at the New Theatre in the Hay-Market* (London, J. Millan, 1731), p. 20

Mongers.'[476] He receives a visit from Sir Maiden Battery, a name which leaves the audience in no doubt where the writer's sympathies lie. 'What does this Bullet headed Knight want now?' says Mortimer. 'I saved his Life but t'other day, for which I had 20,000 Marks — I hope 'is in danger again.'[477] When Sir Maiden appears Mortimer observes, 'I'm glad to see you out of your Confinement.'[478]

Sir Maiden hands his benefactor more money, saying 'Give me leave, my Lord, further to testify my Gratitude for your Interest.'[479]

'Sir Maiden' replies Mortimer, 'you may depend upon me on the like, or any other occasion…'[480]

Walpole enjoyed a little mild satire on himself, but this was more than he could stomach. The actors were forbidden to continue performing the play, an order they ignored. On 21 July, the High Constable and his men twice went to the theatre with warrants to arrest the entire company, but the actors had made their escape.[481]

On 17 March 1732, newspapers carried advertisements for the prints of Hogarth's *The Harlot's Progress*, the first of which immortalised not only Charteris but his toady, Jack Gourlay. The Colonel may well also be the lascivious figure attending the harlot's funeral. This immensely popular series attracted the attention of poets who supplied commentaries elaborating the story.

---

[476] ibid

[477] ibid, p. 21

[478] ibid

[479] ibid

[480] ibid

[481] V.J. Liesenfeld, *The Licensing Act of 1737* (Wisconsin, The University of Wisconsin Press, 1984)

Writer John Durant Breval published a series of poems in 1739 based on the pictures, in which he accords the Colonel a starring role. In plate I, a virtuous country maid, Moll Hackabout, has just arrived in London on the York wagon. Moll's name amalgamates that of Moll Flanders, and the eponymous heroine of Daniel Defoe's 1722 book, and Kate Hackabout, a prostitute and sister of Francis, the highwayman condemned at the same sessions as the Colonel. Mother Needham, lingering by the tavern to seek out attractive girls, has spotted Moll as a valuable prospect. Moll is promised the respectable employment she seeks but her new benefactress intends her to be ruined by the Colonel. It should by now be apparent that in fictional representations of the Colonel, he is either a rampant and virile despoiler of innocent women or a sad, old, impotent has-been as the plot requires. Sometimes, as in Breval's poem, he is both:

> Behind the *Beldam's* Back FRANCISCO plyd,
> With his known *Pander*, and the Quarry ey'd;
> Monsters! Who scarce, of Men, deserve the Name,
> Strangers alike to Honesty and Shame;
> A noted Pair, the Master, and the Man,
> Who use all Arts the Virtuous to trepan,
> This, a sly satyr, swell'd with lawless rage,
> And lewd in spit of Impotence and Age:
> And that, a servile Wretch, whose Study lies
> To spring the Game, and bear his Lord the Prize.[482]

After taking Moll home and softening her up with honest employment, the sly procuress suggests that there might be less arduous modes of life.

---

[482] J. Breval, *The Harlot's Progress. Founded upon Mr Hogarth's six paintings* (Dublin, 1739), p. 9

As the anonymous author of another, more vulgar, poem inspired by Hogarth's prints puts it:

> And whither should the baud and miss go,
> But to the Stallion, *Don Francisco*.
> With muckle ee, like saucers twa,
> He gaz'd, as tho' he'd leek'd her thra;
> With his left hand he tip'd a broad piece,
> And put his other hand in's codpiece.[483]

In this version, he charges her from the rear and overcomes her, 'nolens volens.'[484]

Breval is both more descriptive and less brutal:

> Impatient, fix'd the trembling fair to seize,
> Rank as a Goat, dissolv'd in Sloth and Ease;
> Whose boundless Flame, nor Youth nor Age escapes,
> Fam'd for great Whoredoms, and renown'd for Rapes.[485]

Moll is left alone with the Colonel, who tries to overcome her modesty.

> Fond Looks and Frowns alternately he try'd,
> And Protestations, Vows and Oaths apply'd,
> To gain his Ends, but she all Arts defy'd.
> Gold then he proferr'd, and with the Gold prevail'd.[486]

Moll reigns triumphant for a time, revelling in her new lover's

---

[483] Anon, *The Harlot's Progress: being the Life of the noted Moll Hackabout, in Six Hudibrastick Canto's*, sixth edition (London, J. Dourse, 1753), p. 20
[484] ibid
[485] *Breval*, p. 10
[486] ibid

generosity, but he soon tires of her.

> Strips her of all his former Bounty gave,
> And treats his late-lov'd Mistress as a Slave:
> Yet this was no way strange, for hundreds more
> Had felt like Measure from his Hands before.[487]

Only then does the distressed girl discover from another servant that the Colonel, 'Wretch, detested, vile and lewd',[488] has treated others the same, and she takes her revenge by abandoning him for another.

Colonel Charteris' finest hour on the stage very nearly never happened. In the summer of 1737 Michael Clancy a 33-year-old Dublin doctor with no prior works of drama to his name, lost his sight, due, he said, to a cold. No longer able to practise as a physician he decided to spend summer in the country. While there, a friend chanced to read him Dr Arbuthnot's epitaph of the Colonel, and this inspired Clancy to write some scenes which he later incorporated into a play *The Sharper*. Showing the work to some friends they told him it was good enough to be performed on stage, and encouraged by this, he decided on his return to town to place it before the noted man of letters and friend of Arbuthnot's, Jonathan Swift. He asked a friend, Dr Helsham, who knew Swift, to act as go-between, but to Clancy's surprise, Helsham was so terrified of Swift's temper that he dared not show him the unsolicited manuscript. He suggested that Clancy ask a Dr Grattan whom he believed to be braver than himself, but when Clancy went to Grattan, he too refused, saying he would have the book thrown back in his face, '...or be called a blockhead for my Pains.'[489]

---

[487] ibid, p. 11

[488] ibid

[489] M. Clancy, M.D., *The Memoirs of Michael Clancy, M.D.* (2 vols.,

Fortunately, Grattan's brother was present at this meeting, and volunteered to place the book surreptitiously on Swift's table, on the basis that sooner or later the great man would pick it up and read it. Months passed, but when Swift did read the play and asked his friends where it came from, he omitted to mention what he thought of it and no-one dared own up. Eventually Swift mentioned to Helsham that the play had '...a villain well-painted, and that whoever had written the piece conveyed a good moral.'[490] Helsham now felt able to reveal the identity of the author, and though Swift claimed to have no influence in the theatre, he sent Clancy a letter of encouragement and five pounds. It was Christmas day 1737.The play was eventually performed five times in Smock Alley Theatre, Dublin, '...and on the Author's Night, before the greatest Number of Nobility and Gentry, that was ever seen at one meeting in this Kingdom',[491] Clancy later wrote proudly. Clancy remembered his patron and sent Swift a parcel of tickets, and Swift later sent him two four-pound pieces for some more. The part of the villainous Francisco was played by a noted Irish comedy actor, Luke Sparkes.

In Clancy's play, Francisco is no disorganised drunkard mouthing almost unintelligible curses, or even a gross debauché fuelled by undiscriminating lust. He is a cunning master schemer, an early Hanoverian Mr Big, with the power to control, direct and terrify others even at a distance. He does not, extraordinarily, appear on the stage until Act III, yet his influence is felt from the start. Ralph and Ned are two minor sharpers newly arrived in London. Both are creatures of the Colonel. Ralph has been sent by his master on a kind of

Dublin, S. Powell, 1750), vol. 2, p. 55
[490] ibid
[491] Clancy, vol. 2, pp. 52-3

travelling embassy, to find dupes and fleece them. His target is Squire Fasten, an apparent innocent, but secretly an adventurer every bit as criminal as they. Fasten has received a letter warning him that Ralph is a sharper and one of Francisco's spies, but Fasten thinks he is a match for any man:

> And if the fam'd *Francisco's* Ingenuity proceeds from an early Poverty, a Necessity of Shifting, and the Happiness of having first breath'd the keen Air of *North Britain*, I think I have an equal Title to all those Advantages.[492]

Ralph and Ned hurry away to report their progress to Francisco, who is also revealed to have set up a young heiress, the fair and innocent Angelica under his protection in the care of Mrs Lurewell, an Innkeeper who is also a procuress.

Enter Stephen Darey, father of runaway Susanna, who, having been warned about Francisco by his friend, Trueman, fears above all that '…that Hell-hound, that Flash of Hell-fire smother'd in Human Flesh, that Squib of Brimstone, wrap'd and bound in Leather of the Devils tanning…,'[493] has got hold of his daughter. Trueman asks Darey if he had heard of Francisco before his warning and Darey wails 'Alack-a-day, Sir, hear of him, ay truly, all the World has heard of him; ho!'[494]

'This *Francisco* who now stands on the Pinnacle of Vice…',[495] says Trueman, '…he is now the Standard of Villainy, deep sunk in that lethargic Drowsiness, that stupid Insensibility to all Goodness…'[496]

---

[492] ibid, pp. 8-9
[493] ibid, p. 21
[494] ibid
[495] ibid, p. 22
[496] ibid, p. 23

By the time Francisco actually appeared on stage the audience must have been agog to see him, and they were not disappointed. He is discovered seated at his desk, surrounded by money bags and parchments, writing out his annual accounts, something the real Colonel undoubtedly never did. He calculates that he has extracted over nineteen thousand pounds from a charitable corporation. 'To rob single Persons is but paultry Work; — he who defeats a whole Body, has some Title to the name of a Conqueror...'[497] He made over thirty-six thousand pounds by mortgages on Lord Spendall's lands, 'Glorious Product! from about seven hundred and forty Pounds, lent him at several Times...',[498] eleven thousand on Squire Giddy's estate in Ireland, eight thousand on the rents of his properties in English shires, Scotland, and London, and 'Twenty-nine thousand Pounds upon Bonds, Pledges, Chances of Deaths and Marriage, Lotteries, *York* Buildings, Fisheries, Insurance-Office, Wagers, Chances of *South-Sea* Stock, and *Mississippi*.'[499]

He reveals to Ned (who could have been a rich man if he had worked for himself but remains a poor drudge after ten years in the Colonel's service) how he controls and spies upon those from whom he plans to make money. By lodging Angelica in a house of ill-repute he will destroy her character, make her unmarriageable so her ten thousand pounds will go into his pocket. He has recently ruined a Bishop's nephew, something the world (that is, fashionable society) deplores, but Francisco cares nothing for the opinion of the world. 'The Bishop preaches Conscience, — it's his Trade, and I, as a military Man, preach Plunder.'[500]

---

[497] ibid, p. 38

[498] ibid

[499] ibid

Francisco sends Ned off with instructions to destroy Darey, blast Angelica's reputation, and ruin her admirer. '…Let me repeat the sage lesson which I have often taught you: — All Cheating is fair Play, if not detected; the Highwayman suffers at *Tyburn*, not because he robb'd, but because he was taken.'[501]

The next visitor to Francisco's den of iniquity is Simon Shark, '…the best Fellow in Christendom; — egregious Retailer of feminine Merchandize!'[502] Francisco is trying to engage in affairs with six women all living under the same roof, Lady Thunderbolt, her two sisters and three daughters, something even Shark thinks might be too ambitious a project.

'Look you, *Simon*,' Francisco persists, 'not one of 'em must escape me; when I spread my Net, I take in the whole Covey.'[503] Unlike the real Colonel, the stage Francisco prefers to ruin respectable women of high social standing. 'I have as much satisfaction in taking one of these Booties out of a good and creditable family, as a general can have in demolishing a well fortify'd City…'[504]

In a later scene Francisco has set up a gaming table at his house where he is fleecing wealthy dupes by plying them with drink and laudanum. He lectures Ralph and his servant, Robin, on the art of milking young men of their money:

> …They should be sparingly dealt with; if you draw too large Sums from then at once, you as effectually spoil your good Chap, as an Enemy alarms a City by blowing up the Arsenal; those willing young men are to be manag'd with Art…[505]

---

[500] ibid, p. 41
[501] ibid, p. 42
[502] ibid, p. 43
[503] ibid
[504] ibid, p. 44
[505] ibid, p. 60

Having turned the dupes out of the house with neither money nor clothes, he now demands a report on another sector of his business empire, asking what money his whores have made for him that week. There is only one problem, Robin tells him, Molly Frouse, who was hired the previous day has been stubborn, muttering of '... barbarous Usage — Cruelty — Villainy — a Rape — and such Nonsense ... I could hardly hinder her from roaring out of the Windows, and alarming the Neighbourhood.'[506]

'Damn her,' exclaims Francisco, '...kick her out of the House; the World is come to a fine Pass, when such inferior Strumpets pretend to Modesty and Chastity...'[507]

Shark returns, saying he has '...muster'd a whole Regiment of female recruits...',[508] which sends Francisco into transports of sensuous anticipation. 'I was ever the favourite of the Gods',[509] he declares, 'Now will I triumphantly indulge my Appetites ...'[510]

His pleasures lead to his downfall, as Mrs Lurewell is informed by Hester, one of her women:

> O Madam, dismal and dreadful tidings, *Francisco* is seized for committing a Rape — a Rape, madam, he has ravish'd some Body, and was just now hawl'd along the Streets to *Newgate*. I saw him dragg'd along close bound and pinion'd, the Bayliffs were scarce able to secure him from being torn to Pieces by the Mob.[511]

---

[506] ibid, pp. 63-4
[507] ibid, p. 64
[508] ibid
[509] ibid
[510] ibid, p. 65
[511] ibid, p. 74

'Confusion! Death!' exclaims Mrs Lurewell, 'what, *Francisco* in the Hands of the Mob — Blood he has Money enough to bribe all the Mob in *Europe*.'

'The whole Neighbourhood is in an Uproar,' says Hester, 'you can hear them from the Street Windows tearing all before 'em, and pulling his House to Pieces, — the unmerciful Pack have us'd him barbarously, and what vexes me most, is, that the vile dirty rabble rejoice in his Ruin.'[512]

Francisco's final appearance in the play finds him sitting in Newgate, bolted to the wall, bewailing his fate like Toad of Toad Hall. 'And am I become the Foot-ball of publick Insolence?' he rumbles.

> Was not the World wide enough for the injurious Law to spread her destructive banners? — and must I fall a Prey to that rapacious Harpy? What! Is there an intire Inversion of the very Intent of Justice — were not Goals and Whips, and irons, all invented to torture the vile and wretched poor? — Was it ever meant that Riches should fall under the Verge of legal Scrutiny?... *Francisco*, the great *Francisco* laid in Irons, for a little paultry Rape ... does not prudence teach ye that an Abundance of Money changes the Nature of Things just as the Possessor pleases — my Gold shall dazzle the Eyes of Power, and with shining heaps I'll press down the tottering balance of Justice ...[513]

But Francisco's determination to buy his way out of trouble is short-lived. He is visited by Puzzlesuit the solicitor, who encourages him at first, but then spins legal confusion about him. He consoles Francisco by saying, 'If the sentence be of the severest Kind, I'll engage to change it to a Pilloring, or a

---

[512] ibid
[513] ibid, pp. 77-8

gentle Lashing about the City.'[514] Taking his leave, 'I know where to find you, Sir, and I'll wait on you again when the least Opportunity offers', he mutters aside to the Turnkey, 'The Dog is as close-fisted as an old Usurer: damn him, load him, nail him down.'[515]

Francisco, '[After a long Contemplation]' gloomily observes, 'My Mind misgives me strangely, and dreadful Apprehensions roul in my perplex'd Imagination.'[516]

The turnkey confides that his master, Mr Throttle the Keeper, is a bashful man who never talks of money, and therefore Francisco must sign a blank cheque, or wear heavy leg irons. Francisco, just as Charteris might well have done, loses his temper at this blatant attempt at extortion.

> Extravagant Villains, not a Farthing! load on, destestible Rascals, load on, and press me down — not one Penny will I part with.[517]

He is left alone to contemplate his fall, and rages against the world and everyone in it. One moment he sinks into a deep depression, the next he rouses himself to new heights of determination to survive his ordeal. '...Fly off inglorious Fetters — perhaps you are the just Reward of some unfelt Spark of Honesty, which still lay smothered in my Heart, and lurk'd unknown, and baffled all my Industry when I rooted out the rest.'[518]

Francisco is left to rot in gaol, and is referred to later by Trueman as '...that hideous Beast unworthy to bear the name

---

[514] ibid, p. 79
[515] ibid
[516] ibid, p. 80
[517] ibid
[518] ibid, p. 81

of a Man...'[519] and '...the infamous *Francisco*; he is the scorn of the Great, and the Scoff of the Populace; abandon'd by the worst of men in his well-deserv'd Adversity, as he was despis'd by all good Men in his ill — acquir'd prosperity.'[520]

Clancy, who never recovered his sight, and died in 1776, published two volumes of memoirs in 1750, a collection of poems and another play, but nothing outshines this.

Samuel Richardson's novel *Pamela; or Virtue Rewarded*, published in 1740, is about a servant girl who resists the attempts of her employer to seduce her. It is not based on the Charteris case, but a true story brought to Richardson's attention by a friend some twenty-five years previously, but the notorious trial may have played a part in the novel's success. Charteris as a concept and a man was still very much in the public mind. In Richardson's *Clarissa*, published in 1748, he makes a direct reference to the Colonel's preferences in women when Mr Lovelace, writing to John Belford, recommends 'A fine strapping Bona Roba, in the Chartres-taste...'[521]

Two years later the Colonel was still famous enough to be held up as an example of moral degeneracy. Lord Chesterfield, writing to his son in 1750, to express '...a most scrupulous tenderness for your moral character...'[522] and advising him not to do or say the slightest thing that might taint it, cited Charteris — then almost eighteen years dead — as a warning of the dangers of having a bad reputation. In time, however, the memory of Charteris the man and what he had been,

---

[519] ibid, p. 84

[520] ibid, p. 86

[521] S. Richardson, *Clarissa* (London, printed for S. Richardson, 1748), p. 328

[522] *Chesterfield*, vol. 4, letter no. 1684, 8 January 1750, p. 1483

inevitably faded. Those who had seen him as children, such as Alexander Carlyle of Inveresk and Horace Walpole, Sir Robert's son, still recalled and spoke of him, but when they were gone, and the era of early Hanoverian libertines was replaced with the stricter moral code of the Victorians, the wicked Colonel was forgotten. He was not a subject for decent conversation.

The name still has a connection with crime. In 1926 a young thriller writer called Leslie Yin changed his name by deed poll to Charteris. His friend and biographer W. Lofts commented that Yin decided on the name when he heard of '…Colonel Francis Charteris, the notorious gambler, duellist rake and founder member of the Hellfire Club. The chance of claiming him as a distant or at least a spiritual relative was too good to miss.'[523] In Leslie Charteris' defence it should be said that, like many, he must have seen the rake as an idealised romantic character, and was unaware of what an unpleasant individual the Colonel actually was.

It is many years since Colonel Charteris strode upon the stage, and the *Sharper* at least is long overdue for a revival. After its short run in 1730, *Rape Upon Rape* was not performed again in its original form until 1983, when it was revived by the Soho Rep of New York. In 1959 it was adapted by Bernard Miles as *Lock up Your Daughters* and became a musical, with lyrics by Lionel Bart and music by Laurie Johnson. In 1969, it was made into a film.

Fielding's essential themes, of the wealthy and privileged escaping the consequences of their own amorality, and of highly-placed officials screening their friends from retribution, are as relevant today as they were in 1730. But we still live in

---

[523] W.O.G. Lofts, and D. Adley, *The Saint and Leslie Charteris* (London, Hutchinson, 1971), p. 17

the hope that it is possible, if the law counts for anything in the twenty-first century, for a determined girl with only truth on her side to bring down a monster.

APPENDICES

Appendix 1: When was Francis Charteris born?

From the moment Francis Charteris stepped up to the bar at the Justice Hall, Old Bailey, thus ensuring the rapid appearance of a spate of celebrity biographies, his birth date was subject to intense dispute. The author of *Scotch Gallantry Display'd* declared that Charteris was born in 1666, and poured scorn on the suggestion of the author of *Authentick Memoirs* that his true birth year was 1664. *The History of Col Francis Ch—rtr—s* also gives a birth year of 1666. Jonathan Swift, however, believed that Charteris was seventy at the time of his trial. Charteris himself, when pleading for his life, claimed to be over sixty. By contrast, the obituary published immediately after his death, almost certainly issued by his family, suggests a birth year of 1675. R.C. Reid in *The Family of Charteris of Amisfield*, published in 1938, is more precise, giving a baptismal date of 12 January 1672, with a younger brother, Thomas, baptised on 4 April 1675, about whom nothing more is known. These details also appear in *Burke's Landed Gentry*.

Edinburgh Parish records confirm that James and Mary Charteris baptised their first born son Francis after his maternal grandfather on 12 January 1672, but it also shows that the son they baptised on 4 April 1675 was not called Thomas, but was a second Francis. The most probable reason for the re-use of the name is that the first Francis Charteris died in infancy. This theory is strengthened by the fact that the burial registers for Edinburgh Canongate show that on 9 January 1674, James Charteris buried a child. Unfortunately no details of name, age or gender are given, but there do not appear to have been any children in the family at that date other than the Francis baptised in 1672. It is a reasonable assumption therefore, that the son baptised on 4 April 1675 is the Francis Charteris who is the subject of this book, and that, in the absence of any compelling evidence to the contrary, the ceremony was, according to the custom of the time, performed within a few weeks of his birth.

Appendix 2: Monetary Values
According to the Retail Price Index, the purchasing power of £1 in 1730 would be approximately equivalent to £140 in 2008.

Appendix 3: The Jury
The jurors at the trial of Colonel Francis Charteris were:
Benjamin Forster
John Wilton
Simon Parsons
John Barret
Robert Matthews
Thomas Wise
Richard Wilder
Nicholas Gardener
William Carpenter
Jonathan Halley
John Wells
Richard Powel

Appendix 4: Dates
The Gregorian calendar was introduced in 1582 to correct an error of ten days that had accrued with the use of the Julian calendar since 46 BC. New Year's Day, which had been celebrated on 25 March, became 1 January The new calendar

was accepted on the continent of Europe but not in England, which for the next 170 years used both, referred to as Old Style and New Style. The date of the trial of Francis Charteris, for example, which took place on 26 February was in 1729 (O.S.) but 1730 (N.S.) and would then have been rendered 26 February 1729/30. England finally converted to the Gregorian calendar in 1752.

In this book the days of the week are given as recorded in the documents of the time, which give the Julian date. For clarity it is assumed throughout that the year begins on 1 January.

BIBLIOGRAPHY

Specific sources

Additional Manuscripts (British Library), Add.36138, Add36129, Add33054

Anon, *Calista. An Opera* (London, C. Davies, 1731)

——, *The Case of Col. Francis Chartres, as it appeared at his Trial, at the Sessions held at Justice-Hall, in the Old-Baily, on Thursday the 26th of February, 1729-30; for a Rape committed on the Body of Anne Bond, his Servant, November, 10, 1729* in *A Collection of Remarkable Trials* (Glasgow, Eighteenth Century Collections Online, *c.* 1739) (accessed British Library electronic resources)

——, *Col. Francis Charteris, Appellant. The earl of Hyndford, Respondent, The Appellant's CASE To be heard at the Bar of the House of Lords on 30 March, 17 23/24* (London, 1724)

——, *Culloden Papers, Comprising an extensive and interesting correspondence from the year 1625 to 1748* (London, Printed for T. Cadell and W. Davies, Strand, 1815)

——, *Don Francisco's Descent to the Infernal Regions, an Interlude* (London: Printed for S. Slow, 1732)

——, *The Harlot's Progress: being the Life of the noted Moll Hackabout, in Six Hudibrastick Canto's*, sixth edition (London, J. Dourse, 1753)

——, *The History of Col. Francis Ch—rtr—s*, fourth edition (London, printed for the author, 1730)

Anon (ed), *Letters to and From Henrietta, Countess of Suffolk* (2 vols., London, John Murray, 1824)

Anon, *The Life of Colonel* Don Francisco (London, Printed for the Author, 1730)

——, *Mother Needham's Elegy* (London, *c.* 1730)

——, *The Newgate Calendar, or the Malefactors' Bloody Register* (London, T. Werner Laurie, 1932)

——, *The Political State of Great-Britain* (60 vols., London, Printed for the Executors of Mr Boyer, and sold by T. Warner, 1730)

——, *The Proceedings at the Sessions of the Peace, and Oyer and Terminer, for the City of London, and County of Middlesex; on Wednesday the 25th, Thursday the 26th, Friday the 27th, and Saturday the 28th of February, 1730, in the Third Year of His Majesty's Reign* (London, T. Payne, 1730)

——, *The Reprieve: An Epistle from J—ck K—ch to C—l C—s* (London, A. Moore, 1730)

——, *Scotch Gallantry Display'd, or the Life and Adventures of the unparralel'd Col. Fr—nc—s Ch—rt—s, Impartially related* (London, Printed for, and Sold by the *Booksellers* in *Town* and *Country*, 1730)

——, *Select Trials at the Sessions-House in the Old-Bailey, for Murder, Robberies, Rapes, Sodomy, Coining, Frauds, Bigamy, and other Offences* (London, J. Applebee, 1742)

——, *Some Authentick memoirs of the Life of Colonel Ch—s, Rape-Master General of Great Britain* (London, Printed and Sold by the Booksellers of *London* and *Westminster*, 1730)

——, 'The Trial of Francis Charteris, Esq. for a Rape', in *The Tyburn Chronicle: or, Villainy Display'd in All Its Branches* (4 vols., London: Printed for J. Cooke, at Shakespears Head, No. 10, Pater-noster Row, 1768), vol. 2

——, *The Tryal of Colonel Francis Chartres for a Rape Committed by him on the Body of Mrs. Anne Bond* (London, A. Moore, 1730)

——, *The Tryal of Colonel Francis Charteris for a RAPE Committed on the Body Of ANNE BOND, Who was tried & found Guilty at* Justice-Hall *in the* Old Bailey, *on Fryday the 27th of* February

1729-30 (London, Sylvanus Pepyat, 1730)

——, 'A View of London and Westminster, or the Town Spy' (London, T. Warner, 1728)

Applebee, J. (ed), *Select Trials at the Sessions-House in the Old-Bailey, for Murder, Robberies, Rapes, Sodomy, Coining, Frauds, Bigamy, and other Offences* (4 vols., London, J. Applebee, 1742)

Baker, S., *Prestongrange House* (Prestoungrange University Press, 2000)

Breval, J., *The Harlot's Progress. Founded upon Mr. Hogarth's six paintings* (Dublin, 1739)

Browning, W.E. (ed), *The Poems of Jonathan Swift, D.D.* (2 vols., London, G. Bell and Sons, Ltd., 1910)

Burton, J.H. (ed), *The Autobiography of De Alexander Carlyle of Inveresk, 1722-1805* (Bristol, Thoemmes Antiquarian Books, Ltd, 1990)

Butt, J. (ed), *The Twickenham Edition of the Poems of Alexander Pope* (10 vols., London, Methuen and Co Ltd, 1939-67)

Caldwall, T. (ed), *A Select Collection of Ancient and Modern Epitaphs, and Inscriptions: to Which are Added Some on the Decease of Eminent Personages* (London, T. Caldwall, 1796)

Clancy, M., M.D., *The Memoirs of Michael Clancy, M.D.* (2 vols., Dublin, S. Powell, 1750)

Chamberlen, P. (attr.), *The Perspective, or Calista Dissected. To which are prefixed, A Lock and Key to the late Opera of Calista* (London, J. Dicks, 1731)

Charteris, F., *The Case of Lieutenant-Colonel Charteris* (London, 1711)

——, *The Following Affidavits are for clearing Colonel Charteris of what is falsely charged against him by Hurley and his evidences* (London, printed for F. Charteris, 1711)

——, *The Humble Representation of Lieutenant-Colonel Charteris* (London, printed for F. Charteris, 1711)

De La Chéterdie, T., *Instructions for the Use of a Young Lady of Quality or, the Idea of a Woman of Merit* (Edinburgh, W. Cheyne, 1734)

Dobrée, B. (ed), *The Letters of Phillip Dormer Stanhope fourth Earl of Chesterfield* (6 vols., 1932, London, Eyre & Spottiswoode Limited)

Dreghorn, Lord J.M., 'His Majesty's Advocate, and James Carruthers, Waulker, against Colonel Francis Charteris of Amisfield', in *Arguments and Decisions in Remarkable Cases before the High Court and other Supreme Courts in Scotland* (Edinburgh, printed for J. Bell and E & C Dilly, London 1774)

Douglas, Sir R., *The Peerage of Scotland* (Edinburgh, R. Fleming, 1764)

Fielding, H., *The Lottery. A Farce* (London, J. Watts, 1732)

——, *Rape upon Rape; or the Justice Caught in his Own Trap* (London, J. Watts, 1730)

Fraser, Sir W., K.C.B. LL.D., *Memorials of the Family of Wemyss of Wemyss* (3 vols., Edinburgh, 1888)

Grant, J. (ed), *Cassell's Old and New Edinburgh* (3 vols., London, Cassell & Co., 1884-70)

Hatchett, W, *The Fall of Mortimer. An Historical Play. Reviv'd from Mountfort, with Alterations. As it is now acted at the New Theatre in the Hay-Market* (London, J. Millan, 1731)

Hurly, P., *An Answer to the Affidavits lately procur'd by Lieutenant-Colonel Charteris, about False Musters* (London, printed for P. Hurly, 1711)

——, *An Answer to Col. Charteris's Second Libel which he Calls his Humble Representation* (London, printed for P. Hurly, 1711)

——, *An Answer to the Affidavits lately procur'd by Lieutenant-Colonel Charteris, about False Musters* (London, printed for P. Hurly, 1711)

——, *An Answer to a False and Scandalous Libel, lately stol'n into the world, under the title of The Memorial for Lieutenant Colonel Charteris* (London, printed for P. Hurly, 1711)

———, *The Case of Several of the Persons from whom Lieutenant Colonel Charteris extorted Money for protecting them from their Creditors* (London, printed for P. Hurly, 1711)

———, *Demonstrative Proofs, that Lieutenant Col. Charteris hath by* False Musters, *and other Unwarrantable* Practices, *Defrauded the Queen and Publick of 12*l. 5s. 3d. *every Week since he bought his Company* (London, printed for P. Hurley, 1711)

———, *Fresh Proofs against Colonel Charteris* (London, printed for P. Hurly, 1711) Jackson, W. (ed), 'Narrative of the Trial of Sarah Prydden otherwise called Sally Salisbury, who was convicted of an assault', *The New and Complete Newgate Calendar* (6 vols.) (vol. 1 ,pp. 333-7) (London, Alexander Hogg, 1795)

Langley, B., *An Accurate Description of Newgate* (London, T. Warner, 1724)

Lofts, W.O.G., and Adley, D., *The Saint and Leslie Charteris* (London, Hutchinson, 1971)

Maidment, J. (ed), *Private Letters Now first Printed from The Original MSS* (Edinburgh, privately printed, 1829)

Marshall, J.D. (ed), *The Autobiography of William Stout of Lancaster 1665-1752* (Manchester, the University Press, 1967)

Menary, G., *The Life and Letters of Duncan Forbes of Culloden* (London, Alexander Maclehose & Co, 1936)

Moor, A., *The Genuine History of Mrs Sarah Prydden, usually called Sally Salisbury, and her Gallants* (London, printed for Andrew Moor, 1723)

Mottley, J., *A Survey of the City of London and Westminster* (2 vols., London, J. Read, 1733-5)

Nicolson J. and Burn, R., *History of the Antiquities of Westmoreland and Cumberland* (2 vols., Wakefield, EP Publishing, Cumbria

County Library, 1976, facsimile reprint for Strachan and Cadell, 1777)

Paterson, J., *History of the Regality of Musselborough* (Musselburgh, J. Gordon, 1857)

Patten, R., *The History of the Late Rebellion* (London, J. Warner, 1717)

Percival, M.O. (ed), *Political Ballads Illustrating the Administration of Sir Robert Walpole*, Volume 8 of Oxford Historical and Literary Studies (Oxford, Clarendon Press, 1916)

Percival, Viscount, *Manuscripts of the Earl of Egmont. Diary of Viscount Percival afterwards First Earl of Egmont*, vol. 1. 1730 — 1733 (London, HMSO, 1920)

Pulteney, W, *An Answer to One Part of a late Infamous Libel, Intitled, Remarks on the Craftsman's Vindication of his two honourable Patrons; in which the Character and Conduct of Mr. P. is fully Vindicated* (London, R. Francklin, 1731)

Ramsay, A., 'An Ode with a Pastoral Recitative, on the Marriage of the Right Honourable James Earl of Wemyss and Mrs Janet Charteris', *Poems by Allan Ramsay* (2 vols., London, J. Clarke, 1731), vol. 2, pp. 83-6

Reid, R.C., *The Family of Charteris of Amisfield* (Dumfries, Courier Press, 1938)

Richardson, S., *Clarissa* (London, printed for S. Richardson, 1748)

Roper, W.O., *Hornby Castle, Lancashire* (Liverpool, Thomas Brakell, 1890)

Trapnell, William H., *Thomas Woolston: Madman and Deist?* (Bristol, Thoemmes Press, 1994)

Walker, C., *Authentick Memoirs of the life, intrigues and adventures of the celebrated Sally Salisbury (Sarah Priddon). With true characters of her most considerable Gallants* (London, 1723)

Warrand, D. (ed), More Culloden Papers, 5 vols. (Inverness,

Robert Carruthers and Sons, 1927)

Williams, H. (ed), *The Correspondence of Jonathan Swift* (5 vols., Oxford, The Clarendon Press, 1963)

Wright J. (ed), *The Letters of Horace Walpole* (6 vols., London, 1840)

Microfilm

Complete Hanoverian State Papers, Edition held by the British Library

Online Resources

The Swinton Family Society, www.swintonfamilysociety.org

THE PROCEEDINGS AT THE Sessions of the Peace, and Oyer and Terminer, FOR THE City of LONDON, AND County of MIDDLESEX; ON Wednesday the 25th, Thursday the 26th, Friday the 27th, and Saturday the 28th of February, 1730, in the Third Year of His MAJESTY'S Reign http://www.oldbaileyonline.org/

Records relating to the Barony of Kendale, volume 2, pages 292 and 297 (1924), accessed 24 March 2007, http://www.british-history.ac.uk/

'Townships: Hornby', *A History of the County of Lancaster*, Volume 8 (1914), pp. 191-201. URL: http://www.british-history.ac.uk/ (accessed 24 March 2007)

Archive sources

The Public Record Office, Kew

Order in Council for the pardon of Francis Charteris SP 36/18

Petition of Francis Charteris read to the King in Council PRO/30/29/3/1/4

Petition of James Carruthers SP35/34/151

Will of Francis Charteris PROB 11/650

Charteris v. Wemyss Promissory notes, bonds, bills of exchange, declarations of account and other securities belonging to Col Francis Charteris of Hornby Castle, Lancs. C 104/196

Scottish National Archives

GD/237/20/8/12-13 Letters from George Skene of that ilk to Archibald Stuart 7 April 1730, and 2 May 1730

GD18/4590 Letter to Sir John Clerk from William Aikman 3 December 1723

GD18/5245/4 letter 11, 26 November 1723, Laurence Charteris to John Clerk

CG1/2/3/2/215-226 Church papers relating to the case of Captain Francis Charteris (gross immorality)

GD248/563/68/17 Letter from Countess of Hyndford 13 April 1724

GD1/867/2 Printed information by Robert Dundas, advocate for Mr Francis Charteris and his tutors against James, Earl of Wemyss.

Family History Centre, Hyde Park, London

Parish Records of Edinburgh Canongate, film 1066698

Edinburgh Old Parochial Registers, film 1066663

Burial Records Greyfriars Kirkyard, Edinburgh, film 1066746

Edinburgh Canongate Church baptisms, film 1067741

Parish Registers St Michael Crooked Lane, film 0535712

Parish registers of St Mary Woolnoth, film 0897089

St Michaels Crooked Lane marriages, film 0416712 (3)

Other archives

Marriage Licence Allegations, Faculty Office 1701-1850, 20 April 1730

Westminster Archives
St George Hanover Square Rate Books, Conduit St Ward
C1-C8/433
C1-22/434

General and background sources
Anon, *Low-Life or One Half of the World Knows not how the Other Half Live* (London, printed for the author, undated *c.* 1753)
———, *The Tricks of the Town Laid Open: OR A Companion for Country Gentlemen*, 2nd edn (London, H. Slater, 1747)
Battestin, M.C., *A Henry Fielding Companion* (Westport CT, Greenwood Press, 2000)
Battestin, M.C. and Battestin, R.R., *Henry Fielding, a Life* (London, Routledge, 1989)
Besant, W., *London in the Eighteenth Century* (London, Adam and Charles Black, 1902)
Chancellor, E.B., *The Lives of the Rakes*, Volume III, Charteris and Wharton (London, Philip Allan and Co, Quality Court, 1925)
Cockburn, J.S. and Green, T.A. (eds), *Twelve Good Men and True. The Criminal Trial Jury in England, 1200-1800* (Princeton, Princeton University Press, 1988)
Dingwall, H.M., *Late Seventeenth Century Edinburgh* (Aldershot, Scolar Press, 1994)
Goldgar, B.A., Walpole and the Wits (Lincoln and London, University of Nebraska Press, 1976)
Gordon, C., *The Old Bailey and Newgate* (London, T. Fisher Unwin, 1902)
Hill, B.W, *Sir Robert Walpole* (London, Hamish Hamilton, 1989)
Hooper, W.E., *The History of Newgate and the Old Bailey* (London, Underwood Press Ltd, 1935)

Liesenfeld, V.J., *The Licensing Act of 1737* (Wisconsin, The University of Wisconsin Press, 1984)

Mackay, C., 'The South-Sea Bubble' in *Extraordinary Popular Delusions and the Madness of Crowds* (London, Richard Bentley, 1841)

Laprade, W.T., *Public Opinion and Politics in Eighteenth Century England* (New York, The Macmillan Company, 1936)

Linebaugh, P., *The London Hanged* (London, Verso, 2003)

Lowther, W, M.D., *A Dissertation on the Dropsy* (London, J. Cooke, 1771)

Matthew, H.G.C. and Harrison, B. (eds), *Oxford Dictionary of National Biography* (61 vols., OUP, New York, 2004)

McLynn, F., *Crime and Punishment in Eighteenth Century England* (Oxford, OUP, 1991)

Morley, J., *Walpole* (London, MacMillan and Co Ltd., 1903)

Paulson, R., *The Life of Henry Fielding* (Blackwell, Oxford, 2000)

Pearce, E., *The Great Man* (London, Jonathan Cape, 2007)

Plumb, J.H., *Sir Robert Walpole* (2 vols., London, Cresset Press, 1956-60)

Seccombe, T. (ed), *Lives of Twelve Bad Men* (London, T. Fisher Unwin, Paternoster Square, MDCCCXCIV)

Stanhope, P.D, 4th Earl of Chesterfield, *The Characters of George the First, Queen Caroline, Sir Robert Walpole, Mr. Pulteney, Lord Hardwicke, Mr. Fox, and Mr. Pitt, Reviewed* (T. Davies and T. Cadell, London, 1777)

Thomson, A., *The Disappointed Gallant, or Buckram in Armour* (Edinburgh, printed for the author, 1738)

ACKNOWLEDGEMENTS

I would like to extend my grateful thanks for all the people and organisations who assisted me in compiling the information for this book. I should especially like to mention:

The British Library
The National Archives of Scotland
The National Archives Kew
The National Portrait Gallery Scotland
The Family History Centre
The Scottish Society of Genealogists
The Library of Scotland
Colindale Newspaper Library
The National Gallery of Scotland
Westminster Archives
Stuart Fagan for the tour of Greyfriars Kirkyard

A writer's life is so much easier with a supportive partner, and I must pay a special tribute to my husband Gary, and his enormous patience in the face of my peculiar obsession with long-dead villains.

A NOTE TO THE READER

If you have enjoyed this book enough to leave a review on **Amazon** and **Goodreads**, then we would be truly grateful.

Sapere Books

Sapere Books is an exciting new publisher of brilliant fiction and popular history.

To find out more about our latest releases and our monthly bargain books visit our website: **saperebooks.com**

Printed in Great Britain
by Amazon

56883088R00149